ADVANCE PR[...]
PLEASE GOD LET IT BE HERPES

"If you ever felt smitten, heartsick, lovelorn, or just smacked in the face by Cupid's cruel hand, this book was written for you. Carlos Kotkin's hilarious memoir will make you feel better about the state of your love life because his is so much worse."

—Michael Ian Black

"My diagnosis: Carlos Kotkin's *Herpes* will stay with you for a *very* long time. His remarkably singular voice seems to bubble forth from a truly quirky, shamelessly personal, and desperately deep comedic soul. This wonderfully offbeat book is a rare gift to the 'hopeless romantic' in all of us."

—Tony Shalhoub

"Carlos Kotkin continues to have one of the most original, outlandishly funny minds."

—Mark Johnson, producer of *Rain Man* and *The Chronicles of Narnia*

"Carlos Kotkin has a consistent ability to wring laughter out of everyday, seemingly simple situations through intelligent humor that oftentimes sneaks up on you before delivering knockout laughs."

—Jim Vallely, writer/coexecutive producer of *Arrested Development*

"Carlos Kotkin's stories are hilarious. They're heartfelt, memorable, and perhaps most importantly, they could only have come from Carlos."

—Ben Wexler, writer/producer of *Secret Girlfriend*, *Still Standing*, and *The King of Queens*

continued . . .

"Carlos Kotkin writes stories that are genuine, funny, and endearing and somehow make me feel a little bit better about the world. Plus, they're funny. I know I mentioned that already, but it seems important enough to mention multiple times. I would be happy to lose a weekend with a book written by him."

—Jaclyn Lafer, producer of Sit 'N Spin
at the Comedy Central Stage

"This is a hilarious, extremely satisfying, and poignant read—whether you are searching for love, have herpes, neither, or both. In fact, I couldn't put it down. Physically I could. But I didn't want to. I'm not still holding it."   —Myq Kaplan, comedian

"The awkward, often horrifying misadventures of this seemingly normal man are hilarious. Carlos Kotkin is an engaging, original voice."

—Elizabeth Beckwith, author of *Raising the Perfect Child Through Guilt and Manipulation*

"Carlos Kotkin is so funny. I would never go out with him."

—Nadine Velazquez, actress

PLEASE GOD LET IT BE HERPES

A HEARTFELT QUEST FOR LOVE AND COMPANIONSHIP

CARLOS KOTKIN

 NEW AMERICAN LIBRARY

NEW AMERICAN LIBRARY
Published by New American Library, a division of
Penguin Group (USA) Inc., 375 Hudson Street,
New York, New York 10014, USA
Penguin Group (Canada), 90 Eglinton Avenue East, Suite 700, Toronto,
Ontario M4P 2Y3, Canada (a division of Pearson Penguin Canada Inc.)
Penguin Books Ltd., 80 Strand, London WC2R 0RL, England
Penguin Ireland, 25 St. Stephen's Green, Dublin 2,
Ireland (a division of Penguin Books Ltd.)
Penguin Group (Australia), 250 Camberwell Road, Camberwell, Victoria 3124,
Australia (a division of Pearson Australia Group Pty. Ltd.)
Penguin Books India Pvt. Ltd., 11 Community Centre, Panchsheel Park,
New Delhi - 110 017, India
Penguin Group (NZ), 67 Apollo Drive, Rosedale, Auckland 0632,
New Zealand (a division of Pearson New Zealand Ltd.)
Penguin Books (South Africa) (Pty.) Ltd., 24 Sturdee Avenue,
Rosebank, Johannesburg 2196, South Africa

Penguin Books Ltd., Registered Offices:
80 Strand, London WC2R 0RL, England

First published by New American Library,
a division of Penguin Group (USA) Inc.

First Printing, March 2012
10   9   8   7   6   5   4   3   2   1

REGISTERED TRADEMARK—MARCA REGISTRADA

LIBRARY OF CONGRESS CATALOGING-IN-PUBLICATION DATA:

Kotkin, Carlos.
   Please god let it be herpes: a heartfelt quest for love and companionship / Carlos Kotkin.
   p.   cm.
   ISBN 978-0-451-23571-8
   1. Kotkin, Carlos.   2. American wit and humor.   3. Dating (Social customs)—Humor.   I. Title.
   PN6165. K68   2012
   818'.602—dc23   2011033392

Set in ITC Giovanni STD
Designed by Alissa Amell

Printed in the United States of America

For courageous chickens across the globe

A BRIEF INTRODUCTION

Dear Readers,

Hello, I'm Carlos's mother. I am honored that Carlos asked me to write the introduction to his book. This introduction is going to be short because, to be honest with you, I don't really like introductions in books. They are a pain in the neck. I'd rather go to the beginning of the book. I might read the introduction after I finish reading the book because I like to get to the nitty-gritty. Nowadays, you read a book before you get to the book and that irritates me. I think, "Yeah, right, yeah. I'll come back to you later. I need to read the book." So go ahead and get to the book if you want. The dedications are for the people who they are dedicated to; they probably don't apply to you. The preface—there isn't one—so you don't have to worry about that. Just go to the first official page and enjoy it.

If you're still with me, you have chosen a very interesting book.

In this book, you will find Carlos's history of dating—here, there, and everywhere—as he looked for a nice girl to call his own. Carlos is my only son. I am very proud of him. He is a great writer. He is a great person. Through the years, I have tried to help him. He has had many troubles with dating and finding the right person. Like many of us, you need to kiss a lot of frogs before you find a prince, or in his case, a princess that he can keep forever. To do that I have sent some girls his way, hoping that one of them will click. Some of the girls that I personally introduced to Carlos, I really thought they were the right girl and I could not understand why he didn't like them. A lot of the girls Carlos met on his own. I could see way far away from San Diego to Los Angeles that some of these girls were tushyholes and he should not be involved with them. They weren't all crap; some of them must have been nice. I would best describe the girls Carlos has dated as a bouquet of flowers, of many varieties. Some of them were wilted. Some didn't smell very good. But you go on—you try to find the best rose in the garden. You get what you desire if you try hard.

The stories you are going to read are true stories. Names, places, and other things have been changed for the protection of the characters. I am not sure if Carlos's full name is going to appear in this book, but if so I am going to change my last name. As far as my first name, you can call me "Carlos's mother." The title of the book is very creative; it is a good title. But when I tell my friends about this I am going to call it *The Love Stories of Carlos*. Get a handkerchief because when Carlos first told me many of these stories I could not stop laughing and tears came down. I hope you get to use a handkerchief as many times as I had to and go to the bathroom. You won't get herpes by reading this book, but you might get a stomachache from all the laughing. And you don't need to be intellectual. This is an easy book to read. I guarantee that. English is not my first language.

With all my love I have for my son, I highly recommend this book. Have a lot of fun and good luck to you,

Carlos's mother

CONTENTS

CONTENTS

PLEASE GOD LET IT BE HERPES

SCHOOLYARD CONFIDENTIAL

My blundering and arduous journey of romantic misadventures was set in motion at age seven. That is the age I discovered females would be an inseparable part of my life, even when they weren't in it, and I would spend a dizzying amount of time searching for a good woman. It all began on an ordinary ride home, when I spotted a young mother pushing a stroller and made the mistake of asking my dad where babies come from. His science-fiction explanation, complete with original sketches, was shocking. To this day, I still don't fully understand how sexual reproduction came to be known as *the birds and the bees*. It probably has something to do with birds hatching from eggs and bees distributing plant pollen—a tasteful way of saying plant sperm—available once there has been a plant orgasm. Alligators also hatch from eggs and bats pollinate as well, so baby making could just as easily be referred to as *the alligators and the bats*.

The origins of that expression were the least of my worries the

1

afternoon my dad sat me down at the dining room table and began drawing strange illustrations of tiny serpents with balloon heads. If I'd known anything about drugs at the time, I would have suspected my dad was high. This is where babies came from? Girls were gross. Always had been, always would be. I didn't want to touch a girl's *shoulder*, much less her . . . "Ew!" I responded in disbelief. And to touch it with my . . . "Sick!" I protested. Sex was obviously a surefire way to catch cooties. My dad pointed out there were a number of other things a person could catch while having sex—raising the question, *why would anyone ever be wild and crazy enough to do it?* On its own, the physical act was awful enough. There were diseases involved, too? Of course there were! What did people expect? Piling onto the insanity, my dad also informed me that when I became a teenager, I would hate my parents' guts and masturbate into a sock. In other words, I would become a monster.

The teen years were far off, so I set worries of mutating into a masturbating demon aside. I had enough to contend with. The unexpected revelation that I would someday *like* girls was nothing less than outrageous. Not only would I *like* them, I would supposedly make great efforts to get their attention. If I was to have any success, I would need to be *good* at getting a girl's attention. This was madness. When I returned to elementary school after my father's talk, I returned in a daze. At recess, I was quiet and sober. My world had been rocked. Here I was, in sunny, suburban Anaheim, California, minutes from the happiest place on Earth—the one with the giant, smiling mouse—and all I could think of was uncivilized men and women engaging in riotous orgies. During a regular game of dodgeball, I remained in the background. Usually, I was a star player. But that was before I knew I used to be a sperm. As I repeatedly ran this through my mind, a girl across the schoolyard caught my eye. Her name was Yvonne.

I had known Yvonne since kindergarten. She used to be a sperm, too. Now she was a skinny blond girl. Sometimes Yvonne wore repulsive pink jeans that outlined her pointy hipbones, making her look even more disgusting than usual. She sat next to me in first grade. It was a long year, that year. I watched Yvonne playing with her friends and couldn't imagine being attracted to her. To think that someday I might want to hug and kiss Yvonne the way people did in the boring parts of movies! I had trouble picturing this, not only because the image was so outside the agreed standards of decency, but also because as I began to envision it I was pounded in the face with a big, red bouncy ball. The dangers of not paying attention during a fast-paced game of dodgeball. I was knocked to the ground.

My friends rushed over. Once they stopped laughing, they wondered what was wrong with me. I told them I was tired. The truth was I *knew*. I knew there was a storm approaching. Sure, everything was hunky-dory at the moment. But at some point—somehow, some way—a cloud would appear above us. It would transform us into zombies. Not just regular zombies—horny zombies. We would move faster than normal zombies, desperate to get our hands on girls' icky parts. It was only a matter of time. There was nothing we could do about it. I kept this knowledge to myself, choosing to preserve my classmates' innocence. Besides, if word got out, it could lead to widespread panic.

The tempest started brewing in fifth grade. By this point, everyone knew they used to be a sperm—either through word on the street, their dad drawing them pictures, or a movie our fifth-grade teacher, Ms. Anderson, showed us, which starred a bespectacled bald scientist from the 1950s wearing a white lab coat. The scientist used a pointer on the diagram of an erection to emphasize a tube named Aretha while the class did its best not to burst into laughter. Every now and then a few boys would crack stupid jokes on the schoolyard about snakes in the grass or Mommy wrestling with Santa Claus, but for the most part we didn't mention anything. We just waited. Girls seemed to be struck sooner than boys, making recess a perilous endeavor.

A girl named Mamie was one of the first to go. Mamie and I were playing outfield during a game of kickball. When my classmate Tim kicked the ball toward right field, Mamie ran over and tackled me on left field. She pinned me down and began licking my face like a crazy person. The moment she mounted me, I thought, *It's happening.* Mamie had become a sex zombie. I struggled mightily to break free from what I would later find out was the cowgirl position. Had my older self been able to travel back in time to this moment, I would have advised the fifth grade version of me that there were many lengthy dry spells in the future, and that I should be thankful for what Mamie was doing.

One by one, we all started to turn, including—the horror, the horror—*me.* It was Yvonne, of course, who captured my attention with her hypnotic pink jeans and seductive hipbones. As she had in the first grade, Yvonne sat near me again in Ms. Anderson's fifth grade class. In Ms. Anderson's class, Yvonne sat *facing* me. Ms. Anderson's class had a peculiar configuration. Rather than each of us sitting at our own desks, looking toward the front, Ms. Anderson grouped four desks together, forming a pod. Each group of four students was a team. Teams would compete against each other in the myriad of academic challenges Ms. Anderson foisted upon us.

My team consisted of Tim, Gwen, Yvonne, and me. Tim sat

beside me. Gwen, a trusted friend of Yvonne's, sat facing Tim. And Yvonne sat beside Gwen, facing me. Having to look into Yvonne's eyes each and every day, all day, it was impossible not to fall in love. I kept my desire for her a secret. At a certain point, however, it could no longer be contained. That's when I began pulling Yvonne's hair, calling her "dog breath," and scribbling on her homework. She once had the audacity to join the boys in a game of dodgeball. As Yvonne fled from my aim, I forcefully threw the ball at her, hitting her squarely on her backside. I thought surely after this incident, she would know once and for all that I wanted her to be my girl. But no.

While the rest of us were succumbing to our passions, Yvonne kept her cards close to her budding chest. Midway through the year, Mamie had managed to launch surprise dry-hump attacks on every boy in fifth grade, and a few in the sixth. Fellow fifth graders Mike and Gloria had gone so far as to get married under the monkey bars. Tim and I were groomsmen; Mamie conducted the ceremony. But Yvonne gave no indication of being interested in anyone. How could this be? Had she taken an antidote to the germs referred to as "hormones" by the scientist in Ms. Anderson's movie? She ate a lot of raisins. Maybe that was it.

I finally had to ask. "Do you like anybody, Yvonne?" We were sitting at our desks, facing each other, as usual. Tim and Gwen were sitting next to us. It was supposed to be a quiet study session, but I needed answers and I needed them now. Yvonne blushed at my question. Her eyes darted to Gwen, who smiled knowingly.

Yvonne softly answered with a shy grin, "I might." Her candor surprised me. I asked Yvonne who she liked. "I'm not going to tell you," she quickly responded, in a bit of a huff. Gwen continued smiling. It was obvious she possessed the information I was seeking.

I glanced at Tim, asking Yvonne if she liked him. Before Yvonne could answer, Tim spoke out. "You better not," he scolded her.

Yvonne told Tim she wouldn't like him if he were the last boy on Earth. So Tim was off the list, even in the event of an apocalypse. My curiosity as strong as ever, I bombarded Yvonne with a series of questions systematically designed to pinpoint her secret crush. Is he in this classroom? What color is his hair? Which side of the room is he sitting on? Is he wearing a striped shirt or solid? How many letters in his name? Some of the questions she answered, some she refused. But all of them wore her down. She finally blurted out, "I like *you*, okay? I like you." A hush came over the four of us. This was nearly as big a bombshell as when my dad told me about zygotes.

Yvonne's confession scared me. All of sudden I had a girlfriend. Adjustments would have to be made. I wasn't sure what they were, only that they would have to be made. First things first, I would need to respond to Yvonne's declaration. She stared at me expectantly. I played it cool, thanking her for telling me and then going about my business. My business consisted of looking down at my desk for the remainder of the class. A few days later I realized the honorable thing to do would be to ask Yvonne if she'd go steady with me. Although that's not how we phrased it at our school. We dropped the *steady* part. People didn't *go steady* at our school, people just went—as in "Carlos and Yvonne are going together." Where exactly people were going was anybody's guess. Nevertheless, I needed to ask Yvonne before she started liking someone else; I needed to lock her affections down.

Despite the fact that Yvonne exclaimed to my face that she liked me, I was nervous about asking her to go with me. What if she only liked me *to a point*? Maybe going together was crossing a line. After all, when she blurted out, "I like *you*, okay?" she didn't follow up with, "So why don't you ask me if I'll go with you?" Things would be strained for the rest of the year if I put my heart on the line and she took a flamethrower to it. I'd have to ask Ms. Anderson for a new seat assignment, people would talk, too much hullabaloo. In order to avoid any possible indignities, I decided I would ask Yvonne if she would go with me through an intermediary—her friend Gwen.

Gwen was one of the few students who volunteered to work in the cafeteria at lunch hour. At the end of lunch she would stand by the little window where we were to return our trays. Gwen would take the trays from us and make sure they were stacked in an orderly manner. She did this because she said having it on her résumé would help get her into Harvard. A few days after Yvonne's confession, I handed my tray to Gwen at the end of lunch and whispered, "Ask Yvonne if she'll go with me." Gwen smiled broadly, nodding her head. Class resumed a short while later. I sat across from Yvonne wondering what her answer would be and if she had already provided one. For all I knew, we were already going together. I was anxious, but true to form, played it cool.

The next day, as I handed Gwen my lunch tray, she flashed that broad smile again and informed me Yvonne had agreed to go with me. It was official. The process of obtaining a girlfriend had unfolded seamlessly. When Ms. Anderson's class resumed after lunch, Yvonne and I made no mention of our romance. But both of us knew our hearts now belonged to each other. It was an exciting time, one that would require important decisions. After all, I knew there were only two things a girlfriend could become: an *ex*-girlfriend or a wife. When I'd attended fellow classmates Mike and Gloria's nuptials under the monkey bars a few weeks earlier, I never would have guessed that Yvonne and I might be next to tie the knot. I'd need to check to see if the monkey bars would be available in the near future for a possible upcoming wedding, just in case.

I was moving fast because, unfortunately, the only reference point I had when it came to personal relationships was the one between my mother and father. My American father met my Mexican mother while vacationing in la Ciudad de México. She was working the front desk at his hotel. Her English, while not perfect, was far better than my father's nonexistent Spanish. Apparently check-in went well, because my mother offered to be his tour guide. A few days later, my father proposed. Legend has it, my mother responded with, "Of course." So my parents were clearly out of their minds, but as a fifth grader I did not know that. It didn't help that my parents' love for each other, like their marriage, was unbreakable. This was the template I had to work with. You liked someone, you married them. End of story.

I was prepared to move fast, but maybe not as fast as my parents. Our engagement could wait a few weeks, rather than a few days. I thought it best for Yvonne and me to initially keep our relationship on the down low—to let us figure things out on our own without outside interference. Official announcements would be made at the appropriate time. But Yvonne had other plans. She told the world. The day after Gwen helped facilitate our commitment, Yvonne showed up to class wearing a badge that read I LOVE CARLOS. The badge made me feel self-conscious. Where did she get it? At the I Love Carlos store? And just *how* did she obtain it so quickly? She couldn't drive, to my knowledge. She must have told her parents she loved me and her parents then obviously said, "Okay, we'll take you to the mall and get you a badge."

This meant her parents knew about me and most likely were

expecting to meet me. Unless Yvonne had snuck out of the house and either ridden her bike or taken the bus or hailed a taxi or gotten someone's older sister to drive her, or, if her love was strong enough, she'd walked to the mall and bought the badge on her own, using funds from her allowance. Most likely, her parents were expecting me for dinner soon, along with *my* parents. The adults would shake hands, smile courteously at one another and say things such as, "We'll be getting to know each other pretty well, I'm sure."

I'd have to dress nicely. Yvonne's dad would sit me down in the living room and ask me all kinds of questions like, "Where do you see yourself in the next twenty years?" All of this made my head spin. I wasn't ready for a meet and greet with Yvonne's parents, nor did I want my own parents involved—which is why I didn't mention Yvonne to them. I certainly wasn't about to ask them to drive me to the mall so I could buy an I Love Yvonne badge.

There were other matters to address. Since Yvonne and I were now going together, it seemed logical that we should actually go somewhere together. Like on a date. Perhaps on a weekend or after school we could go to the mall. Maybe catch a G-rated flick or have an ice cream. Going on a date would be tricky, due to our mutual lack of driver's licenses. Again, the parents would need to get involved. My parents were not in the equation since I did not want to discuss my new girlfriend with them and answer all of their inevitable questions. I suppose I could have asked them to take me to the movies and suggested we pick Yvonne up on the way because it turned out she wanted to go to the movies on the same day and her parents were having car trouble, no big thing. Not a girlfriend, just ride sharing. But my folks would undoubtedly have gotten suspicious. On the ride over my mother would probably ask Yvonne, "Do you enjoy sewing? I like to sew. It would be nice to sew sweaters for my grandchildren someday." Too risky.

I had no desire to sit next to Yvonne's father in his truck (I pictured him driving a truck) as he took us to the movies, prodding me with more imaginary questions along the lines of, "What kind of grades do you get, son?" My grades were excellent—that was not a concern—but the thought of being interrogated by her father made my forehead sweat. For the time being, I decided the best course of action was to not bring up the subject of going on a date and hope Yvonne would stay mum about it as well. She did.

Besides the prospect of meeting her parents, the issue of physical contact also made my forehead temperature rise. Now that we were boyfriend and girlfriend, everyone probably expected us to hold hands and kiss and maybe Yvonne would even need to get on top of me during a game of kickball the way Mamie had. I was willing to consider hand holding after school for a few minutes when no one was looking. Anything beyond that was unreasonable. Kissing and sex were one and the same. At the tender age of ten, I didn't feel ready to raise a family. Between my father's talk and the scientist in the movie, I had somehow come to the conclusion that when people had sex, the girl *automatically* got pregnant. In all likelihood, couples began discussing baby names minutes after they were done rolling around in bed. You could determine the number of times a couple had had sex by the number of children they raised. If Yvonne and I had kids, they would need to live with my parents—at least part of the time—since I did not yet possess my own home or social security number. Living at home with my parents and my kids would be too much chaos. How would I ever be able to finish my schoolwork? Because kissing inevitably led to sex, kissing was off the table too.

Not wanting kids was an excuse, albeit legitimate. Truth be told, the thought of touching Yvonne terrified me.

If there were to be no public or private displays of affection, there were other actions I could take to show my feelings for Yvonne, and I took them. I could represent us as a couple, make her proud to be my girlfriend. Also, I could stand up for her should that become necessary. The standing up part I wasn't too keen on. Thankfully, I didn't have to do it often. A few days into our relationship, Yvonne dropped her pencil. As she reached down to pick it up, Tim suddenly began to laugh, gleefully proclaiming, "Yvonne's getting boobies! Her boobies are coming in. I just saw them down her shirt! Boobies! Boobies! Boobies!" Tim was borderline special needs. Yvonne clearly felt embarrassed about Tim's comment, as if she was being ridiculed. She looked to me and I realized I needed to say something. I turned to Tim and mustered as much fake anger as I could, demanding he shut up. Hopefully my show of force would be enough, as I had no desire to engage in physical combat with Tim or anyone else.

Gwen looked at Yvonne, observing, "Carlos is defending you." This pleased Yvonne, but upset me. Why did Gwen have to make a *thing* out of it? Tim did in fact shut his trap, but now that Gwen had opened hers, maybe Tim would start blabbering again, escalating the conflict. I wasn't a lover *or* a fighter. There was no way I was going to throw Tim on the floor and punch him in the nose just because he pointed out Yvonne's brand-new boobies. I saw Tim consider saying something else, but ultimately he remained silent, to my relief.

Stupidly, I seized the opportunity to warn him, "Yeah, you better not say anything else." Then I prayed he wouldn't. My prayers were answered. Yvonne flashed me another appreciative smile. She leaned over to grab a paper, flashing me more than just a smile in the process. I caught a glimpse of her alleged boobies. They scared me.

While defending Yvonne required backbone I barely had, making her proud was much easier. Ms. Anderson held a geography challenge in which our group of four went up against the other groups in pursuit of academic glory. I was chosen to stand at the front of the class, pitted against rival students, each of us representing our respective teams. When Ms. Anderson asked, "What is the only country in the world that is also a continent?" I was the first to yell out the correct answer. Australia! My team clapped and cheered, happy we'd won another meaningless gold star—giving us more meaningless gold stars on the meaningless gold-star chart than any other competitors. No doubt Gwen would be alerting the Harvard admissions board about this.

I didn't care what Gwen did, but I did take special notice of Yvonne, my one and only. She was glowing, nodding her head, clapping enthusiastically, as if to say, *That's Carlos. He's my boyfriend. I love him. You can tell by the badge I'm wearing.* It felt good to make Yvonne happy to be associated with me. Australia! What a glorious moment. I took a seat, staring at Yvonne. We smiled warmly at each other.

If we ended up getting married under the monkey bars, I imagined someday Yvonne and I would travel to Australia. I would need to get a job—perhaps as a paperboy or pizza maker. Probably by the time I was eighteen I'd have enough saved up. The two of us would fly in a private plane. When we got there, we would overlook Sydney Harbour. I would gaze into Yvonne's eyes and tell her, "Australia is the only country in the world that is also a continent. And also they spell *harbor* with a *u* here." We would laugh, remembering our youth. I would take Yvonne in my arms and hug her tightly, followed by a kiss on the cheek. We would smile affectionately in that moment and know waiting all those years as a married couple for our first kiss was worth it.

The next time I stood at the front of the class, competing against other students, my performance was not as magnificent. It was a spelling competition. Ms. Anderson would say a word and we were to spell it on the chalkboard. The first person done spelling the word correctly won the meaningless gold star. Just before Ms. Anderson spoke, I made the mistake of looking over at Yvonne. She was staring at me with her trademark pride, ready for me to blow away the competition once again. Suddenly I felt the weight of Yvonne's expectations. It made me feel off balance. Ms. Anderson loudly voiced the word *roofs*. Everyone got to spelling. I was the first to finish. In my rush, I spelled it *roffs*. Not realizing my mistake, I threw the chalk down and raised my arms triumphantly. But Yvonne did not give a proud nod to anyone. This time she laughed and uttered, "*Roffs.*" There were laughs from others, but Yvonne's laughter hurt the most. I sat down in embarrassment, my forehead again with the heat. Though I had made a fool of myself—and in front of Yvonne—she still gave me a pleasant smile. She thought my mistake was endearing. In the worst of times, Yvonne was still happy to be by my side. *Roffs.* How could I be so stupid?

As if working out the particulars of my relationship with Yvonne wasn't stressful enough, my father added an extra layer of pressure by making a momentous announcement. We were moving to San Diego. My dad was a Navy man, and as such he had been transferred. We would be moving a couple of hours down the freeway, from Anaheim to San Diego. A small, rustic suburb in eastern San Diego County known as Lakeside, to be exact. When I started the sixth grade, it would be at a new elementary school. Without the ability to drive, Lakeside might as well have been Mongolia. Damn the state of California's driving laws! Those laws had no compassion for young romance trying to blossom in this unfair world. Maybe I could take the train up to Anaheim on the weekends. I could imagine some stranger sitting next to me in a passenger car, asking if I was traveling to Anaheim for business or pleasure. I'd respond with a swagger, "Going to see my lady." (I pictured myself wearing a fedora while stating this.)

Living in Lakeside would undoubtedly place a heavy burden on Yvonne and myself. I wondered if we could survive a long-distance relationship. I also wondered what my new school was going to be like. Would the students there be friendly? And the girls? Would there perhaps be a girl who would try to steal me away from Yvonne? I didn't want to think about it. Yvonne didn't want to think about my impending move either. When I told her the news, she gave me a blank stare of uncertainty, finally nodding her head with a quiet "Okay." That was the most we discussed it. From there we went on with our daily lives, choosing to ignore the elephant in Ms. Anderson's room. Though the elephant was subconsciously trumpeting every day, reminding me: *Lakeside, Lakeside, Lakeside! You're going to Lakeside! I'm an elephant! I'm trumpeting! That's what elephants do!*

One afternoon it was announced all the boys in class would be given a second recess, while the girls would remain inside to watch a *very special* film. I assumed this *very special* film starred the scientist in the previous production. He was most likely going to instruct the girls how to wear bras. That's what I figured. I didn't really care that I was missing the movie; I was excited about a second recess. A second recess was unheard of. On the playground, we gathered for a game of dodgeball. It was one for the ages. Pumped by the adrenaline of an added recess, everyone played their hearts out. The ball went flying at record speeds. As I remained on the battlefield, I realized that when the ball was being thrown at me, it was no longer simply being thrown at *me*. Symbolically, it was being thrown at me *and Yvonne*, even though she was inside the classroom watching the scientist explain how to put a bra on. If I went down early, no doubt Yvonne would find out about it. The two of us would be judged by my poor athletic performance. With this in mind, I played with the ferocity of a warrior.

I was the last man standing on my team. At one point, I lost my footing and was not able to distance myself in time from Tim, my opponent. I was inches away from him. He could have gently tossed the ball against my leg and neutralized me. Instead, wanting to exert his masculinity after I had told him to shut up about Yvonne's boobies, he threw the ball at me as hard as he could. The ball drilled straight into my gut. And I caught it! I caught it for Yvonne. There was a roar of approval and admiration, acknowledging my display of invincibility. I went on to win the game single-handedly, a triumphant gladiator. My performance was epic, destined to become a part of our school's dodgeball lore. I couldn't wait to tell Yvonne.

Yvonne was not interested in my amazing victory. She looked downtrodden, defeated. All the girls did. They were downright pale. I could not understand what was so distressing about having to wear a bra. Maybe they hadn't watched a movie with the scientist after all. Judging by their expressions, they looked more as if they had been subjected to a screening of *Slumber Party Massacre*. In a way, they were. The *very special* film the girls had to watch starred their Aunt Flo. Had I known the actual subject matter of the film, I would have cried and fainted. Praise the Lord my dad did not include those details in his educational drawings.

The last day of school was soon approaching. My relationship with Yvonne had undeniably reached a plateau. There was only so much distance a couple could traverse wearing affectionate badges and catching dodgeballs in the name of love. Even if I hadn't been moving away, things had run their course. But *especially* because I was moving away, I knew the time had come to end things. There would be no monkey bar wedding. With only a week of school left, I handed my lunch tray to Gwen and soberly asked her to let Yvonne know we were no longer a couple. Gwen nodded, her expression glum.

Yvonne's I LOVE CARLOS badge was gone the next day. Enough said. Rumors abounded as to why things didn't work out. Yvonne and I never spoke directly of our downfall or how we could have salvaged things. (A vehicle would have helped.) We were cordial to each other during the final days of school, choosing to remember the good times like "Australia!" On the last day of school I thought about giving her a good-bye hug. But we were no longer boyfriend and girlfriend. This would have been scandalous. Instead I chose to protect her reputation with a friendly wave, telling her to have a good summer. She wished me luck next year at my new school. We were done. It was on to Lakeside.

Sixth grade was rough. I had a lot of trouble making friends at my dreadful new school. The student body was a cold, tight-knit group who had known one another since kindergarten and kept to themselves like the North Korean government. Nobody made any effort to be friendly. I wanted to tell these punks that where I came from, people wore I LOVE CARLOS badges. My mother would drop me off each morning. She could tell I was not a happy camper not only because of my facial expression and body language, but also because every morning I would tell her, "I hate this school—it sucks."

My mother would flash an encouraging smile, promising me things would get better. Then she would give me a kiss on the cheek and advise me not to forget my jacket because it was chilly outside, noting the temperature was in "the late fifties." Since moving to California from Mexico, my mother's English had improved significantly, but every now and then she'd lose her grasp of the language. (She was stunned the day she learned how the word *people* was spelled. "*Peh-oh-pleh?* You're kidding!")

Despite my mother's promises, things did not get better. Finding a pal was such a challenge that one morning, when my mother dropped me off, she got out of the car with me—much to my surprise and dismay—took my hand, led me to a pudgy, freckled boy sitting by himself at one of the lunch area picnic tables, and proceeded to make introductions by saying, "Hello, this is Carlos. I'm his mommy. Carlos doesn't have any friends. Would you be his friend?" I'm not sure whether my mother was genuinely trying to help me forge new friendships or, perhaps as a life lesson, trying to help me get my ass kicked. Whatever the case, with a slight nod, the pudgy, freckled boy agreed to be my friend, and for the whole rest of that school year . . . we never exchanged a single word. (The dude wasn't even in the sixth grade—he was a *fifth* grader. *Come on, Mom!*)

Since my parents were unable to help me find new human friends, they did the next best thing. They bought me five pet chickens. My parents purchased them at the local feed store. Initially, I was amused by the idea of having pet chickens. But when I looked into their eyes, I saw their souls. For the record, chickens are extraordinary beings. When they're not busy being fried or sautéed or barbecued, chickens are curious, daring, protective . . . the list of a chicken's admirable qualities goes on and on. One thing I learned firsthand, however, is that chickens are not *chicken*. They are tough, feathered mofos. While no one at my new school seemed interested in socializing, the chickens welcomed me with open wings. I was proud to be a part of their posse.

I got along famously with all five chickens, but my closest friend was the Gray Chicken. (None of the chickens had names— our bond transcended names.) The Gray Chicken was the alpha hen of the group. We would go for walks around the expansive backyard. She would follow me as I lifted rocks so she could gobble up whatever innocent pincher bugs and roly-polies were placidly living out their lives underneath. One day I lifted a rock and revealed a large scorpion. The Gray Chicken swooped in and gulped down the scorpion before I could stop her. I panicked, expecting her to cough up blood or explode. She didn't. Instead she calmly waited for me to lift the next rock so she could eat the next scorpion, as if it were a potato chip. Like *all* chickens, the Gray Chicken was a badass.

My friendship with the chickens made getting through the school day much easier. However many cold shoulders I received, I knew the chickens were waiting for me at home, ready for the next adventure. I would often put the Gray Chicken on my shoulder and pretend I was a pirate. She gladly played along. One time I brought the chicken inside the house, perched on my shoulder. My mother instructed me to take the chicken outside immediately because it was "giving her looks." Then the Gray Chicken promptly flew off my shoulder and landed squarely on my mother's head, digging its talons deep into her scalp while it comfortably preened its feathers. My mother began to whimper, asking for help. I laughed and laughed and laughed. How different life was in Lakeside! I went from popular dodgeball superstar to outcast chicken wrangler. If Yvonne could see me now. I wondered how sixth grade was treating her and if she ever thought about me.

After months of attending my new school, the students began to realize I wasn't going away. I formed begrudging acquaintanceships, getting to know my fellow classmates by name. As the fog of isolation began to clear, one classmate in particular emerged from the darkness. Jenny Gokenbach. Her name rolled off my tongue. She was by far the prettiest girl in school. One morning, as she walked into class, Jenny greeted me with a bright smile and cheerful hello. That was all it took. With this simple action, Jenny Gokenbach made me forget how much I disliked my new surroundings. This new school wasn't so bad after all. I forgot all about Yvonne. Yvonne who? All I wanted was Jenny Gokenbach.

The problem with liking Gokenbach was that every other guy in school liked her, too. I was the fresh fish, so my chances were slim to none. Since I didn't know her that well, I assumed pulling her hair to get her attention would not be effective. Besides, I was beginning to grow out of that phase. I was looking for more in a relationship. I was hoping to maybe put my arm around a girl. My chosen tactic was to be the silent, mysterious type. In class, I was lucky enough to sit near Jenny. Hoping to draw her in, I would dreamily look out the window in a daze. The plan was for her to wonder what I was thinking. What made me so special and different? She'd have to talk to me to find out. The plan didn't work. It was a stupid plan. A lot of pointless staring out the window. I kept my crush on Jenny Gokenbach a secret, telling no one. No one that is, except my only true friends—the chickens. As I fed them scratch inside their coop, I quietly informed them, "Hey, chickens. I have a crush on Jenny Gokenbach." It felt good to get it out in the open. The chickens would look at me wide-eyed and tilt their heads in fascination. Either they wished they could help, or they wondered if what I was saying had anything to do with food.

Not long after Jenny's watershed hello, I wound up standing beside her during recess while we waited our turn to play handball. No one played my favorite game of dodgeball at this school, because they were losers. I regally stood beside Jenny, hoping she would turn and talk to me—at least bestow me with one of her rapturous *hello*s. (There had been no additional hellos since the first one, but I kept hope alive.) Jenny was caught up in a conversation with a girlfriend of hers. At one point she confided to her girlfriend, "I like Jimmy." Then she gasped and turned to me, as if realizing I was standing there for the first time. She was mortified by the fact that I had overheard which boy she had her eye on. I didn't know Jimmy personally. I knew he was one of the more popular dudes on campus and that he was a lucky guy. Jenny asked me—pleaded with me—not to tell Jimmy or anyone else. I promised her I wouldn't.

That afternoon, I arrived home in a morose mood. Jenny Gokenbach didn't like me. I was so forlorn, I wrote a song about this in my head. The song was entitled "Precious Secrets," sung to the tune of any ballad performed by Sting. My lyrics were simple. They were: "Precious see-crets . . . precious see-crets." That was it. I sang this over and over to the chickens. I was being serious. The chickens looked at me wide-eyed, tilting their heads in fascination. Either they wished they could help, or they wondered if what I was singing had anything to do with food.

I kept Jenny Gokenbach's secret a closely guarded one, but Jenny leaked it herself. Consequently, Jenny and this Jimmy character ended up becoming an item. It crushed me to see them together. I had been right about my new school the first time. It was a prison camp. While fifth grade brought me my first girlfriend, sixth grade delivered my first heartache. What an emotional roller coaster women were. I had experienced the soaring heights of Yvonne's exclaiming that she liked me, only to sink to the depths of despair with this Jenny Goken-bach disaster. It didn't seem fair, liking someone who didn't like me. What kind of ridiculous system was that? Was this common? Did people often fall for others who didn't feel the same way? I couldn't imagine *more* girls besides Jenny Gokenbach not liking me. That would be terrible. Jenny's lack of interest was bad enough.

If pursuing girls meant sometimes failing, I was going to have to reevaluate who I became attracted to. It would be helpful if the post office could deliver a list of females who liked me or *would* like me in the event we met, and also the post office would need to include the addresses of these women, otherwise the list would be useless. That would be much better than continuously having to mend a broken heart. The one Jenny Gokenbach was responsible for felt like getting run over by a lawn mower—not a push reel mower, a riding lawn mower a person could drive along a golf course or to a liquor store. No more broken hearts for me. No, sir. Or so I thought. Jenny Gokenbach was merely a false alarm. True heartache would not arrive until senior year of high school. When it did, I would know what it felt like to be run over by a steamroller—not a steam-roller used to give a girl's hair more volume, a steamroller used in heavy construction. To flatten highways.

MY FIRST PROM

Senior year of high school, I was in love. With Isabelle Cambria. *Isabelle Cambria. Mmm.* We were a beautiful couple. Isabelle was unaware of this. We were not together. Still, I was positive Isabelle was the only woman in the universe for me. I had developed bumbling, unfulfilled crushes on other girls in junior high and my earlier high school years. But by senior year, Isabelle was it. My search was over. I would never be interested in another girl no matter how strong her feminine wiles. Granted, I was seventeen, and lacked a few life experiences here and there, but I knew. The first week of school when I discovered Isabelle's locker was next to mine, I knew immediately I wanted to spend the rest of my life with her. I wanted to share my most intimate secrets with Isabelle, visit far-off exotic locales with her, give her hot-oil massages—but not too hot. The reason I knew Isabelle would be an ideal lifelong partner was because she had perfect breasts. What more could a guy want?

Besides our adjacent lockers, Isabelle and I were in two classes together. In one of those classes, Ms. Miller's economics class, Isabelle sat next to me. I spent most of the hour whispering sweet nothings to her, such as "Can I borrow a pen?" or "Do you have some gum?" There was no doubt being born during the same time period, living in the same city of all the cities on Earth—these were cosmic forces at work. Even though Isabelle never acknowledged it, we were drawn to each other like moths to a flame, only we didn't burn to death.

One afternoon, as I was shoving some school books into my locker, Isabelle walked up behind me, pushed her enticing pelvis in my direction, pressed her enchanting bosom against my back, wrapped her delicious arms around me, and rested her perfect chin on my shoulder, purring, "You're in my way." I wanted to buy a house for us right then and there.

Remaining true to my modus operandi, I intentionally played it cool around Isabelle, keeping my emotions in check, not wanting to seem too eager and consequently scare her away. I figured if I brought up marriage and children as we walked to class, she would run. Leaving talk of our family for another occasion, I decided to take things slow and first casually ask Isabelle to be my prom date. She laughed, hard, when she heard this. "It's only March. Prom isn't until June," she pointed out.

"Has somebody already asked you?" This was my greatest concern and the very reason I chose the month of March. I wanted to make sure to get ahead of the pack.

Again, she laughed, even though we were discussing serious business. "No. Nobody's asked me. Nobody's asked anybody. It's *March*." We were sitting in her car in the school parking lot at the end of the day. This was the first time I had ever asked Isabelle out, so it *was* kind of peculiar, asking if she wanted to go on a date with me three months in advance. But it had to be done—first dibs. In my mind, priority went to the boy who asked the girl first, not the one she liked. Essentially I was officially confirming I had more than a passing interest in her; I was officially placing my heart on the chopping block. I was sure she already knew. There were a number of subtle hints she'd probably picked up on.

Shortly after the school year began, we were assigned a group project in economics class in which four students had to work together and create a business plan. Isabelle was in my group. Ms. Miller, pimp daddy that she was, instructed each of the four group members to exchange phone numbers. When I heard this, my eyes lit up, I inhaled sharply with excitement, and grinned widely. I was about to get Isabelle's phone number, without even asking for it! Isabelle noticed my exuberance—I did not corral it in time. She flashed a knowing, amused smile. I explained to her I was really excited about the class assignment; it sounded like a terrific assignment—I had tackled plenty of assignments in my day and I could tell this was a doozy. Isabelle nodded, a perceptive smile still on her face. "Mm-hmm," she sarcastically murmured as she handed me her phone number. It was written with sensual penmanship, a small heart drawn above the *I* in Isabelle. The *I* was capitalized. She had to *want* to put a heart over it.

When I got home, I immediately threw the other group members' phone numbers away and placed Isabelle's number securely under my pillow. I even called her that weekend—not to discuss our economics project, but to see if she was interested in a movie or a hike—a bold move, to be sure. But I was a bold guy. As Isabelle's phone rang, I felt a panic attack coming on. I kept the ship steady, though. When an older woman answered the phone, her mother I presumed, I somehow managed to ask if Isabelle was home.

"No, she isn't. Not at the moment," her mother informed me. She sounded nice.

"Okay," I said, and hung up. That was literally a close call. What if Isabelle *had* been there? Then I would have had to talk to her, ask her out, and then she would have known *for sure* that I liked her. What was I thinking?

The tipping point finally came in March. It was the point at which my desire for Isabelle outweighed my fear of telling her about it. That is why I had walked Isabelle to her car at the end of the day, taken a seat inside, asked her to be my prom date, and was now anxiously awaiting a joyful yes or a disheartening no. I was confident there was a chance Isabelle liked me too. She had thrown her fair share of subtle hints my way as well, such as laughing at my dumb jokes—especially if I told one while tickling her. There was also the close, physical proximity at our lockers, not to mention the dotting of the *I* in her name with a heart—that was huge. Based on that alone I thought the odds of Isabelle agreeing to be my prom date were fairly strong.

After shaking her head and repeating numerous times that it was only March, Isabelle placed her hand on mine and said, "I have to think about it." Not the answer I was expecting, but still, much better than a flat-out no. She patted my hand as if I were a child. It was time for me to go. I smiled pathetically, got out of the car, and stood there for a bit, thinking Isabelle was perhaps considering whether or not to attend prom with me and would let me know momentarily. When she drove away, I determined she needed a little more time to decide. Standing in the parking lot, watching her sleek red compact sedan disappear in the distance, I hoped for a positive outcome.

There is a famous episode of the classic television show *The Twilight Zone* in which a young boy with special powers holds his family hostage. The family caters to his every whim for fear of incurring the wrath of his telepathic dominance. This is what became of my relationship with Isabelle once I asked her to the prom. She now had the ability to destroy me. I walked on eggshells around her, not wanting to upset Isabelle in any way as she contemplated going to prom with me, afraid she might turn me down. Every once in a while, with hesitance, I would bring up the big dance. She would dismissively let me know she was still thinking, and I would respond with a quick "Great" or "Cool" or "No problem," which actually meant, "I'm dying, you're killing me, this is Hell." It was agony, the waiting. But it only made me want her more. While she made up her mind, I did not ask her to go out on any additional dates. I didn't want to rock the boat or overwhelm her. She obviously already had a lot on her plate.

March rolled into April, April rolled into May, May rolled into June. Isabelle was still thinking. By this time, all of my friends had prom dates. All of my friends knew I was waiting on Isabelle. Even though I hesitated to bring the prom up to Isabelle, I talked about the predicament all the time with my friends, family, and whoever else would listen—including random customers in the Hardware Department at Sears, where I worked. I told anyone within earshot of my troubles, whether they were interested or not (some people just wanted to buy a hammer).

One person always happy to lend a helpful ear was my colleague

Valerie. Valerie sold blenders and such in the Housewares Department at Sears, located just across the aisle from Hardware. This was the ideal department for her. She was a blond girl-next-door type with a sunny disposition. I'd known her before my stint at Sears because Valerie attended my high school freshman year until she transferred to a rival school. Whenever I would come in to work, Valerie would ask, "Did you hear back from Isabelle yet?" Eventually, Valerie didn't bother to ask. She would just look at me and I would shake my head. Then Valerie would shake hers, in solidarity.

A week before prom, I still did not know if I had a date. By now, people were divided into two camps in their views of Isabelle Cambria. There were the people who thought Isabelle Cambria was trash, and then there was me. One of my closest high school friends, Chuck Lundy, did not approve of Isabelle's behavior at all. Chuck was super easygoing. He usually approved of everybody. After a lengthy lesson on gravity, Chuck once famously asked our tightly wound physics teacher if people in public restrooms were supposed to rip the middle part of public toilet seat covers by hand or to let their crap drop out and have the paper tear that way? He was a valued friend. I listened intently when he told me, "It's like you've stumbled onto this pile of garbage and for some reason you're really happy about it. You're stepping in it on purpose, and then you're rubbing your hands in it, and then you're rolling around on the ground in it. Isabelle is the pile of garbage, by the way."

I respectfully disagreed with Chuck. Yes, it would have been nice if Isabelle had given me an answer two or three days, weeks, or months earlier, but I felt we still had a special rapport. I didn't want to go to prom with anybody else, so however long Isabelle took didn't matter—aside from the fact that with each passing day, another piece of my heart was chipped away. No big deal. I could sort of take it. Plus, Isabelle and I were the only ones who didn't have dates, as far as I knew. Who else would Isabelle go with at this point? Somebody who wasn't from our high school? That would be crazy.

There *were* the practical matters that needed to be addressed. If I was going to the prom, I'd need a tuxedo. One would have to be rented and fitted in time. I also needed to tell my group of friends if I was joining them for dinner, with my date, so they could have an accurate head count for a reservation. And I was pretty sure I'd have to bring flowers or something for my date. It was these considerations that led me to seek an answer from Isabelle once and for all.

I walked Isabelle to her car at the end of the day, as I had when I first asked her to prom so long ago, when I was younger. In a gentle tone of voice, I nudged her. "Isabelle, I don't mean to rush you, but I kind of need to know if you're going to prom with me. There's all the stuff I need to do to get ready, if I'm going. I mean it's not even really me asking. It's my friend Chuck. Chuck wants to know. He's organizing things. He hopes you're coming with me; he's a fan of yours. He wants to know, for the restaurant and the limo and things like that. I don't mean to pressure you. Sorry. I'm just kind of passing Chuck's questions along. He's the one who's really wondering."

Isabelle's facial expression was impossible to decipher. Either she was about to give me an answer, she was going to laugh, or she had indigestion. Suddenly, she took a deep breath. A verdict was imminent. She stared intensely and said, "I'll tell you tonight at Air Band." More waiting. But there was now a light at the end of this never-ending tunnel. I nodded. Tonight at Air Band.

Air Band was a show students put on each year in the high school auditorium. It was always well attended. At Air Band, people would dress up like popular singers and lip-synch to a chart-topping song. I had secretly flirted with turning in a performance for Air Band. At the beginning of the year, I gave significant thought to buying some flashy clothes, a wig, and shoes with knee-high heels at the local thrift store and portraying James Brown, lip-synching to his signature piece, "I Got You (I Feel Good)." If I had decided to go through with it, I would have given it my all. I'd work just as hard on my dance routine as I did on my studies, which would shock the community at large and probably make the local news—considering I wasn't known for dancing, nor was I known for walking fast or breathing fast. I would have blown the roof off of that auditorium. It would have been awesome. But it was not to be. I'd decided against tackling the role of James Brown due to the uncertainty of the Isabelle Cambria situation. I would not have been able to concentrate onstage, wondering the whole time whether she was going to prom with me.

Air Band was packed. I went by myself, but quickly found Chuck and a few other friends in the audience. Isabelle was nowhere to be seen. Hoping to run into her, I told my friends I was going to walk around the auditorium for a bit. The show itself was very good. Fellow senior Erik Wren and company performed a memorable version of Van Halen's "Hot for Teacher," which Erik was—for his Spanish teacher, Mrs. Flores. Who could blame him? Erik was great as David Lee Roth with his crazy wig and his jumping off the desk and chair. Even so, I could have taken him as James Brown.

Isabelle found me by the drinking fountain during intermission. She looked somber when she greeted me. I asked her if she was enjoying the show. She said she was; she especially liked Erik's performance of "Hot for Teacher." I agreed he was good, thinking of how much better I would have been as James Brown. There was a heavy silence between us. Isabelle broke it by informing me, "I can't go to prom with you. I'm sorry."

I knew this had always been a possibility, but now that the possibility became reality, I had no idea what to say. With a courteous nod, I settled on, "Okay, well, thanks for letting me know."

"It's my parents," she explained. "My parents. And my church. We belong to a really strict church. There's been all these rules I've had to deal with ever since I can remember. My parents won't let me go to prom with you. Or on any kind of date. I'm really sorry."

I asked Isabelle how long she had been a member of this strict church. She told me her entire life. I ran the numbers through my head. I wasn't the greatest at math, but according to my calculations . . . last March—when I initially asked her to be my prom date—that time frame fit within the span of her entire life. Technically, she could have provided this information two seconds after I asked her to prom and saved me months of hanging on tenterhooks. I was too disappointed to argue, so I didn't bring up this minor detail. Instead, I grasped at straws. "What if I went to some of your church services?" I suggested. "I wouldn't join, but just to show your parents, you know, respect, and that I'm a good person, I'd be willing to maybe sing in the choir on Sunday. I'll put on a robe, shake a tambourine, and sing *Jesus! Jesus! Jesus!* Would that work?"

She gave me a weak smile and shook her head. That would not work. I double-checked that we could not even go out on a regular date. No, we could not. So even just a casual dinner, just the two of us, on prom night somewhere else, was out of the question? Yes, it was. I accepted my fate, advising her, "On prom night, when you're at home watching television, think about me. I'll be at home too. Maybe we could even watch the same television show. What show do—"

Isabelle stopped me. "You have to go to prom. That way we can see each other."

"Say what?"

"I'm going to prom. My parents are letting me go. Just not with *you*. I'll be going with a boy from my church. You have to go too. I want to see you in a tuxedo. Please go." She squeezed my arm affectionately and walked away.

I feel good! blasted through my mind, mocking me. James Brown was mocking me. I definitely would not have been able to pull his song off this night. But I could have performed a kick-ass rendition of any Megadeth, Iron Maiden, or Black Sabbath song. Any of those. I would have amazed people with an Ozzy Osbourne performance and gladly would have bitten the head off of any real bat, like Mr. Osbourne himself supposedly once did. Forget bats. I could have bitten the head off of a pterodactyl right then. Stupid pterodactyls. What a bunch of idiots.

When I returned home from Air Band, my mother sensed my profound disappointment. "Cheer up," she said. Like everyone else, she knew of my yearning to be Isabelle's prom date. She consoled me with an understanding hug, aware by my sullen expression that I had finally received an unhappy answer. "It's okay. Everything will be okay. How about this? Why don't you invite all of your friends over for a nice dinner? I'll set up a buffet for them in the dining room." Somehow my mother thought a homemade buffet would make up for losing the girl of my dreams. A buffet sponsored by my mother. I know she wasn't intentionally trying to socially assassinate me. Still, I needed to keep an eye on her lest she rope me into the kind of embarrassing situation that might scar me for life.

The next night, I went to work at Sears and saw Valerie in

Housewares. She gave me a look, wondering what the latest was. I shook my head, a little more slowly than usual. Valerie was surprised, "Still? She *still* hasn't told you? Isn't your prom in a couple of days?"

I reported my breaking news. "I'm not shaking my head this time because I don't know Isabelle's answer. I'm shaking my head because *this* is Isabelle's answer." I shook my head one more time for dramatic effect.

Valerie brightened upon hearing this. It seemed as if she was trying to hold back a smile when she asked, "She said no?" I confirmed, she said no. "I'm sorry to hear that. I know you really wanted to go with her. When did she tell you?"

"At our high school's Air Band show."

Valerie nodded. "That's right. You guys had Air Band last night. I heard Erik Wren performed an awesome Van Halen."

"Whatever." Perhaps I was a little rude to Valerie, but whatever.

Valerie didn't make any effort to return to her register in the Housewares Department. She stayed with me in Hardware and asked, "So, who are you going to take to prom then?" I told her now that Isabelle had run my heart through a meat grinder, I wasn't planning to go. "That's sad," she commented. Even if I wanted to go, I explained, everyone had dates now—including Isabelle. There wasn't anyone available for me to take, and I wouldn't want to go stag. That would be even sadder. "I'm sure you can find *someone* who's still available," Valerie encouraged, while batting her eyes. A girl had never genuinely batted her eyes at me before. This was a first. It appeared Valerie was offering to be my prom date. Testing this hypothesis, as a knee-jerk reaction, I asked if she would like to go with me. Valerie brightened again, and immediately—as in *as soon as I asked the question*—replied, "Yes! If you want me to." So this is how it normally worked when asking a girl to prom. Interesting.

I smiled at Valerie and said, "Let's go then."

My tuxedo felt weird. It was uncomfortable and abnormal, wearing these threads. I felt like an astronaut, or a bullfighter. But this was the costume for the evening, so I tolerated it. I went to pick up Valerie with Chuck, who was dressed like a butler. The plan was to pick up Valerie and then pick up Chuck's date, my former elementary school infatuation, Jenny Gokenbach, before heading to prom. When we arrived at Valerie's house, I was greeted by a gruff-looking man in an oily T-shirt working on a motorcycle in his front yard. He was Valerie's dad. Her dad was not friendly, but not mean—he had just the right amount of distaste for me. He told me Valerie would be out in a few minutes.

When Valerie came out, I thought there had been some kind of mistake. I didn't recognize her. She was stunning. Her blond hair was stylish, her makeup worthy of a magazine cover, and the tight-fitting white gown she wore revealed curves I had not been aware of. For a second I thought maybe I was at the wrong house. This could not possibly be the average girl who worked in the Housewares Department. She was smiling at me, walking toward me, so she had to have been. Chuck spoke first, saying, "You look beautiful, Valerie."

I followed that up with, "Uh-huh." Then we got in the car and went to pick up Jenny Gokenbach.

Jenny Gokenbach also looked ravishing. I wondered why girls didn't walk around like they were going to the Academy Awards all the time. As I greeted Jenny, I remembered sixth grade. How I'd longed for her back then, to the point of serenading my five pet chickens (two of which were still alive) with ballads of my unrequited love for her. Now she was just a friend. Someone else had me under her spell—a spell far more powerful and devastating than anything I had experienced in sixth grade.

Jenny and Valerie were happy to see each other, remembering the freshman year Valerie spent at our school. Valerie was very excited, looking forward to the evening ahead. She was especially looking forward to seeing her friend Debra and catching up with her. When I heard this, I made a face as if I had just swallowed a glass of rotten prune juice. Valerie noticed this and asked if there was a problem. "Kind of," I told her. "Could you maybe *not* spend time with Debra? Debra is really good friends with Isabelle Cambría. If we hang out with Debra, we have to hang out with Isabelle and her . . . date. I don't really feel like—"

Valerie raised a hand and interrupted. "Don't worry. I get it." She flashed a reassuring smile.

We met up with a large group of friends at a fancy restaurant on the San Diego coast. It was the kind of restaurant one would expect to host prom dinners. The food was all right, as was the conversation. Valerie got along well with everyone at the table. I put my most cheerful face on, trying to suppress any thoughts of Isabelle. But it was difficult. She was with her date, somewhere, at the same time. I knew she was extremely religious, but I couldn't help but imagine she was having sex with her prom date at this very moment. Everyone knew the more religious a person, the freakier they were in bed. Her date had probably rented a hotel room in advance. They were there, in the shower. I aggressively broke a bread stick in half at the dinner table. Valerie placed a gentle hand on my back and asked if I was all right. "Great, great," I told her in a positive tone of voice. The check came and everyone threw in the money our parents had given us. We amassed a large mound of crumpled dollar bills and left it that way for the waiter because we were zany teenagers. As we walked out of the restaurant, I made a mental note to one day tell my future children about this crumpled mass of cash. I'd say, *"That's how crazy we were back then."*

Our prom was held in the ballroom of a luxurious hotel overlooking the San Diego Bay. It was a good spot, though being here made me feel uneasy. As we walked into the ballroom, my eyes scanned the area, searching for her. She was hidden, the same way she had been at Air Band. Isabelle was a true fox, only seen when she wanted to be seen. I did spot a classmate named Linda, who stormed out of the ballroom in tears, loudly exclaiming, "This is the worst night of my life!" I half expected to be doing the same thing a little bit later, but so far so good. Valerie and I joined more friends at the prom and all of us appreciated how magnificent we looked. We steered clear of Debra, as requested.

I socialized, posed for casual and later formal pictures, enjoyed appetizers and sodas. I even did a little mechanical dancing. Not my specialty, but I did it. My friends were happy to have my company. They welcomed Valerie with open arms. I was beginning to have a genuinely good time. Isabelle must have sensed this, because that is when she finally appeared. I saw her across the ballroom. She looked incredible, her arm on the guy she'd had sex with in a sauna before arriving. The guy was tall, athletic, and well groomed. I could tell by his dapper tuxedo and shiny shoes he was a scumbag. Isabelle and her date were chatting with Debra and Debra's date. Everybody was laughing and smiling, except for me. Isabelle didn't see me; at least she wasn't looking at me. I turned away and forced myself to focus on my own group.

Even without seeing Isabelle, I sensed her presence. It forced me to recalibrate. I was here to have a good time, damn it. And I was determined to do just that. Everything was going smoothly until Valerie left to visit the ladies' room. For a moment, I found myself standing on the edge of the dance floor, alone. My eyes reluctantly drifted back to Isabelle, as they would to a car accident. I had to look. She was with her man, but she was focused my way. Leaning into her date, she quickly said something to him, and began walking over to me.

My body went on red alert. I heard internal sirens. *Mayday! Mayday! Isabelle Cambria is headed toward us. Repeat: Isabelle Cambria, headed toward us.* I gave my eyes the order to look away, my feet to run. But they did no such thing. Then there she was, right in front of me with a bittersweet smile. She tenderly adjusted my necktie and drew closer. As her soft cheek caressed my own, I heard her whisper, "You look very handsome."

"Thanks," I replied in a barely audible, shaky voice. Then she walked back over to him.

Valerie returned on cue. She told me she was thirsty. I took the opportunity to go get us more drinks, and collect myself in the process. The sodas seemed to be taking an absurdly long time. I sulked at the bar, still reeling from my close encounter with Isabelle. The drinks finally arrived. I grabbed them, turned around and headed toward Valerie. She'd disappeared for a second, but then I found her. There she was, sitting at a table with Isabelle, just the two of them, in a gabfest. Very good, very nice. I decided to wait at the bar for Valerie to make her way back to me. As I sat at the bar, I took a good, long look at Valerie and Isabelle, making sure it was indeed Valerie. Maybe it was a clone? Maybe she had a twin sister who coincidentally was someone else's date tonight? I studied her outfit. It was definitely Valerie, definitely shooting the breeze with Isabelle. I guess earlier when I'd mentioned I didn't want to hang out with Isabelle, and Valerie told me, "Don't worry. I get it," that actually meant, "I will be sure to find Isabelle when she is sitting by herself at a table and I will talk to her at great length as if we are best friends forever." That was cool. The bar was comfortable enough.

After a while, Valerie joined me at the bar. She was in a good mood. "Got our drinks?" she asked, as she helped herself to one. I didn't ask, she didn't tell. We went on with the evening as if nothing happened. The last time I saw Isabelle that night, she was leaving with her date to go have more sex in the hotel swimming pool. As she reached the exit of the ballroom, she stopped, turned, and gazed at me. She had a strange look on her face. Perhaps regret? Maybe she was just mirroring my own expression. She finally looked away and left with the scumbag. If I were to say anything to that guy, I would have said, "I asked her in *March*, creep."

Valerie and I left a short while later. We made a brief appearance at a mild hotel after-party and then decided to call it a night. Valerie was asleep when we got to her house. I woke her up. She gave me a car hug. I kissed her on the cheek, thanked her for being a wonderful prom date, which she had been—except for when she bonded with Isabelle, but minor blip—and told her I would see her at work. I did not make a move on her. Shattered though it was, my heart belonged to another girl, a girl undoubtedly having crazy, nasty sex in the back of her date's car. For me, prom was in the books.

The following Monday, as I was walking to my physics class, I noticed someone walking beside me. It was Isabelle. I didn't normally run into her this time of day. The emotional roller coaster she'd placed me on was so draining, when I saw her, I instantly felt fatigued. I gave her a courteous hello and asked if she'd had a good time at prom.

"Prom was wonderful," she cooed. They'd definitely had sex all night long on a trampoline. "My favorite part was talking to your date."

"Oh really? What did you guys talk about?" I asked.

Isabelle took a deep breath, as if she had a lot on her mind. "She told me what a bitch I was. That I was completely selfish and self-centered for stringing you along the way I did. She said that I didn't deserve you, and that I needed to learn how to treat people with respect. That basically I was a really bad person." In an accusatory tone, Isabelle ended with, "I wonder who told her to say all those things."

It was impressive. Prior to this, I'd thought Isabelle had brought me down as low as I could go. But hearing this made me feel as if I had passed the Earth's core on my way to China. I was quick to clear my name, or attempt to. "I did not tell her to say any of that. I had no idea that's what she said. As a matter of fact, I specifically told her to stay away from you."

Isabelle gave me a self-righteous "Mm-hmm." She did not believe me. Once again, I was her puppet. I followed her to her class on my knees, begging and pleading for her to hear me out.

As she walked into her class, I implored her to stop. "Please, Isabelle, let's talk about this. I'll do whatever you want if you just talk to me. I'll buy you jewelry. I'll paint your nails. I'll wait in line for you at the DMV. Please."

"Your date said enough for you," she responded. Then she

slammed the classroom door in my face. Right in my face. Here I was trying to clear the air, trying to show her how I really felt because I cared so much about her, and she was making me eat a door. The door tasted like anger. I was so mad, I decided to do what any self-respecting high school student would do when he was angry with someone—I decided to stop talking to her.

There were only a couple of weeks left before the school year ended, before high school ended. It would be easy enough to freeze Isabelle out. In Ms. Miller's class, the class where we sat next to each other, I was very good about not turning my head in her direction. I used two techniques. One, I imagined I had been in a severe car accident and was wearing an invisible neck brace that made it impossible for me to move. Secondly, I told myself that if I looked at Isabelle, I would turn into salt. I don't know how she reacted to my boycott of her existence because I never saw her. Who wants to turn into salt?

The first intimation my actions were having some sort of effect came a few days after they were implemented. Ms. Miller decided to devote the entire hour to having students sign one another's yearbooks, which had just come out that day. There was a huge pile of yearbooks on my desk; demand for a written note from me was high. Imagine if I had performed as James Brown at Air Band; then requests for me to sign people's yearbooks would have tripled. It was probably for the best I hadn't gotten onstage as James Brown. I'd never have been able to live down that glory. I would be like a former high school quarterback who never stopped reliving that one spectacular touchdown pass. Only instead of a touchdown pass I'd be reliving the time the spotlight turned on and there I was, dressed as the hardest-working man in show business, with the crowd going wild.

As I continued to write in people's yearbooks, someone lifted the other yearbooks on my desk and placed her own yearbook underneath. It was Isabelle. When I got to hers, without signing my name, I simply wrote: *Next time someone shows an interest in you, and you cannot reciprocate, let them know right away.* I was pleased with my use of the word *reciprocate.* The school bell rang and I was off like a prom dress, still refusing to look at Isabelle.

Later that day, when I was home, the doorbell rang. I was the only one home and wondered who it could be. It was Isabelle. She appeared distraught and tired. But still gorgeous. Her presence made me tremble. "What are you doing here?" I asked, reining in my emotions. Isabelle began to cry. She couldn't take my ignoring her. She said she was sorry for the way she'd treated me and really, truly wanted to go to prom with me. Those three months I waited for an answer she had spent trying to convince her parents to let her be my date. In between sobs she told me she'd had a miserable time at prom with that guy and was even more miserable seeing me with another girl. She said she loved me.

This was uncharted territory. It seemed as if I had the power here. I wasn't sure what to do. I'd spent the vast majority of senior year pining for this girl, dreaming of this girl, clamoring for her attention. She destroyed me. And now here she was in the doorway, in tears, begging me to forgive her. Not having had an experience like this before, I couldn't confirm it, but I had a feeling that perhaps . . . I was a stud? How had this happened? It almost felt like I had been promoted. Now that I had been elevated to the rank of stud, did this mean I was *forever* a stud? From here on out, would any and all future dealings with ladies be conducted with the confidence and expertise of an official stud? (No.) First things first, as a stud, what was I supposed to do in my present situation? Having no other experiences to fall back on, I thought of what might occur in the movies.

I took Isabelle in my arms. We kissed passionately. It was straight out of a Hollywood romance. Except it would have been better under the moonlight, during a rainstorm, with stirring violins in the background. We kissed in the afternoon. It was hot. The loud twang of country music was playing out of somebody's garage down the street. I had not yet mastered the art of kissing. My tongue flopped around in Isabelle's mouth like a fish out of water. Her face was messed up from all the crying; there was a little bit of snot coming out of her nose. We did our best, continuing to embrace and kiss in the doorway. Isabelle told me our relationship would have to be kept secret. If her father found out about us, he would shoot me with his shotgun. She couldn't stress enough that this was not an exaggeration—her father *really* had a shotgun, and he *really* would shoot me with it. I was moved by her warning. Isabelle cared so much about me, she was willing to risk my own life. I told her not to worry. It would take more than a shotgun blast to keep me away from her, which was a nonsensical statement, but that's what I said.

That summer, we saw each other sparingly, whenever Isabelle could sneak away from her parents. We met up at locations that were quite a distance from our own homes, at restaurants or movie theaters where the love police wouldn't spot us. Even outside the city limits we couldn't hold hands or kiss or show any affection toward each other. Isabelle was too afraid of getting caught. We were fugitives is what we were. I felt like a dog that has a treat placed on his nose and patiently waits for the okay to eat the treat. Only I never got the okay, not in public anyway. There was one three-day weekend when her family went out of town to visit relatives in Nevada. Isabelle stayed behind, pretending to feel ill. We spent that weekend at her house. I saw her father's guns with my own eyes. It was a glorious, yet terrifying weekend.

In September, I moved to Los Angeles and started college. Isabelle and I exchanged lovelorn letters. She gave me some bizarro address to send them to, some sort of nursing home where she volunteered, somewhere her parents couldn't discover them. About a month after I moved to Los Angeles, I received a letter from Isabelle letting me know she had finally told someone about us. She could not keep the secret to herself any longer, so she told her best friend, Margo. Margo was a member of their strict church. When Margo heard what was going on, she declared that Isabelle was spiritually sick. If we didn't end things, Margo would tell Isabelle's parents as well as the church leaders. Isabelle would be disowned by her family, kicked out of the house, and banished from the church—all because she went to the movies with me. Isabelle's letter was not a breakup letter. She was just letting me know how things were going. I read the letter several times and concluded things were going badly for her. It was my fault. I'd never considered myself to be the root of all evil, the cause of someone having to suffer eternal damnation on account of sharing a sandwich with me, but I guess I was. You learn something new about yourself every day.

Isabelle and I were on very different paths. We could never stay together. I realized our "love" was a teenage love, not strong enough to survive the light of day. The consequences Isabelle faced just for keeping in contact with me were irrevocable. As difficult as it would be, I knew going our separate ways was for the best. We could cherish what memories we had. For instance prom, we would always have prom—except not really. But the summer we spent together, I would look back on it fondly. It was time to move on, for both of our sakes. This is what I informed Isabelle in the letter I wrote back. With the heaviest of hearts, I sluggishly marched to a campus mailbox. I stood in front of the mailbox, staring at it, hesitating to put my letter inside. If I sent the letter, would I get a response? Would I ever see or hear from Isabelle again? I did care about her very much and wished her well. I always would. Taking a deep breath, I placed the letter in the mailbox. With the loud clang of the mailbox closing, the Isabelle chapter came to an end.

MARCIA NADEL

Doing my best to forget about girlfriends past, or rather girlfriend, I focused on college life. For many people, college is an opportunity to become more independent, to gain greater social confidence, and to expand one's horizons both intellectually and, more important, sexually. For me, college was like high school except I had to do my own laundry and there was a guy in my dorm cell always sitting in front of his computer. I didn't want it to be that way, but apparently the University of Southern California did. For starters, I was assigned to live in Trojan Hall, which sounded more tantalizing than it was. It was not a dorm in which Trojan condoms were being utilized around the clock. I wish. From what I heard, that dorm was actually Pardee Tower, a dorm that *was* appropriately named. Trojan Hall was the dorm for smart students, otherwise known as nerds. I have no idea how I got mixed in with this crowd, other than that I was valedictorian of my high school. Punished, for being valedictorian. As if cohabitation with nerds wasn't bad enough, Trojan Hall was a coed dorm, but segregated by floor. It was all males on my floor. The floors below and above us were all female nerds. This meant if I was interested in any kind of interaction with the women in my building, which I was, I had to make a concerted effort to meet them. I had to go upstairs or downstairs and literally troll the floors in hopes a girl would come out of her room. I wasn't a troller.

On rare occasions, I would cross paths with a random girl or two in the stairwell. The girl or girls would smile at me, maybe say hello, and that was it. What was I supposed to do? Introduce myself? Find out what their major was and how they were enjoying college life so far? These weren't appropriate stairwell questions, at least not in my book.

One time, I was walking down the stairs on my way to class and, to my amazement, an incredibly beautiful long-haired brunette joined me. She looked like someone who should be on her way to a bikini calendar shoot rather than some college class. I didn't speak to her on account of I was too intimidated and also I was shocked that this girl was supposedly a nerd. Huh? When we exited the building, there was a man waiting for her. A man—not a young adult like I was. A real man, with a beard, parked right in front of the building in a yellow Volkswagen van covered in bumper stickers. The bikini model nerd was overjoyed to see him. She rushed into his arms, then into his van, and he whisked her away. I couldn't compete with a bearded man in a van.

On another occasion, as I was heading down the stairwell, I heard footsteps below that were decidedly female. By the sound of it, she was also heading downstairs. I picked up my pace to catch up to this mystery girl. Maybe I would go out on a limb and talk to her.

At the very least, it would be nice to *see* a girl in my building. When I reached her, I had to make a deliberate effort not to cringe. She was huge. For some reason, she was wearing shorts that showed off her thick, hairy gams. The woman was in desperate need of a shave. The hair on top of her head was frizzy, as if she had recently been struck by a Taser. And her pimples were simply out of control. I couldn't believe I had *rushed* down to see her. She wasn't necessarily unattractive, just not my cup of tea. We walked out of the building together, without a word. There was no man in a van waiting for her. This encounter pretty much encapsulated my experiences with the opposite sex during my college years, or more specifically, college year.

Maybe I would have seen more action if my roommate had been a player. If he'd known what he was doing, I could have swum alongside him, like those little opportunistic fish that swim with sharks. But the University of Southern California gave me a computer science major as a roommate. A *computer science* major. If ever there were two words that screamed chick magnet, those two words were not *computer* or *science*. His name was Dan. He was a courteous, mild-mannered, considerate Midwestern roommate who became a true friend, but a polished lover boy with game he was not. If anything, *I* was the wild one of the two of us. Dan spent most of his free time playing video games on his computer. We were doomed.

For a fleeting moment I considered joining a fraternity to get a social life. But my favorite drink of choice was hot chocolate. I'd never acquired a taste for alcohol. Additionally, I didn't feel like being forcibly stripped to my underwear and made to swallow live goldfish, so a fraternity was out of the question. I once attended a football game with some nerds who lived on my floor. There was too much sun, and I wasn't very good at yelling, "Fight! Kill them! Destroy!" or whatever the chant was. I didn't like yelling. Football games were off the list. There were other various campus social clubs I could have joined. The problem with these social clubs was that they were too social. My roommate, Dan, joined a special effects club. It was a club where people could talk about how much they enjoyed the special effects of a particular movie. I went to a meeting with Dan once. It was extremely officious, and all men. Dan was the executive vice president of the club or some such title. It surprised me how formal the proceedings were. Sure, I liked special effects, but I didn't need to go to a meeting about them.

Since I failed to participate in the numerous extracurricular activities college had to offer, my greatest chances of meeting that special someone ended up being in the classroom. Most of my academic classes were painfully dull. The professors would say things like, "And that is why the process of eating, of consumption, serves as a daily reminder of our mortality." I discovered that when it came to discussing the obscure reading assignments we were given, pointing out that the main character was a Christlike figure was always a safe bet. Most of the classes were mind-numbing. When they were finally done, I didn't want to meet girls. I wanted to take a nap. A normal day consisted of me listening to yet another boring lecture featuring words such as *pathos* and then marching back to the hermetically sealed dorm I was regulated to for some hard-core loafing. College was a blast—not so much.

There was one class that offered a bit of excitement, a film production class. I was a film production major, interested in pursuing a career in motion pictures. That was the main reason I was attending this university—to learn how to be creative and use my imagination. My fellow aspiring auteurs were an eclectic bunch from all over the country. There were even girls in the class, but unfortunately none of them made my heart go pitter-patter. Even so, student filmmaking offered an excellent opportunity—my only opportunity—to meet women. What a fantastic excuse to approach the most attractive women on campus! I could ask them if they'd be interested in acting in my short film about a group of sorority sisters who get into an extreme pillow fight. Maybe there could even be a sequel about a group of sorority sisters who get into an extreme food fight, with strawberries and honey. Finally, a way in.

The film professor was a thin-haired, bespectacled man in his fifties who often wore clothes in need of ironing. He was quick to inform us he had been the associate producer of an independent film released eons ago that had been nominated for two technical Academy Awards. We would often be reminded of this. When the professor announced each of us was to write and direct a ten-minute character sketch and that the short film was only allowed to feature *one* person, I felt like he'd punched me in the stomach. *One person.* The cast of sorority sisters was suddenly whittled down to a lone wolf. My film professor was obviously part of the greater conspiracy to keep me from having fun. To rub salt in my wounds, the professor also firmly declared that for each additional human being who appeared in our film, we would be docked a grade. Meaning if some- one ended up making something far superior to *Citizen Kane*, but it had another person in it—the short would receive an automatic B. Our stern professor ended by warning us that if anyone produced a snuff film or something with pornographic content, he would shut off the projector and we would be given an F.

The concept of grading our short films bothered me. Art, in any form, cannot be graded. If it could, the *Mona Lisa* would earn a C minus. In my opinion, her smile is not enigmatic at all. She is amused, thinking, "Look at these people, obsessed, because I have no eyebrows and I'm really a man." It didn't take long for me to figure out a clever way to break the professor's stingy one-person rule without actually breaking it. My second cast member would be a blow-up doll. The blow-up doll would be named Marcia Nadel. I don't know why I chose this name. Chalk it up to divine inspiration— the will of the film gods. Now that I had a name, all I needed was the doll herself.

My soul was still somewhat pure at this time. Consequently, I had no clue where to purchase adult paraphernalia. Buying a blow-up doll was the same as buying enriched uranium. My search began using the same source I would have used were I actually seeking enriched uranium—the phone book. I thumbed through the pages, first through the *B*s, hoping to find *Blow-up Doll*. Where it should have been there was only *Blood Test* and *Blueprinting*. Next I looked under *Sex* as in *Sex Doll*, but only found *Sexual Assault Counseling*. I considered calling the sexual assault counseling offices to see if anyone there could point me in the direction of a doll, but realized this would not be appropriate. It was finally the *A*s that provided a breakthrough. Under *Adult Products*, I learned of a store called The Pleasure Chest, located in homosexually controlled West Hollywood, or WeHo as it is affectionately known (pronounced the way grammatically incorrect prostitutes might identify themselves).

I nervously called The Pleasure Chest and asked the person who answered the phone if they happened to have any blow-up dolls in stock. They did. For some reason I found it necessary to inform the person my name was Carlos and I would stop by on

Friday evening to purchase one of those dolls. The sex shop employee registered this information with an affable, "We'll see you on Friday, Carlos." Suddenly college life had gotten interesting.

When I pulled into the busy parking lot of The Pleasure Chest that Friday night, my pulse began to race. The nondescript building was large and pink, without any windows. I imagined all sorts of heathen madness raging inside. The clientele would be riding each other, whinnying like horses. They would probably be covered in lubricants, wearing feathered thongs, cracking leather whips. When I walked into the crowded store, I was surprised to find that the customers didn't look deviant at all. They reminded me of people I saw at Sears when I worked in the Hardware Department. Granted, this place sold a different kind of hardware, but in general these people, of various ages and backgrounds, appeared wholesome.

While I got my bearings, an employee approached a conservative-looking man who had just entered. The employee cordially asked him, "Can I help you?"

The conservative man, equally cordial, stated, "Yes. I'm looking for something evil."

"Right this way," responded the employee. And off they went to the evil section.

I inconspicuously strolled the aisles without assistance, hoping to find Marcia Nadel on my own. In the few minutes I wandered through the store, I learned more about sex—sexual awakening, liberation, experimentation—than in all my years of formal education combined. The search for Marcia Nadel was illuminating. I saw things. Things I had never imagined, but now would never forget. There were rings for sale, intended to be worn on an appendage other than a finger. A very different sort of promise rings indeed.

Beads were displayed, designed for jamming deep into an individual's rectum. This seemed invasive, but apparently to some it was the highlight of their day. I saw portable vaginas for people on the go. One item I did *not* find, however, was a blow-up doll. Marcia Nadel was missing in action.

I had hoped to keep social interaction to a minimum while at The Pleasure Chest. But my perplexing inability to find the inflatable doll aisle forced me to seek guidance. I reluctantly approached an androgynous employee standing behind the checkout counter and deduced she was female, judging by the badge pinned to her vest, which read YES, I'M A DYKE. Another difference between this establishment and Sears.

When the self-proclaimed dyke asked if she could help me, an internal monologue began running through my mind. I stood there with a hint of shame, about to explain, "I need a blow-up doll—it's for a film. Not for my own personal use. I'm not going to get biblical with her. I'm not a pervert. I'm just a film student. I'm not making a porn with the doll. I don't even really like porn; I think it's kind of boring, like soccer. If you're not directly involved, then who cares what's going on, right? My student film, it's a character piece. We're going to start shooting in the morning. This is my first time in a sex shop. A lot of interesting jewelry you've got here." Rather than say these things, I simply asked, "Can you please show me where the blow-up dolls are?" I figured the second she heard, "It's for a film," I would have seemed even guiltier.

The genial dyke nodded and smiled, no doubt convinced I was going to bang the doll's brains out. She led me to an area I had somehow missed, loaded with dolls, and explained the differences as if she were selling cars. The low-end models ran at twenty dollars.

They featured a drawn-on face with ruby red lips and a permanent wink. The higher-end dolls began at five hundred dollars. They had real human hair, in all the places real humans have hair, and were capable of hugging back. On a tight budget, I decided to go with the twenty-dollar model. I also purchased an inflatable sheep I spotted at the last minute, defiantly adding a *third* character to my film. With a sly grin, Yes, I'm a Dyke rang up my items and said, "Have a good night, sweetie." Without a word, I grabbed the sex toys, leaving any last vestiges of innocence behind.

As soon as I returned to my dorm room, I began inflating my new friends. Dan was at one of his special effects meetings so he missed the show. It only took a few minutes to get the sheep ready for action. I named him Alan Cartwright. No reason, other than he needed a name. Alan looked like he was in a good mood. On deck was my star, Marcia Nadel. She was not as easy to fully inflate. Like many women, it was taking a ridiculous amount of time to get her even halfway there. Nearly out of breath, I examined Marcia and discovered a fatal flaw. Her left leg was severely torn. My actress was seriously injured. I grabbed some tape and carefully sealed her. Her wound fully covered, I started inflating her again. This time it worked. But not for long. She leaned against the wall, her momentarily taut body on display. I heard the distinct sound of hissing. It was coming from the tear, which had not been completely sealed. There were microscopic openings, allowing the air to escape, and Marcia's life with it. I hastily covered the area with more tape. But no matter how much tape I applied, I could not properly complete the job. She continued to steadily deflate every time I blew her up again. It became apparent I needed a new leading lady.

With Marcia Nadel stuffed in my backpack, I left my dorm

room and ran into a fellow student filmmaker in the corridor—Matt, from Utah. On the first day of class, Matt announced he wanted to make films to spread the Gospel through cinema. He smiled when he saw me and asked what I was up to. I told him I was on my way to return some defective equipment for my upcoming film shoot. He asked if he could join me. I agreed.

We arrived at The Pleasure Chest, and Matt began to hyperventilate. I pulled the crumpled sex doll out of my backpack, informing Matt that Marcia Nadel was injured. Matt eyed the store in shock, declaring it was a dirty place for sinners. And yet, he still went inside. The Pleasure Chest was even more crowded than before. Whereas during my earlier visit I had been a prude, feeling embarrassed and unsure of myself, I was now a sex shop veteran. I didn't care who was there to buy what to insert into whose orifice. I just wanted my doll. Matt and I got in line at the main checkout counter. The dyke was still there, helping a young couple select the perfect vibrator. The boyfriend mentioned this was their first vibrator. His girlfriend added it was their first vibrator *together*.

With his arms folded, Matt leaned toward me and whispered, "I thought you were returning camera equipment." He looked convinced his presence here meant he was headed straight to Hell, which must have been disappointing.

The young couple purchased their desired vibrator. It was now my turn. I placed a flaccid Marcia Nadel on the counter. The dyke remembered me, sympathetically asking, "What happened? Is she not The One?"

Everyone in line behind me listened intently as I explained, "This doll isn't working. She has a tear in her leg."

The dyke consoled me, advising, "Don't worry. We'll take care of you." She called out to a colleague named Leo, who was packing shelves nearby. Leo was a chipper man, right at home in this world. I recognized him as the employee who had earlier led the conservative man to all things evil.

When Leo heard I was having trouble with my doll, he said, "I'm so sorry to hear that," as if offering his condolences. "We'll get you back in the saddle in no time." He headed toward the blow-up doll aisle.

"Leo will help you, baby." The dyke gestured I should follow him. I did. Matt joined me, making it clear with his facial expression that he disapproved of everything and everyone around him.

Leo retrieved a new box, scribbled something on my receipt, and took the old Marcia Nadel from me. I thanked him for his help and said I didn't want to drive all the way back to USC, only to discover the new doll was also critically injured. I thought it best if I blew the doll up in the store. "That's understandable. You want to make sure she's got the goods." He stayed there, ready to watch me inflate Marcia. Leo's eagerness to watch made me self-conscious. I asked if he could give us a moment. "Sure, sure. No problem. Just holler if you need a hand." Leo walked away, leaving me with the new Marcia Nadel and unhappy Matt from Utah.

I opened the box, removed the doll, and began blowing with purpose. Anyone in the store who decided to focus their attention on me at this moment most certainly viewed me as incredibly sex starved—to the point where I refused to inflate the doll in the privacy of my own home, or car for that matter. People probably thought I was going to have my way with her in the parking lot, if not in the store. I needed it *now* and I needed it badly.

It no longer mattered what anybody thought. I didn't care.

Marcia Nadel gave me the strength to move beyond whatever potential public humiliation I might face. In the future, I would utilize this strength more than I expected or wanted. At the moment, I successfully blocked out all judgmental assumptions, concentrating on the mission at hand. I was in the zone, ignoring those around me and my own heavy Darth Vader–like sounds of sexual rhythmic respiration.

Slowly but surely, the new Marcia Nadel emerged. First, her right arm popped out. Then her left leg became more defined. She did not appear to have any defects, at least not yet. As I continued to blow, there was only one person I could see out of the corner of my eye. The mortified, forever frowning Matt stood beside me with his arms permanently crossed. The more Marcia Nadel became fully formed, the more Matt began to distance himself from me. He was subtly, slowly heel-toeing away. By the time Marcia Nadel appeared in nearly all her glory, Matt was gone.

A few breaths from meeting the latest incarnation of Marcia Nadel, I unwisely decided to take a look around, out of curiosity, to see if any customers were looking at me. All of them were. Some were pleased, some seemingly disgusted. Leo was proud. He gave me two thumbs up, way up. All of these faces, with their mixture of delight and wonder and disdain, were suddenly hilarious. I almost declared, "It's not what it looks like," but instead I started laughing. And laughing and laughing. This may have been partly due to fatigue and lack of oxygen from all of the heavy breathing. The Pleasure Chest patrons now most likely thought I was incredibly stoned in addition to being exceptionally lustful. Again, it didn't matter what anybody thought. However, it *was* problematic that my uncontrollable laughter allowed precious air to escape from Marcia Nadel.

Those last few breaths, bringing her to life, were like the last few breaths climbing to the top of Mount Everest, I suspect.

The moment arrived. Marcia Nadel arrived. She looked as vibrant and robust as could be. Remembering the microscopic openings that gradually led to the first Marcia's demise, I held her close and began listening for the sound of hissing. No hissing. To be especially certain, I thoroughly groped her entire body, carefully inspecting every inch of her. A jovial, balding, shorter man walked by as I examined Marcia. He asked, "Are you inspecting her for holes?" and then pointed out, "She's supposed to have holes. That's what she's for." He was obviously a television sitcom writer.

Ignoring the man, I stared into Marcia Nadel's eyes. There was a twinkle about them. Her playful wink seemed to be expressing joy at meeting me, as if asking what took me so long. Her whole manner had an energy unlike the first Marcia Nadel. As soon as I looked at her, I felt like I knew her. This time was real; this time would last. And she knew it too, judging by her look of approval. With Marcia Nadel securely under my arm, a new search began—this time for the long-since vanished Matt. I found him salivating over a sixteen-month lesbian calendar, decrying every page with over-the-top scorn. Matt, Marcia Nadel, and I left The Pleasure Chest, a curious threesome. Marcia comfortably sat in back on the ride home, her ever-present wink at the ready. When we returned to our dorm, a shell-shocked Matt politely stated it had been a memorable night. He wished me luck with my short film assignment and then scurried back to his room, holding the calendar he had quickly purchased before we left The Pleasure Chest.

Production began on my epic that weekend. Dan played the part of Marcia Nadel's leading man. I had cast Dan a couple of days earlier. It had been a much easier process. When I offered Dan a role in my short, I explained he would be performing with a blow-up doll, engaging in all sorts of depraved acts. It was a character piece.

Dan stopped playing games at his computer long enough to say, "Okay." That was that.

Rounding out the crew was ultra-low-key fellow film student Brian. I had met Brian in my production class. (Most people called Brian "BJ," but he was determined to transition to Brian on account of his displeasure with the connotation of the letters *B* and *J* together. Throw in a *P* before the *B* and *J* and it makes a world of difference!) Other than the sensitivity about his name, Brian was a cool cat. At least that's the impression he gave with his soft-spoken, quiet demeanor that either struck people as that of a serial killer or someone on horse tranquilizers. I didn't feel threatened by him. He was always in an affable mood whenever we interacted. I noticed if Brian ever found himself part of a group of three or more people, he would immediately become an observer, hardly ever adding to the conversation. This seemed to stem from shyness more than anything. Though I wasn't so shy that all of my systems would shut down, I could relate. Early in the semester, a girl in my production class asked me how I was doing. I told her, "The same." This was true. I was the same. But it was also an attempt at humor. The girl did not laugh. Brian did. That is when Brian and I became friends.

Brian was happy to help me out with my short film. He was particularly pleased to discover I was breaking the professor's one-person rule by adding a blow-up doll and also delighted to be associated with a forbidden porno. I pointed out the professor was prohibiting additional *human beings*, not blow-up dolls. As for the porn, I didn't consider it porn if one of the characters was made entirely of plastic. No bodily fluids were going to be exchanged. Nevertheless, Brian felt I was pushing the limits. To be working as a production assistant on what he viewed as a felonious, erotic film was an honor and a privilege.

To film, we went to my cousin's house in West Los Angeles. My cousin was away for the weekend, but had very kindly agreed to let us shoot there. It was just the five of us: Marcia Nadel, Dan, Brian, Alan Cartwright the sheep, and me. Though we were five, Brian did not hide in his shell. As promised, I did record a number of carnal acts between Dan and Marcia Nadel. Marcia was a trooper. She was much more free-spirited with her body than Dan, who always kept his boxers on. I couldn't help but think of the influence Marcia was having on my life. She lowered the velvet curtain of my inhibitions, emphasized the value of taking chances, and presented the world in a different light. She was a true muse.

The scenes weren't all Triple X. We grabbed shots of Dan and Marcia (wearing a charming flowery blue dress) sitting on a couch, gazing into each other's eyes, softly caressing each other's faces. They spooned each other in bed. There was also a tender slow-dancing scene between Dan and Marcia. While Marcia embraced Dan during their dance, it really looked as if she cared. Brian deftly held on to Marcia's ankles off-camera, maneuvering her feet so she gracefully twirled at the right time. It was hopelessly romantic. After the dancing, we took a break.

Perhaps it was the setting, perhaps the tone of the scene we had just filmed, but something caused Dan to lean back with a wistful smile and comment, "I wonder if I'll ever get married."

Dan surprised me. His remark made me think of my future wife. I told Dan, "I'm sure you'll get married. Most people do." Brian informed us his wife hadn't been born yet. He then admitted he was kidding. In reality he wanted to marry one of the USC cheerleaders, but the closest he had gotten to talking to her was the time he was standing atop one of the university parking structures and saw her walking across campus. Here we were, three college freshmen without girlfriends, in the sexual prime of our lives, sitting around a table with a blow-up doll talking about marriage. Still taken by this topic, I pondered aloud how I would meet my wife. I wondered what she was doing at that very moment.

Brian matter-of-factly responded, "She's probably screwing a football player or taking a dump."

While both of those actions were certainly within the realm of possibility, I preferred to imagine her writing in a journal, pining for her future husband. Maybe she was sitting around a table with her girlfriends, joined by a male blow-up doll, talking about me. My thoughts drifted to Isabelle Cambria, the high school love I had broken up with several months earlier. I wondered how she had reacted when she read the good-bye letter I sent. Was she able to keep whatever emotions she felt from her parents? Was she angry with me? Did she understand? Had she already completely moved on? I'd never know. Thoughts of her continued to surface, though they would gradually fade in time. I knew she wasn't meant to be my wife.

Whether or not my future wife was thinking about me at the precise moment I was shooting my blow-up-doll masterpiece, she *was* thinking about me on occasion. We *were* going to meet. Of that I had no doubt. I just didn't know how or when. Perhaps I would reluctantly attend a college pep rally. Amidst the crowds and noise and celebration, we would accidentally bump into each other. I'd offer my apologies. She would flash a hopeful smile and say, "I hate being here." In that moment, I would know she was meant for me. Stirring from my thoughts, I glanced across the table at Marcia Nadel. She gave me her trademark wink. With her wink came clarity. I wasn't making this short film to break the professor's rules. I was expressing my own personal desires. I wanted to be with someone. I didn't want the beer drinking and hollering. No toga parties, no casual hookups. That wasn't for me. I wanted a girl to hold, someone I cared about, who cared about me. I sought to share the kind of intimate moments only two people in love could have together. I wanted someone who made my experiences that much more rich and vibrant and meaningful. *That* was for me. I kept these thoughts to myself, knowing the kind of response they would illicit from Dan and especially Brian. Our break ended and we began to film Dan buggering the plastic sheep.

The completed character piece premiered the following week in my production class. Everyone continuously darted their eyes to our professor during the screening to see if he was going to turn the projector off. I suppose they expected the screen to go dark, given the oral copulation, fisting, and bestiality. When Dan took Alan Cartwright the sheep from behind there were audible gasps (and one big laugh from Brian). I didn't feel my short was all that shocking; I saw it as a portrait of a lonely young man who only wanted to love and be loved. The professor must have agreed, because he let the picture run in its entirety.

My film divided the students. Half were inspired, half were appalled. Brian was as proud as ever to be associated with it. A handful of students decided they would boycott my subsequent projects. In Matt from Utah's mandatory written review in which we had to list seven qualities exhibited by the character in my short, he listed the seven deadly sins. His review was fair. Our professor had the last word. He nodded slowly, with approval, and decreed, "Excellent. I'm giving you an A on this. Because there is no doubt about what kind of individual your character is. We learned a lot about him. And we learned a lot about *you*." Yes. We did.

CHECKER LOVE

College wasn't my thing. Which is why I dropped out after a year—which is why I never experienced any college romances or cheap one-night stands or smoked marijuana for that matter. I was tired of school and so I decided *no more*. My mother nearly had a heart attack; my father asked me, "What took you so long?" This was an accurate distillation of the contrast between their personalities. Despite my mother's protestations, I pursued my cinematic aspirations by joining the workforce, taking a grunt job at a production company located on the lot of a major motion picture studio. Rather than sit in a classroom, I opted for the trenches, deciding to work my way up the Hollywood food chain.

I was now twenty-two years old, still a buffoon in many ways. If meeting girls in college had been a challenge, the real world was like being stranded at sea. It was difficult for me to strike up natural conversations with girls. This was due to a number of reasons. One,

I was an only child, not accustomed to heavy social interaction. Two, I'd spent a great deal of my young adulthood communing with chickens. Three, I hadn't been in college long enough to give my people skills a proper honing. And four, I was inherently introverted. Still, I somehow managed to overcome all these factors and go on an occasional date, usually with a coworker. But there were never any fireworks—not even a sparkler.

On the professional side of things, I had made a smidgen of progress in the entertainment industry. I had gone from grunt to *executive* grunt, personally bringing tea and gourmet coffee to a number of Oscar-winning filmmakers on various high-profile productions. On the food chain, I went from guppy to minnow. Occasionally, my mother would suggest I go back to school. "Think of where you'd be if you graduated," she liked to offer. I knew where I would be. My friend Brian did graduate. We had kept in touch. He was now asking me for help finding a job. That is where I would be. Presently, I was in a landmark Los Angeles deli, waiting for Brian to show up. We were going to have dinner.

Brian was running late so I took a seat in the PLEASE WAIT TO BE SEATED area. People were everywhere—in the dining room enjoying corned beef sandwiches, in the bakery buying mandelbrot or other pastries that sounded similar to characters who might live in Middle Earth. An elderly gentleman using an oak cane, wearing a blazer and a tweed cap, slowly made his way into the deli. He took a seat beside me, resting both hands atop the cane. We said hello to each other. He looked like a man who had led a life well-lived—someone who possessed knowledge that could only come with age. In a halting voice, the elderly gentleman told me he was taking a break from his daily walk. Since we were explaining ourselves, I told him I was waiting for Brian. The gentleman sighed. It was a sad sigh. I felt compelled to ask if something was wrong.

With a heavy heart, the elderly gentleman said, "I used to take this walk with my wife. She was the love of my life. I met her after the war."

I was curious about his battlefield experiences, but it seemed an inopportune moment to say "I need to know *which* war." Whatever specific conflict he'd fought in, his wife had recently passed away. He was on the verge of tears as he spoke of her.

If I had a dime for the number of times strangers have decided to cry in my presence, I would have thirty cents. The elderly gentleman reined in the waterworks, but was still clearly crushed by the weight of his grief. I did my best to console him, telling him he was blessed to have found such a meaningful love, fortunate to have shared the time he had with her. She would always be with him in spirit and in his heart. My ability to sound like a greeting card came out of the blue. Every now and then my mouth would speak without me knowing what it was going to say. The elderly gentleman looked downward, nodding in agreement. Then he turned to me and asked, "Is there a special lady in your life, young man?"

I told him there wasn't, not really, no. He seemed disappointed by my answer. I explained it was difficult to meet people in Los Angeles, pointing out that people were in their cars most of the time. (Anyone walking was not to be trusted.) Aside from that, I worked crazy hours as a production assistant, etc., etc. The elderly gentleman refused to accept this. "There must be *somebody*," he insisted. There kind of was. Since he was pressing, I decided to tell the elderly gentleman about my weakness for girls behind a cash register, especially one in particular. . . .

I was living on my own, in a modest one-bedroom West Los Angeles apartment. For all intents and purposes I was a legal adult, though sometimes I didn't quite feel like one. It still surprised me on occasion that I drove a car. I could get in a car and drive wherever I pleased whenever I wanted. That seemed so adult. One of the locations I would regularly drive myself to was the grocery store. I would buy food to place in my adult refrigerator.

Grocery shopping was a tremendous chore. There were many things that bothered me about it. First of all the music, or rather the Muzak. It was punishment. Listening to it made me feel like I was stuck in a giant elevator. Every time I stepped foot into a grocery store I wanted to change the station. There was something untoward about being forced to listen to generic upbeat melodies while people slowly pushed their shopping carts around. The spectacle of random citizens cruising the aisles with their carts was disturbing enough on its own. Everyone looked like members of an unnamed cult. The elevator music made it all the more macabre. I especially hated it when someone was traveling the opposite direction from me and then I would pass them again in the next aisle. There was no escape from certain folk.

To top it all off, of the twenty or so aisles in the grocery store, only about two were really of any use. I didn't know how to cook, and even if I had, nothing was sold in single portions. Single people were second-class citizens—forced to buy more bread and milk than they could reasonably consume on their own before the expiration date. Learning to cook excited me as much as the prospect of getting my teeth cleaned or looking for a new apartment. Consequently, I would always walk out of a grocery store with things like bananas, cereal, a TV dinner or two, and peanut butter. I would still browse all the aisles, conforming to society. It was a dismal exercise in futility.

One heavenly night, everything changed. Grocery shopping became my favorite pastime. After stocking my cart with the usual, I got in line behind various cult members, somberly waiting to pay for my goods. That is when I saw Naya. There were fireworks the moment I laid eyes on her. I had never noticed her before. She was behind the register, ringing up items with the grace and elegance of Audrey Hepburn. A tacky instrumental version of a saccharine love song from another era began to play throughout the store as I gazed at Naya. I recognized the song as "Lady in Red." Naya was dressed in red. This was destiny. Her manicured fingers lightly passed each item beneath the laser, her brown eyes sparkled under the shine of the fluorescent lights, and her long black hair flowed in the breeze of the air-conditioning. Never had there been a sexier checker.

An old woman in front of me holding a thousand crumpled coupons struggled to find the correct one for a bottle of detergent. Naya helped her. Once everything was rung up, the old woman took out a checkbook. Everyone behind her groaned in disgust—a check-book! Everyone but me, that is. I didn't mind waiting. As I watched Naya compassionately help the old woman, I realized I was in the presence of a celestial being.

The old woman waddled away with her detergent and the rest of her bags. It was now my turn. I studied Naya, happy to be closer to her. Her name tag was securely fastened to her color-coordinated clothes. She carried herself with confidence, pressing buttons on the register like a pro. When Naya smiled at me, I felt special.

"Paper or plastic, sir?" A pimply-faced teenage bagger was ruin-ing the moment by talking. At first I didn't catch his blubbering because I was so focused on Naya. I asked him to repeat himself. "Paper or plastic?" I told the bagger to surprise me, doing away with him. Or so I thought. "I need to know. You have to choose, sir. You could go with both if you want." Choosing plastic seemed the simplest thing, so I did, hoping never to hear his grating voice again.

My attention shifted back to Naya. She asked, "How are you?" We didn't even know each other and still she wondered how things were going. Naya was obviously a caring young woman. She probably asked everyone how they were doing, but there was something in the tone of her voice—something that in my case made it seem like she *really* wanted to know.

Certain that most people said they were fine when Naya asked this question, I decided to mix things up by replying, "I'm doing all right." I shrugged to emphasize my casual nature, showing her that I was simultaneously different and indifferent. Because Naya was so good at her job, she rang my items up almost as quickly as I had placed them down. I wished I had purchased more if for no other reason than to lengthen our time together.

"Would you like some help outside, sir?" It was Pimple Face, butting in again. I don't know why this dude kept calling me *sir.* I was twenty-two—I'd only been driving for six years. And I had two bags of groceries. If I needed help outside with two bags, I wouldn't have had the strength to go shopping in the first place. I almost told him, yes, I did need help. This would give Naya a window into my sense of humor. But I could see Pimple Face using that as an opportunity to have another extended conversation with me, so I tersely replied, "No, thank you." Naya gave me my receipt. Our hands touched. I swooned. She told me to have a nice day, and I'm pretty sure she meant it.

Suddenly grocery shopping mattered. It was an event. I would pick out specific clothes for buying milk. My shopping patterns were completely influenced by Naya. If Naya wasn't working, I'd promptly turn around and come back another day, though sometimes I would take advantage of Naya's absence to make purchases I'd rather Naya not be privy to—like toilet paper or deodorant. I didn't want her knowing I used such things. On rare occasions, even if Naya *was* there, I would choose a different checkout stand, one right next to her. I'd make sure she saw me, letting her know that she did not have me under her thumb, no, she did not. I was a wild card.

Every so often I would make repeated visits to the grocery store on the same day, conveniently "forgetting" to buy batteries or tooth-paste or gum. Naya appeared happy, and somewhat amused, to see me each time. It was encouraging. Of course I could have asked Naya out during any of those visits. But that opened up the possibility of her saying no.

There was a method to my madness. It was all part of a plan. Rather than getting in Naya's face at the checkout counter and bra-zenly asking if she would like to have dinner, I thought it best for her to first become emotionally invested in me. That would increase the chances of her accepting my dinner invitation when the time came. I'd have to play things just right. After all, the checkout coun-ter wasn't exactly an ideal location for courtship. Pimple Face would be there watching, not to mention the line of customers behind me. If they got mad at old ladies writing checks, imagine their wrath at having to stand behind someone wooing the checker. The customers would throw their arms in the air, complaining, "Great! He's wooing her. We're going to be here another half hour." If Naya rejected me I'd have an army of witnesses to revel in my humiliation. And who could blame her for rejecting me if I was just another customer, if I didn't give her a chance to see the *real* Carlos? Better to go slowly.

Naya gained insight into the content of my character through the purchases I made—and in some cases did not make. For example, she could glean I was someone who cared about my health through my choices of oatmeal and fat-free yogurt. I was also someone who believed in compromise. This was evident by my selection of chocolate-vanilla swirl pudding. Naya learned that I was not a heavy drinker, given that alcoholic beverages were seldom placed on the conveyor belt. If I did buy a bottle of wine or a six-pack of beer, I'd let her know I was headed to a party and in so doing demonstrate that I had friends. Because only someone with friends would be invited to a party. Sure, I could have been crashing a party. But I was confident Naya assumed I had friends. We developed that level of trust.

One of those friends, Dave, nearly destroyed everything. I knew Dave from a low-budget slasher film we had both assisted on. When I told him about the wonders of Naya, he wanted to see for himself. I did not like the idea of Dave scoping Naya out. Dave promised we would just be there for a second and he wouldn't talk to her. He would just pick up some snacks and be on his way. Against my better judgment, I went to the grocery store with Dave. He walked in and immediately strutted past Naya, actually *slowing down* as he approached her. I was not far behind. Dave gave her a thorough once-over. He was the most blatant ogler I knew, making no effort whatsoever to be subtle about his actions. If anything, he would go out of his way to be obvious. Often, when an attractive girl caught his eye, Dave would clean his glasses in front of her and then put them back on to get the clearest view possible. He gave Naya an asinine nod as he continued walking past her. Naya glanced at me. She smiled in recognition and uncertainty. I waved at her in embarrassment as I followed Dave out of the store. We didn't even bother to buy anything.

"She's hot. You should totally ask her out," Dave concluded. I informed Dave that I'd intended to, but now that he had ruined my chances, I probably wouldn't. Dave played dumb. "What are you talking about? She didn't even notice me." Uh-huh. Again, he encouraged me to ask Naya out. I explained it was difficult to find the right moment. Dave suggested I wait for her in the parking lot and follow her to her car. I thanked Dave for the advice, telling him I might try that—as soon as I bought a ski mask. Then I made a mental note to stop being friends with Dave.

In spite of Dave's best efforts to sabotage me, Naya continued treating me kindly. I decided the time had come to ask her out. Since there would probably be a number of pesky customers in line, I thought the best way to go about things would be to inconspicuously slip her a note with my phone number. That way I wouldn't put her on the spot. She could read it at her leisure and get back to me when it was most convenient. And I wouldn't be subjected to possible rejection on the supermarket gallows under the hostile eyes of demanding customers. A note was definitely the best way to go.

It took several drafts before I got the note just right. The first version was a lighthearted attempt at humor. In an homage to grade school, it simply read: *If you like me, check this box.* I drew a square and provided my phone number below it. But I scrapped that note, in case she thought I genuinely wrote like a first grader. Plus, it wasn't obvious I wanted her to call so we could schedule dinner. I took a more formal approach on my next attempt, writing: *It's been great getting to know you. Give me a call if you'd like to have dinner some-time. That would be fun. Here's my number* . . . That seemed too dry and academic. I wanted my note to have more panache. *Curious to see what you look like when you're not behind a register. Give me a call sometime, we'll grab a bite.* That was it; that was the keeper. Casual, yet assertive. Smooth, but genuine. It took five Post-its before I got my penmanship just right. The *y*'s in *you* and *you're* looked too sloppy. But I finally nailed it.

Naya was working the fifteen items or less checkout stand. This added to the pressure. I thought of coming back another day when she was at a register that carried less urgency. But enough was enough. This was going to happen. I bought six items, none of which I needed—a mozzarella cheese stick, a box of cereal bars, and so on. The line was long, but moving fast since it was the express lane. Behind me, a mother attempted to quiet her unruly children who were angry because she wouldn't buy them chocolate bars. The kids were making me nervous . . . *more* nervous. A tall, dark, and hand-some stud was in front of me. He was purchasing alcohol for a party. Apparently he wanted to show Naya he had friends as well. Naya seemed taken by him. He said something witty to her, though I didn't hear it because one of the kids behind me banged into the back of my leg and his mother shouted, "Bruce! Watch it!" Naya laughed at whatever the stud told her. I wondered if I was but one of many suitors who wanted to win Naya's heart on any given day. Probably. Had she become emotionally invested in someone else? Was I too late?

The stud gave Naya a good-bye wink. She smiled at him, the way I had seen her smile at me. He left. It was go-time. Naya looked at me with a bit of surprise, as if she hadn't initially noticed I was there. She wasn't overly excited about my presence. I nodded at her without a word, keeping my hand in my pocket, grasping the note I had so carefully crafted. The plan was to give her the note when she handed me my receipt. I broke into a cold sweat as Naya rang up the last item. The register sounded louder than usual as it coughed up the receipt. She ripped the paper from the machine. Naya turned toward me. I slowly began to remove the note from my pocket.

A handful of chocolate bars slammed onto the counter in front of us, one of them falling off the other side at Naya's feet. It was Bruce, demon-child. He had thrown the chocolate bars down in protest. He wanted them no matter what. The mother scolded her son, apologizing to Naya. Naya remained unruffled. She told the mother not to worry about it as she placed the chocolate bar beside her register and began ringing up the mother's groceries. Naya glanced at me one last time, telling me to have a good weekend. I nodded with a bittersweet smile. This was not the right moment. Another day.

A few weeks passed. When I returned to the supermarket, I did not come with a note. I genuinely needed to go grocery shopping. Naya wasn't there. This was somewhat of a relief. It was nice to be able to shop without feeling so emotionally vulnerable. I casually went up and down each aisle, perusing all the items I had no use for. As I turned a corner to venture into the next aisle, there she was. At first I didn't realize it was Naya. She was not behind a register. She was standing next to the strawberries, holding a basket. Naya had removed her name tag. She was shopping, like any other civilian. Naya was more beautiful than ever. Strawberry was her color.

She did not notice me. I weighed my options. Naya was by herself. There were no shoppers requiring attention. No obnoxious children demanding chocolate bars. No stud winking at her. No nothing. It was just Naya and the strawberries. This was the moment I had been waiting for—for almost a year. All the groundwork had been completed—all the cheerful conversations, the friendly waves, the pointed stares—it all came down to this.

I casually pushed my shopping cart over to the strawberries. Naya flashed her trademark smile. I asked if she could help me. This was just my opener, my fastball straight down the middle. I hoped she would run with it, that she would playfully ask me something along the lines of "How can I help you?" One thing would lead to another and we'd end up talking about our favorite movies, places we'd traveled to, and ultimately make long-sought plans to go out.

As soon as I asked Naya if she could help me, she laughed and responded, "In produce? I don't think so." She called out to a colleague, a stout guy named Joe. Naya informed Joe I had a question and then abruptly walked out of my life. She had no desire to talk to me any longer than necessary.

Before I knew it, Joe was standing directly in front of me, wondering how he could be of service. I spotted a pile of whole watermelons on display and asked, "How come there are only *whole* watermelons on sale? Why aren't there any presliced, in the small plastic containers?" Joe appreciated the question. He launched into a detailed explanation about how presliced watermelon was sold only certain times of the year. I stood there and listened to his entire ridiculous speech, pretending to be enthralled. Once he finished, I thanked him for his time and decided I needed to find a new grocery store for all future shopping excursions.

It had been nearly a month since my final encounter with Naya in the produce section. I had not returned, nor did I plan to. The checkers at my new grocery store did not grab my attention the way Naya had, which was probably for the best. I had not given Naya much consideration until the elderly gentleman walked into the busy deli, sat beside me, and asked if there were any special young ladies in my life. She was no longer in my life—but she recently had been—so I told the elderly gentleman all about Naya as I waited for Brian to show up. Brian had still not arrived. I had enough time to share pretty much the whole story with the elderly gentleman.

When he had first sat down he was bereaved, missing his dearly departed wife. After hearing my experiences with the sexiest checker alive, the elderly gentleman was no longer sad. He was pensive, quiet. I waited for him to tell me something profound, something about how if things were meant to be, they would have happened. The elderly gentleman adjusted his cap, rose to his feet and smiled. Before walking out, he said, "So that's your pathetic life." I laughed. He was right.

Maybe it would be good to get out of Los Angeles for a while. My social life was unintentionally stuck in a rut. I had gotten used to the grind of going from home to work and then back again, with bland meals in between. I was slumbering, alone, and somehow I was okay with that. This was not okay. Part of the reason I had been lulled into accepting life in a trancelike state was because so many of those around me had accepted it as well. Deep down, I wanted more than that, always had. Above all, I still wanted companionship. When my closest shot at finding a partner was an off-duty grocery store checker standing by the strawberries, it was clearly time for a shake-up. A change of scenery might prove just the trick. I wasn't sure where I'd like to go other than *away*. I needed somewhere energizing, a place that would inspire me to be more proactive in my personal life. Traveling might actually be the thing that led me to true love. Perhaps I needed to follow in my father's footsteps, do what he did to find a wife. As soon as I got my things in order, I would take my search for a bride international. Yes, a trip would do me good.

NOMANCE IN PARADISE

When I told my mother I wanted to visit some other part of the world in the not-too-distant future, her response was unexpected. "We're going to French Polynesia—come with us! It'll be fun." My parents had been married twenty-four years and were still going strong. Their twenty-fifth wedding anniversary was coming up and they were making special travel arrangements. It seemed as though getting engaged after a few days wasn't so crazy after all. If only I could find somebody to do cartwheels over. I was ready to get married and do married people things, like argue. Arguments were appealing because of my understanding of what happened *after* an argument. I wanted to *make up* with somebody. The thought was comforting. What was discomforting, however, was the fact that I was beginning to form the slightest doubt as to whether or not I'd ever meet the right person. After all, I was the same age as my parents when they got married and yet I had no viable prospects.

I kept this doubt to myself because I knew if I complained out loud, "I'm *never* getting married!" I would have to change my name to Carla.

My mother couldn't understand why it was so difficult for me to meet someone. She was always ready to help, offering to host a singles party at my parents' house. "You could invite all your friends; they could invite their friends. I'll make flan. Everybody can dance in the living room." She was ready to organize this at a moment's notice.

"You want me to ask all of my single friends and all of their single friends to drive down to San Diego County so they can dance at your house and eat some flan?"

"Why not?"

"That's not going to help," I concluded. "Besides, I don't dance. Anywhere. Especially not in your house with you there and my friends watching."

"No wonder you're not married." I knew she was only trying to help. She wasn't pressuring me—she never did. My dad didn't either. They just didn't want me to be alone. Neither did I, unless the alternative was *Dance Party USA* at my folks' house. Then I was cool being alone. "Don't worry, Carlos. You'll find somebody when the time is right." I told my mother I was thinking of going on a trip. I wasn't sure where yet, only that I wanted to see another part of the world. That was when she offered her invitation. "We've decided to go to Tahiti for our twenty-fifth wedding anniversary, to visit the Tahitian islands. Why don't you come with us? Maybe you'll meet a nice, pretty girl on one of the islands."

When I imagined taking a trip, I did not imagine taking it with my parents. Actually, my friend Brian and I were talking about taking a vacation somewhere. Brian was single and looking for a good woman too. He seemed like a compatible traveling companion. In all the time I'd known him, we'd never engaged in mortal combat. I never knew him to raise his voice or break down in tears. Come to think of it, I'd never known him to show much of any emotion. He'd be great to travel with. My plans were to go somewhere with plenty of available women. Brian could be my wingman. And I could be his when the circumstances required.

Brian said he needed more time to save up for a trip, but when he was ready he thought it would be fun to visit Italy. He wanted to visit Italy because he heard Italy had sexy billboards and allowed nudity on regular TV. Italy could be fun, but Australia also seemed full of potential. It had piqued my interest ever since the fifth grade when I exultantly stated that Australia was the only country that was also a continent. Its distance enticed me. It seemed bold to travel so far, far away. From what I could tell, the women were just as sexy as the Italians. Plus—and this was a big plus—Brian and I would be able to understand Australian women when they spoke, most of the time. We wouldn't have to learn Italian—what a drag that would be. Brian agreed speaking English to Australian women was a bonus, though he expressed concern about the length of the flight. We did ultimately decide upon a future trip to Australia to meet some sheilas (that was Australian for women—I looked it up), but Brian said it would be a while yet before he could afford the trip.

In the meantime, I thought of going somewhere on my own. My mother was trying to talk me into visiting Tahiti with them for their silver anniversary. I wasn't sure. "Listen, take advantage of this opportunity," my mother advised. "Do things while you can. You remember that woman, Lois, who I used to work with? She died last week of a massive hemorrhoid."

"Do you mean hemorrhage?"

"Come with us." Despite Lois's fate, I thought my parents' anniversary would be more satisfying if they went without me. "Don't be silly, you're my only child," she responded. I didn't quite get her point, but the more she made it, the more inclined I was to visit the South Pacific with them. She made the deal sweeter, offering to pay my way. That seemed like a lousy anniversary gift, but who was I to turn down a free trip to French Polynesia? I finally relented. Who knew? Maybe I *would* meet a nice, pretty girl over there.

The first leg of the trip did not begin comfortably. My parents and I took a flight from Los Angeles to Papeete, the capital of Tahiti. It was a seven-hour flight that illustrated how much more slowly time travels when one is smelling rancid body odor. The flight had originated from France. Either the people already on board used extremely low-grade deodorant that wore off somewhere over the Atlantic, or they weren't wearing any deodorant to begin with. Whatever the specifics, these people weren't doing their part to dispel the cliché that Europeans don't believe in showering. Because of them, my parents and I journeyed to Heaven on Earth in a flying locker room. The stench caused me to pass out at regular intervals. That is how I managed to endure the journey. When we finally landed, the hot humid air of Papeete was a relief. Before I met a girl, I would need to shower.

From Papeete, we hopped on a smaller propeller plane and took a short flight to another link in this chain of picture-perfect islands—the island of Huahine (I assumed it was pronounced *Wa-hee-knee*, but the hospitable male receptionist at the front desk of our hotel informed me the correct pronunciation was *Ho-ah-hee-nay*, so the island is misspelled.) Huahine was a three-dimensional tropical postcard in every direction. After dropping off our luggage, my parents and I took a walk on the peaceful grounds of our welcoming hotel, ending up on the edge of a pier overlooking a glistening lagoon. A gust of wind blew my baseball cap off and it fell into the water. It was quickly recovered by a raven-haired siren swimming nearby. With a friendly smile, she tossed me my cap. I caught it, learning something about these islands in the process—going topless was a common practice. The instant I realized this woman was exposing her supple breasts, I maintained careful, constant eye contact as I thanked her for returning my cap. The woman swam off to join an athletic man waiting for her in the water, instantly making her redundant. Throughout the trip, I spotted numerous liberated women—each of them with proud men—who had no qualms about prancing around seminude. It was challenging to catch a good glimpse of them in the presence of my mother and father, not to mention the women's male counterparts, but I did my best.

It quickly became apparent these islands were not the place to meet someone. I was in a honeymooners' paradise, the only single guy within a four-thousand-mile radius. While I was drinking guava juice with my parents, young couples were making passionate love in moonlit bungalows above the water. I was my parents' roommate. None of us would be getting any action on this trip. I decided this trip was a location scout, for a separate visit with my future wife. (I hoped that upon someday returning to this wondrous part of the world, my future wife would keep *her* top on. The thought of some jerk, traveling with his parents, ogling her bothered me.) While on the islands with my mother and father, I would note the best places to eat, snorkel, sunbathe. Then one day I would return with my wife, either for our honeymoon or anniversary. I would be her chivalrous guide, knowing exactly where to go, what to do, when to do it—thanks to the earlier location scout. My wife would be incredibly impressed with my knowledge of the islands and how I managed to make every day an amorous surprise. She would say, "Honey, this is *amazing*. You know the islands so well. Did you grow up here or something? I'm having the best time. How was I lucky enough to end up with a husband as intelligent and adventurous and caring and strong and sensitive and handsome and sensational as you?" That was the plan.

On Huahine, my father woke us up at the crack of dawn. "Time to visit the family of sacred eels. Get ready." This was very much like my father. He enjoyed adventures, especially if they were spontaneous, unpredictable ones with a hint of danger. While in high school, I was studying for a test one afternoon when he arrived home from work and asked if I'd like to go for a drive. We ended up visiting Lake Havasu, Arizona. He called my mother from Arizona and told her we'd be late for dinner. Another time he took my mother and me on what he said would be a casual day hike. We climbed to the top of Southern California's highest peak, Mount San Gorgonio, reaching the 11,503-foot summit just as the sun was going down. And now, sacred eels. We had to be careful around my dad. He'd probably have us swimming with sharks next.

After a quick breakfast, we joined a small group of tourists waiting in the hotel lobby for our guide. It was all couples—and me. One of the couples was from France. The French couple looked to be about my age, and if the woman hadn't already been taken, she would have been the one I ended up bringing back to the South Pacific someday. I imagined her name was Camille. She was so pretty I had to make a concerted effort not to stare. Thank goodness she was wearing a top. Camille was petite, with honey-blond hair, a tanned complexion, and hazel eyes. She gave me a playful look, seeming to empathize with my status as *the kid* in this group. Her beefcake partner eyed me with a condescending smirk. He chose not to wear a shirt in order for his six-pack abs to taunt me. Also, he gave Camille a passionate open-mouthed kiss to show me he could.

Our guide arrived, with a mane of wavy black hair and distinct Tahitian tattoos covering the entire left side of his body. He was a boisterous, charismatic native named Charlie who greeted us with booming hellos. Charlie told us the history of the sacred eels we were about to encounter. As Charlie explained it, a valiant eel first crawled across the mountains from a pool on the north coast of Tahiti thousands of years ago, looking for a mate. He was tired of being a bachelor. Apparently all the desirable female eels were taken, having married beefcake eels with six-pack abs who reveled in giving public open-mouthed kisses. They had probably married too young and would end up unhappy, but no matter. The valiant eel relocated to the south coast of Tahiti, near the village of Mataiea. It was here he met and married a maiden, a human one. The night of their wedding, much wooing and writhing in the water took place between the eel and his bride. Charlie informed us, with a straight face, that everyone who currently lived on the Tahitian islands was a descendant of this eel and the maiden. So in the South Pacific it was possible for different species to commingle. There was hope for me yet. Maybe I would meet a nice eel.

We hiked to an inland bridge that crossed a shallow freshwater river. Looking down from the bridge, the water appeared to be no more than two or three feet deep. The riverbed was easily visible, though any signs of eels were not. "Do you see them?" asked Charlie.

I shook my head. Charlie smiled patiently. He walked over to a large white bucket at the end of the bridge that had been purposely placed there earlier by some anonymous Tahitian citizen. Either that, or some anonymous Tahitian citizen had lost their bucket filled with sliced tuna steaks. Charlie brought one of the steaks over and dropped it into the river. As if by magic, several freshwater eels surfaced from the riverbed and immediately tore into the steak. Charlie laughed, asking again, "Do you see them?"

They were ghastly. Long and massive, their bodies mold-colored green with translucent blue eyes. I would definitely not be dating any of them. The way they fought over the tuna, wrapping around each other, splashing violently, ripping the steak to shreds, reminded me of alligators in a castle moat chomping on villains. Until the tuna steak had been placed in the water, there was no hint it was teeming with these powerful creatures. Had I gone exploring on my own, I could have easily wandered into this shallow river. A posted sign reading CAUTION: MONSTERS CROSSING would have been helpful.

Charlie walked back to the bucket for more steaks. Instead of returning to us on the bridge, he went down the embankment to the river's edge. The monsters sensed his presence and swam to meet him. He began feeding them *by hand* as our group watched in amazement. Next, Charlie stepped into the water. Suddenly his story about the eel marrying a Tahitian maiden made perfect sense. He was insane. Charlie continued feeding the eels by hand as he stood in their midst. With a beaming smile, he looked up at us on the bridge and gestured for the group to join him. My dad was first to go down there, of course. The rest of the group followed, except for my mother and me.

My mother and I watched from the safety of the bridge, wondering what was the matter with everyone. They were acting as if they'd won a prize. My dad's behavior I could understand. But Camille, the dainty, delicate flower with whom I might have had a future had she not ruined things by getting married before we met although technically we hadn't met and Camille probably wasn't her name, looked very much out of place. An eel near her ankles lunged upward, taking a massive bite out of her tuna steak. She played a brief game of tug of war with it before the eel prevailed. Then she looked up at me on the bridge, standing next to my mommy. Camille smiled, amused by my fear of giant river serpents. Her man also looked up at me. He laughed, muttering something to Camille in French. She chuckled at his comment. I did not speak French but had a pretty good idea I was being referred to as a sissy.

With newfound false valor, I decided to have a close encounter with the sacred eels of Huahine. My mother blanched as she saw me head down the embankment toward the water. She called out in a fright, nervously advising me to be careful. I thought it peculiar my mother felt it necessary to remind me that when in the presence of enormous eels, it's important to be careful. I kind of already knew that. Masking my white-knuckled fear with a macho squint, I walked down to the river, removed my thongs (thong sandals, not underwear—although if I had gone on this hike wearing only thong underwear that would have been fantastic), and stepped into the water. A number of eels quickly swam over to me, circling my ankles. They felt heavy and slimy.

Charlie handed me a tuna steak, and I handed it to one of the eels. It ravenously yanked the entire steak from me in one fell swoop, which was not my plan, but who was I to argue? Charlie laughed.

However, his expression turned serious when the eel I had just fed seemed to take more than a passing interest in my foot. It began thoroughly inspecting my foot, determining whether or not any part of it was edible. Charlie grabbed my wrist, whispering, "Don't move the toes."

I did not move the toes. Or the rest of the foot, or the leg, or any other part of the body. Instead I froze, waiting to see if the eel was going to turn me into an hors d'oeuvre. For the first time in my life, I regretted that I had good-looking feet—feet that probably tasted like caviar to sacred eels. Camille stared at me. She seemed concerned, sensing I was in grave danger. I returned her gaze, knowing full well she might be the last person I ever saw alive. If the eel did bite me, if I bled to death through my big toe, Camille would always carry that traumatic memory with her. In a way, she and her pompous husband would be partly responsible. Whatever guilt they felt would be deserved. Thankfully, Charlie took the last piece of tuna steak and used it to distract the eel. When it swam to Charlie, I seized the opportunity to reach the safety of dry land, which was one step away. Whatever happened in my life from this moment on was gravy. I was relieved my future wife was not present to see me a bit shaken up. It was important to be strong for her. She deserved someone strong.

Feeding Gigantor eels was not the type of activity I envisioned participating in with my one true love. I saw us more resting in a hammock near the lapping shore. My wife would sip on mai tais while reading a bestselling novel, and I'd listen to music on my headphones as I enjoyed a virgin piña colada. Maybe, *maybe*, we would go parasailing in the afternoon, but probably not. Better to watch other people do it. Rather than wrestle with savage water beasts, I thought it would be more helpful to explore the more leisurely options, like snorkeling in shallow water or lying down under a palm tree. My parents and I were next headed to nearby Bora Bora, the crown jewel of the South Pacific. I was confident I'd find plenty to do there with my future wife.

Our first morning on Bora Bora, I was awakened at sunrise by the sound of my father's voice declaring, "Time to swim with sharks. Get ready." He wasn't speaking metaphorically. My father actually signed us up for swimming in the ocean alongside sharks. After another quick breakfast, we joined a group of about twenty or so people waiting in the hotel lobby who were stupidly eager to swim with sharks as well. It was all couples—and me. I was familiar with one of the couples. Camille and her six-pack husband were there. It seemed they were stalking me from island to island. Camille and her man flashed a familiar smile, remembering the run-in I had with a sacred eel who nearly sucked the life out of me. Our shared experience with the eels brought Camille and I (and her man, sigh) closer together. Now that we were off to kibitz with sharks, our bond would become that much stronger. I could only imagine what might develop in the unlikely event we exchanged words.

Our shark guide greeted us with the same energy and enthusiasm as Charlie back on the island of Huahine. This guide's name was Jack. He looked as if he could have been Charlie's cousin. Jack had two friends with him who would be assisting. They never introduced themselves, but I'm guessing they were named Manny and Moe. Before we boarded the boat waiting for us on the hotel dock, Jack explained the procedures. We were going to ride out to the reef, Jack and his friends would pour buckets of bloody chum into the water, everybody would jump in, then the sharks would arrive. This didn't sound like a good idea to me. Jack sensed my concern. He told me not to worry, explaining that the sharks were friendly.

Everyone hopped in the boat and thus began the ten-minute ride to the coral reef surrounding the island. I ended up sitting directly across from Camille and her clingy husband. He was all over her, way too much for my taste. Camille studied me as we headed toward the reef. I could tell she was wondering what my story was. My story was I had too much wax in my ear. This must have been the case, because while Camille inquisitively stared, my mother poked her pinky finger into my ear and began to groom me. My mom, such a cockblocker. Camille's husband uttered another one of his snide French remarks. Camille grinned. I attempted to contain my embarrassment, casually playing off my mother's attention. But inside it pained me, my mother cramping my style in front of this gorgeous married woman I had less than zero chances with, minutes before we were all about to be devoured by sharks.

My embarrassment was forgotten once we arrived at the reef. It acted as a natural breakwater. Waves from the open ocean crashed into the reef, keeping the water on the inside of the reef calm and clear. We were going to stay on the inside, where the sharks were benevolent. The other side of the reef, the open ocean side, was a different scenario. Jack warned us *never* to swim on the other side. A swim in the open ocean would not be pleasant due to its resulting in being eaten, which was the opposite of pleasant. It seemed the sharks on the other side of the reef were not as friendly, nor did they care about whatever hopes and dreams we might have been harboring or how much our families and future wives loved us or were going to love us. I heard this warning a number of times from various locals during my stay in French Polynesia. Never swim on the other side.

Jack's assistants immediately dove into the water, each of them holding on to opposite ends of a red rope. Wooden stakes were attached to both ends of the rope. They embedded the stakes into portions of the coral, creating a lengthy red line. With the rope line securely established, Jack explained its purpose: the sharks would stay on one side of the rope, and we would stay on the other. Somehow someone had sent a memo to the sharks notifying them of this. If a shark happened to disobey the rules by swimming over to the human side of the rope, Jack instructed us to punch that shark in the face and everything would work out. I had never punched a human, much less a fish. As I contemplated getting into fisticuffs with a shark, Jack poured several buckets of bloody chum into the water and told everyone to jump in, as promised.

Camille's husband, Captain Courageous, was the first out of the boat. Camille seemed proud of his daring. Everyone else soon followed, including Camille, including—what the hell?—my own mother. My father must have pushed her when he took his dive. The last one in the boat, I reluctantly chose to jump, preferring to risk death than the possibility of Camille's husband making another snarky comment I could not understand.

As I snorkeled near the boat, on my side of the rope, I scanned the underwater terrain and saw nothing but small, colorful fish and a cloud of the bloody chum not far away. Floating in the water, all I could hear was the sound of my breathing through the snorkel. The anticipation of the sharks' arrival was nerve-racking—like being on the plains of the Serengeti, waiting for lions to appear. I'm not sure how my mother dealt with the tension because I was in survival mode. It was every man for himself out here, including my mom. I used Camille's husband as my primary wall of defense. It's not that

I wanted any harm to come to him. He was a big, muscular guy; he made me feel safe. I blinked, and suddenly there were more sharks in the vicinity than people. They were about my size, with black-tipped tails. Some were a little larger than me. Their teeth, though admirably clean, did not make them look docile.

The sharks methodically circled the bloody chum before suddenly gorging themselves like the wild carnivores they were. One of them looked at me from about ten feet away. I started swinging underwater punches to show it I meant business. It stayed where it was. All of the sharks remained on their side of the rope, for the most part. Occasionally they would cross the red rope boundary, but still kept their distance from us. They were like stray dogs who distrusted humans. It was the tourists who were the problem. Camille's husband crossed into shark territory in order to demonstrate how much braver he was than me. His showmanship was irritating. He'd already gotten the girl; he didn't need to prove anything. I absolutely most definitely did not want any serious harm to come to this man. But I would not have objected if a shark took the tiniest morsel out of his shoulder. Just the gentlest, slightest breaking of the skin to put him in his place.

Our guide, Jack, swam over to the husband and herded him back to the humans. These shenanigans drove a shark away from the pack, in my direction. It quickly swam past me and then looped around, heading straight for me. We made eye contact. I couldn't be certain because I wasn't an expert at reading shark faces, but judging by its expression alone, I believe it viewed me as top sirloin. The shark drew closer. My heart raced. I didn't punch it, but as it came within striking distance, I swung my hand out. My fingertips grazed its side as the shark deftly moved away from me, joining its brethren. Sharks feel like sandpaper.

Through the mob of swimmers, I saw Camille. She was watching me, having witnessed my close encounter. We both knew in that moment I was a stud. A stud who almost cried and nearly had an accident in his swimming trunks, but a stud nonetheless. Sure, she was going back to France with Mr. Six-pack, but on that day—in that moment—I was the biggest badass of the sea, even if it was on the calmer side of the reef. Now I had two activities on my list I knew I would definitely not participate in during my honeymoon. It was a shame my wife hadn't seen the shark encounter. Had she witnessed it, she would have thought I was just as big a badass as Camille did. I would let her know. That's the kind of thing my wife would want to know—that I was a badass.

My parents and I did not engage exclusively in death-defying activities while on Bora Bora. We also went for relaxing bike rides, took in a show of Tahitian dancers, and enjoyed a savory seafood dinner at the world famous Bloody Mary's, a festive yet relaxed restaurant in which patrons dug their bare feet into a fine white sand floor under a thatched roof. Like everywhere else, inside Bloody Mary's it was all couples—and me. I reminded myself that it wouldn't always be like that. I'd make a point of coming back to this very restaurant and proudly telling the host I was a party of two. Someday. The food at Bloody Mary's was delicious, but the seats were extremely uncomfortable. They were hard palm tree stumps. If you sat on them for more than five minutes, your ass began to cry for mercy. Preparation H was probably an oft-requested after-dinner treat. Still, I looked forward to eating here again on my next trip.

Though not without its embarrassing moments, the vacation with my parents was an enjoyable one. I was glad to have spent the quality time with them. When we boarded BO Airlines and headed back home, I had enough knowledge of the islands to ensure my second trip to the South Pacific, with a lovely young goddess by my side, would be a success. I looked forward to it, wondering when I would be back. Hopefully sooner rather than later. Regardless of how much time it took before my triumphant return to Bora Bora, I was in the mood for more traveling. It was rejuvenating to see a different part of the planet. I wanted to go somewhere else. Australia was still in my sights. Maybe someone was waiting for me over there, someone who would love French Polynesia.

Two years passed before Brian, still single, announced it was time to take Australia by storm. I had not traveled anywhere since the trip with my parents. Nor had I met anyone. I had gone on a smattering of dates, but each of them were as memorable as *Police Academy 5*, if that movie exists. (There was one girl who stood out by constantly belching like a rhino without ever saying excuse me, but that wasn't enough for a second date.) I was more than ready to visit Australia. Just as when we first discussed flying to Australia, Brian mentioned he didn't really feel like sitting on an airplane forever. He suggested we stop halfway so we could stretch our legs for a few days and then continue on to Australia. We looked at a map to figure out what was located about halfway between California and Australia.

On Bora Bora, I showed Brian the best places to eat, snorkel, and sunbathe. He was impressed. This second trip to French Polynesia didn't count. It was a pit stop. That's all it was. A place to rest for a few days and then get back on the plane. Since I was on my second South Pacific *adventure* as opposed to romance, I signed us up for the shark feeding. This time I looked forward to visiting the sharks, wondering what had transpired in their lives over the past two years and if they might remember me. The hotel staff informed us shark-feeding excursions were sold out until our third and final day on Bora Bora. In the meantime, we took part in other recreational activities, such as a bumpy four-wheel-drive jeep tour of Bora Bora.

Brian and I sat in the back of a sturdy open-air jeep. It was all couples on the jeep—including Brian and me. Our guide drove us to one of the highest points on Bora Bora, giving us a breathtaking view of its expansive bays and the surrounding tranquil ocean. It was a sublime backdrop for a picture. I handed my camera to our guide. Brian was standing off to the side, taking in the view. The guide looked around and asked, "Where's your wife?"

"I wish I knew," I answered, calling Brian over. The guide studied us, quickly jumping to conclusions. My senseless insecurities got the best of me. I wanted the guide to know Brian and I were two buddies who just happened to be visiting one of the most romantic destinations on Earth. I explained, "We're friends from college, on our way to Australia. This is just a rest stop. This is like pulling off the freeway for a bathroom break and maybe picking up some M&M's from the vending machines." Our guide smiled at me. He had no idea what I was talking about.

Throughout the duration of our stay on Bora Bora, people assumed Brian and I were an official couple. This was evident not just by the looks we received, but also from the statements. It seemed not an hour would go by without someone at the hotel or in some restaurant referring to Brian as my wife. Somehow, Brian was always the wife. I took this as the slightest bit of consolation, the slightest. It got tiring explaining over and over again that Brian and I were just friends, especially because I was the one doing the bulk of the explaining. Brian did little or nothing to clear up people's misconceptions.

What became more tiring than explaining ad nauseam that Brian and I weren't in love was constantly seeing all the people around us who were. Nothing against Brian, but I got tired of his face. I'm sure the feeling was mutual. Our surroundings left me with a yearning for female proximity. It was with this yearning that I looked upon our attractive waitress at the world-famous Bloody Mary's restaurant, where Brian and I sat down for dinner.

Remembering the hard palm tree stump chairs from my previous experience at Bloody Mary's with my parents, I suggested to Brian we take seat cushions from our hotel to the restaurant. Yet another benefit my wife, Brian, reaped from my prior knowledge of the area. As we sat down, there was no mistaking the other tourists' envy or their opinion of our sexual orientation. I'm sure bringing in our own personal, plush seat cushions didn't make us look gay at all.

Our cute waitress smiled when she saw the cushions. I explained we just wanted to be comfortable. She nodded, responding in a thick French accent, "*Oui, oui.* You take rest, from too much loving."

"What? No. No, no," I protested. "We're not in pain from too much loving. I've been here before, with my parents, and I remember these seats got really uncomfortable. So, cushions. That's all." She smiled knowingly, saying something in French. I had taken a six-week French language course between my last visit to Bora Bora and this one, because I wanted to understand the next time someone's arrogant husband called me a coward. Despite my studies, I didn't quite catch the waitress's words. The gist was she probably wondered how long Brian and I had been married. She introduced herself as Naomi. Naomi appeared to have been born and raised on the island. She was shapely, with smooth tanned skin and long flowing black hair. I liked Naomi. She was fun. Though I struggled to understand her French and she my English, it was pleasant to talk to someone with breasts.

When we finished our meal, I decided to ask Naomi if there was a place on the island where people danced and, if so, would she and perhaps a lady friend like to go dancing with me and Brian? Back home, I'd sooner clean out a septic tank with a toothbrush than dance. But these were desperate times. In French, asking someone to dance was a mouthful for me. The only phrase I retained from my six-week course was, *"Le stylo est sur la table,"* meaning the pen is on the table. I did however remember a popular radio tune entitled, *"Voulez-Vous Coucher Avec Moi"* which of course meant would you like to sleep with me? By process of elimination, I surmised *coucher* was the word to avoid, unless I was seeking a possible slap in the face.

I gestured to Naomi, as one would gesture during a game of charades, signaling I was going to attempt to communicate with her. She nodded, ready. I spoke slowly, careful not to accidentally ask if she would like to have sex. *"Voulez-vous"*—I paused, shimmying my shoulders simulating a dance move, and then continued with—*"avec moi?"* My run at French ended with me pointing at Brian and another waitress to demonstrate I was not asking for Naomi to participate in a threesome. Brian sat silently, perfectly still, like a street performer who remains supernaturally motionless for hours on end in front of a bucket, hoping passersby will leave change or dollar bills in said bucket. All he lacked was being covered in silver paint. As a wingman, he was about as effective as my mother.

Naomi smiled readily. She nodded her head in recognition of

my question. Then she said a bunch of French gibberish as she showed me the engagement ring on her finger. My consistent lack of ability to spot a ring on a woman's finger never ceased to amaze me. Man, I was good at that. I immediately offered apologies. Naomi shook her head, making it clear none were necessary. The bill was settled, I said good-bye to Naomi and went back to my hotel room . . . with Brian. I asked him if he'd noticed the ring on her finger. He told me he had, right away. I wondered why he hadn't stop me from asking her out. "You were trying so hard," Brian sympathetically commented. Bora Bora had not changed. It still was not the place to meet single women. We might as well have been on the lookout for giraffes.

If giraffes were in short supply, there were sharks aplenty. Our third and last day on Bora Bora, we set out to feed them. We met some fellow tourists in the lobby, just as before with my parents. Only this time the group was much smaller. It was me, Brian, and a couple a little older than us from Texas. That was it. The wife was attractive, but she was no Camille. She did all of the talking while we waited for our captain to arrive. Her husband seemed ill at ease. Making the assumption everyone else on Bora Bora made, the wife asked, "How did you two meet?"

"We're not gay," I matter-of-factly responded. My answer was too knee-jerk, too defensive. I followed up with, "Not that there's anything wrong with that. It's just that we're not. But if we were, Brian would be a great catch." Brian remained quiet, as usual. So did the woman's husband. He was not pleased. I could have been completely wrong, but his silent, disapproving stare gave me the impression he was concerned Brian and I might turn him gay simply by being in his very presence. That would have been an impressive if not useless feat.

The captain arrived. He was not the same captain as before. This man was younger and did not have a firm command of the English language. He introduced himself as Frank. I found it curious how exotic these islands and their people were, and yet Charlie, Jack, and Frank lived here. Frank's assistant was a child, nine years old. His son. I never caught the boy's name, but it was probably Mike. Frank and his son led us to their boat. Instead of a large vessel that fit twenty or so people, his smaller boat barely fit the six of us. As we headed out to the reef, Frank attempted to provide information. Brian asked him how many sharks we would see. Frank started to answer but then abruptly slipped, as if on a banana peel. He then did an accidental backflip *completely* out of the boat into the waters of the South Pacific. Were I judging, I would have given him a 9.5. Frank's jettison from the motorboat happened so quickly, we wondered if he had done this intentionally. He swam back to the boat and pulled himself aboard. Ready to put this incident behind him, Frank declared, "It's fine, it's fine. One of you asked me a question . . ."

A few minutes later, we arrived at the large coral reef where I had previously participated in a shark feeding. But this was not our final destination. Frank steered the small motorboat onward to an opening in the reef leading out to the greater ocean. He took us to the other side of the reef and then stopped. The dangerous side of the reef—the side of the reef I had heard so much about during my first trip. The *never swim on the other side* side of the reef. I mentioned this to Frank, the fact that I was repeatedly told there were large man-eating sharks on this side of the reef guaranteed to swallow us whole. The Texans reacted to my statement with alarm, particularly the husband. But Frank shrugged off my comment, saying, "No, no. It's fine." He then threw a bucket of bloody chum into the water and told us to jump in. Frank did not provide the safety of a red rope, clearly delineating where the sharks should be and where the people should be.

I became concerned that Frank was not our actual guide, that the real group was somewhere else—on the inside of the reef—and Frank was some sort of rogue who hated tourists and was trying to get rid of them one shark attack at a time. None of us jumped into the water. Frank encouraged us again to do so. I suggested he jump in first, to show us how it was done. He smiled at me, accepted the challenge, and took a dive near the bloody chum.

Brian and I sat across from the Texans. We were in a stare-down, wondering who would have the guts to jump in next. The husband, who had yet to say a word to either Brian or myself, kept a steady, challenging gaze on me. He reminded me of Camille's husband, two years earlier. Camille, so sweet and feminine, and her smug husband. I wondered how they were doing, if their marriage was going strong or were they perhaps having intimacy issues. If Camille's husband had been here, he would have no doubt already been in the water, establishing himself as the alpha male. He would have demonstrated that there was no man braver, more confident, or mighty. Remembering Camille's husband, I jumped out of the boat.

I immediately found myself staring into the eyes of an uncaring barracuda, or at least some kind of fish that looked like a barracuda, and definitely uncaring. With concern, I came up for air and called out to Frank, "I think a barracuda is swimming with us."

"No, no. It's fine." This was Frank's answer for everything. Perhaps it was the only phrase he remembered from a six-week English course he took years ago. He didn't seem concerned. Since he was swimming in the same body of water as me, I figured we were safe.

Either that or we were both about to be dismembered. Brian was next to jump into the water, followed by the Texan wife. Her husband remained in the boat. Frank urged him to join us, but he decided against it on account of he was a wimp, and also possessed common sense.

The sharks arrived a few moments later. They were reef sharks as before, but there weren't very many of them, and they were smaller this time around. Because there was no red rope marking the border, the sharks swam all around us. They were in front and behind, to the right and to the left, keeping things interesting. Also interesting was the depth of the open ocean. Last time around, the water hadn't been more than five or six feet deep. You could stand on the ocean floor. This time it was at least a hundred feet deep. The crystal clear visibility allowed us to see all the way to the bottom. I noticed a fish twice my size loafing on the seabed, not interested in our antics.

Looking away from the reef, out to the vast ocean, I saw an endless array of blue. I was very much aware that a shark, bigger than whatever kind of fish was hanging out below me, could introduce itself at any moment. Perhaps punching a great white shark in the face is effective, but I didn't want to try it. I got back in the boat, joining the husband who was prepared to race the boat back to shore in the event one of us was attacked. Brian and the Texan wife followed my lead after a few minutes. My second shark-feeding excursion might not have been quite as exciting as the first, but it was unquestionably more perilous. In all likelihood, there was a massive great white—probably a school of them, probably hundreds of them—swimming nearby, checking me out. I was basically swimming alongside them. Once again, I was a manly man. My wife—not Brian, my *real* wife—was missing so much!

With our legs adequately rested, Brian and I bid farewell to Bora Bora, heading to Australia, where we hopefully would not be so overwhelmingly outnumbered by honeymooners. As our plane departed, I stared out the window at the effortlessly beautiful island of Bora Bora. It struck me that I had now unexpectedly visited French Polynesia twice—and never gotten any action. While others came here to toast the beginning of their lives together, to make memories, bond with and love one another, I had come to feed tuna steaks to eels, nearly punch sharks in the jaw, and be mistaken for Brian's husband. Through the airplane window, I continued to watch Bora Bora grow smaller in the distance. I would return some-day. With my woman. Just as soon as I found her.

A GOOD TIME IN OZ

I was excited about visiting Australia. It would be fun to explore a part of the world so far away from home. Before I left, my mother called to warn me about the deadly spiders, snakes, jellyfish, sharks, and crocodiles. To hear her describe these animals, it was a wonder anyone survived in Australia more than a day. She advised me, as usual, to be careful. As if I was going to be gallivanting with these creatures, singing "Zip-a-Dee-Doo-Dah" while a carefree funnel spider kept tempo on my shoulder and a happy-go-lucky saltwater crocodile harmonized at my feet. Additionally, my mother cautioned me not to trust kangaroos or koala bears. She had heard, through the grapevine, that kangaroos were expert prizefighters, given to knocking people out with solid right hooks. Hopefully I'd get a chance to see that. Koala bears had a penchant for dropping from trees onto the shoulders of unsuspecting victims whom they would then attempt to strangle. According to my mother, koala bears were cute but sadistic.

The idea of being attacked by a koala sounded entertaining. I could take a koala. As much as I would have welcomed a koala bear fistfight, I told my mother such an occurrence was probably rare—as in it had never happened in the history of relations between man and koala. She did not appreciate my disregard for her advice. "Don't go anywhere near the animals," she insisted. "You need to take me seriously. Otherwise you'll end up in the hospital with your legs ripped apart or your eyes scratched out. Oh, and if you see a nice wool sweater, buy it for me."

Interacting with Australian wildlife would be interesting enough, but that was not the purpose of this trip. The purpose of this trip was to meet a warmhearted, caring, genuine girl whom I could sweep off her feet. Or to hook up with someone super hot. Either/or. Casual encounters never strongly appealed to me, but after my inadvertent honeymoon with Brian on Bora Bora, I would not have objected if the opportunity presented itself. To help me communicate with the female population, I studied the Australian language online before I left. During the course of my studies, I learned things such as in Australia when people want to find out how much something costs they say a woman's full name—*Emma Chisit*. I was anxious to try my Australian with the local sheilas.

Chances were high of encountering a charming young lass. Brian and I had signed up for a two-week Australian bus tour operated by the Rikki-Tikki-Tavi Company or some name like that. The tour was specifically designed for fit people in their twenties. In the company's brochure, there were photos of numerous smiling attractive men and, more important, women having the time of their lives. They were shown participating in the kinds of exhilarating activities often featured in herpes commercials—parasailing, river rafting, horseback riding. If there was at least *one* girl in the tour group I clicked with, great! And if I could click without catching a venereal disease, all the better!

Following our stop in French Polynesia, Brian and I arrived in Sydney a couple of days before the Rikki-Tikki-Tavi tour began. By chance, some married friends of mine, Geoff and Diana, were also visiting Sydney at the same time. Not only were Geoff and Diana in the same city, they were staying in the same hotel. We discovered this remarkable coincidence one morning in the lobby. Amazed at having found one another on the other side of the planet, we agreed to meet back at the hotel at the end of the day for dinner. We then parted ways to leisurely sightsee.

Brian and I went to Sydney Harbor (or *Harbour* if you're Australian, which I am not—so forget the unnecessary *u*). As I admired the harbor, the famous opera house, and the harbor bridge, I remembered again that Australia is the only country in the world that is also a continent. Answering this question correctly, way back when, had brought me fifth-grade academic glory, as well as the affectionate admiration of my first girlfriend, Yvonne. It had been years since I'd seen her. I remembered imagining the two of us overlooking Sydney Harbor, hugging and kissing—on the cheek, like respectable adults. Now, here I was. With Brian. Brian approached, telling me he was ready to see more of the city. I remained on the walkway for a few moments, looking around. How incredible would it have been if Yvonne, appearing vivacious and youthful, suddenly strolled up to me the way Geoff and Diana had run into me in the hotel lobby? She didn't.

Toward the end of the day, not long before our scheduled dinner with Geoff and Diana, Brian and I wandered into a popular downtown Sydney club. The place was packed with women, gorgeous women. Gorgeous single women. They were all incredibly friendly and social and inquisitive, wanting to know what our lives were like in America and if we were having a good time in Oz. A lot of the women were scantily clad. Some wore nothing at all! This was in large part due to the fact that the club was a strip club. The women were following a strict non-dress code. I'm not sure how we ended up in there, but somehow we did. I think it was because we had five minutes to spare before our dinner with Geoff and Diana. We were curious to see if Australian pole dancing was similar to American. (It is. Like the language of cinema, the language of pole dancing is universal.)

A stripper, or rather an exotic dancer, named Caramel (apparently her parents loved sweets) sauntered over to us while we sat in the back. She approached me first, offering a lap dance in a delightful Australian accent. Seizing this opportunity, I asked, "Emma Chisit?"

Caramel immediately answered, "Twenty duluhs."

I was pleased by successfully speaking Australian. But I remained calm. I didn't want a lap dance, I just wanted to ask, "Emma Chisit?" So as not to hurt Caramel's feelings, I explained that first of all, I wasn't much of a dancer. Second, my friends were expecting me for dinner—I was going to have to leave momentarily. The third part I did not mention. It was torturously refreshing to be surrounded by so many undressed ladies. But the idea of going in a back room, fully clothed, in order for someone to writhe so close and yet so far while a cash meter ran as if we were in a taxi—that did not appeal to me. Brian didn't have a problem with this concept. When Caramel asked him if he'd like a lap dance, he sprang to his feet. Caramel took his hand, seductively leading him to the private caverns of this distinguished gentlemen's club. I assumed Brian would be right back. One song and we'd be out the door. We *really* did need to leave momentarily if we were going to be on time for dinner with Geoff and Diana. Brian did not return after the first song or the second or the third. Caramel must have been Ginger Rogers to Brian's Fred Astaire. After the *fifth* song, Brian finally reappeared, disheveled but blissful.

We hopped in a cab and rushed to the hotel. Geoff and Diana were waiting in the hotel restaurant. They seemed more than slightly irritated on account of us being about fifteen minutes late. I apologized profusely as Brian took a seat beside me, explaining we had gone to a movie and the movie lasted longer than expected. This was partly true. We had taken in a movie that afternoon. It was a boring Australian feature about lawn bowling and an emotionally distant father. After the movie, we'd stumbled upon the gentlemen's club. I left that part out, not wanting to bore Geoff and Diana with unnecessary details.

But Geoff and Diana wanted details, lots of them. They would not stop asking us questions about the movie. What was it called? What was it about? Who was in it? Who directed it? How was the cinematography? Had I known we were going to be grilled, I would have taken copious notes during the screening. We finally moved on to other subjects, including the group tour Brian and I were about to embark on first thing in the morning.

Dinner ended; we said our good-byes. Geoff shook my hand, bringing up the movie one last time, "Don't forget to e-mail me the title. I'd really like to see it." I told him I would, not understanding his fascination. When I got in the elevator with Brian, I suddenly realized why we'd been so closely interrogated. The elevator had mirrored walls. In Brian's reflection I noticed something I had not seen the entire dinner. He had a glaring bright red lipstick kiss on his neck, planted there by none other than Caramel during their marathon dance session.

I was sitting next to Brian in the restaurant; I could not see the incriminating side of his neck. But Geoff and Diana, who were sitting across from us, that's pretty much all they *could* see. No wonder Geoff wanted to check the movie out. That lipstick was flashing like a neon billboard the entire meal. When we sat down, huffing and puffing, apologizing about some boring lawn bowling film, the kiss on Brian's neck was screaming at them, "Liars, liars! They're lying! They're lying perverts who lie!" Brian looked at his reflection. His face turned beet red—as red as the mark on his neck. I tried to make him feel better by assuring him whatever sense of shame he felt was appropriate.

The next morning, we met our Rikki-Tikki-Tavi tour group at a scenic spot near the bridge. There were as many unencumbered ladies as there were men, perhaps a few more. It was such a refreshing sight after just having spent a number of days trapped on the rest stop island of Bora Bora with a legion of honeymooners. This was an oasis. I almost felt like crying. Our tour group, consisting of about twenty-five travelers from around the world, excitedly stepped aboard the comfortable bus, ready for a trip along Australia's eastern seaboard, from New South Wales into Queensland.

The tour guide was a matronly woman named Janice who appeared to be in her early thirties. As we began our travels up the highway, Janice stood at the front of the bus with a microphone. She announced each of us would take the microphone one at a time, say our name, and share something unique about ourselves. This would give everyone a good chance to check everyone else out and decide who wanted to hump who. Janice didn't say that, but it was the subtext. The energy on the bus was similar to that of a singles meat market. It was sort of like summer camp, without the mosquitoes or s'mores or acne. Just a bus full of randy young adults, thousands of miles from home. There would be love connections, oh yes, there would. After Janice informed everyone that going number two on the bus was prohibited, she handed the microphone over for formal introductions.

First to catch my eye was a perky, busty redhead named Tabitha. I was not normally drawn to her type, but there was something about her energy, her character, that I found appealing. She spoke into the microphone with a confident tone, telling her fellow passengers the unique thing about her was that she was the only Australian amongst our group. She reported she was from the island of Tasmania, adding, "And, no, gentlemen, you won't be seeing my map of Tassie." This did not elicit much of a reaction, since no one really knew what she meant by *map of Tassie*. Realizing this, Tabitha explained the map of Tassie was Australian slang for a woman's pubic area. The island of Tasmania had a similar shape, at least similar to the way women groomed themselves in the 1970s. I thought it considerate of Tabitha to educate us on such matters and hoped for a chance to get to know her.

A man and a woman walked up to the front of the bus together, sharing the microphone. They looked like they were about to sing a duet. The man spoke first. He was American, from Oregon. His name was Steve. He was traveling with his wife, Cynthia, who gave us all a friendly wave. The unique thing about them was they were just married. This trip was their honeymoon. This trip, on this bus, with this group of virile men and nubile women, was their *honeymoon*. I immediately thought of my travels through French Polynesia as the lone bachelor surrounded by couples. My how the tables had turned. In Australia, I was riding on a bus full of singles surrounding the lone newlyweds. It was tempting to call out, "Now who's the loser? You are, Steve and Cynthia!" Instead I clapped perfunctorily, along with the rest of the group, as Steve and Cynthia returned to their bridal seats.

A passive, unassuming, self-conscious woman nervously took the microphone and introduced herself as Kate from Bermuda. She was slim, with lengthy dark hair and a sweet voice. Kate from Bermuda was pretty. A pretty holistic animal therapist. That was the unique thing about her. I would have guessed she was a librarian or quilter. But no. She treated cats and dogs for migraines. I had noticed her before she went up to the front of the bus. While everyone else was traveling with a friend or two, Kate was on her own. I was curious to find out more about her. Hopefully there would be a chance to have a stilted conversation before the tour ended.

Perhaps the most memorable introductions were the briefest. There were two pale blond men traveling together. They were both from Germany. They looked similar, with cropped haircuts. One was slightly taller than the other. The taller one walked to the front of the bus first. In a humorless tone, he said, "I'm Detlef from Hamburg," and then sat down.

His companion took the microphone next, saying, "I'm Ralph, from Hamburg," and then he sat down. The unique thing about them was at some point they were probably going to take over the bus and hold us all hostage until the nine members of the Asian

Dawn Movement in Sri Lanka were released. Hopefully there was an undercover tour bus marshal on board, keeping an eye out.

Our first stop and overnight stay was Coffs Harbour (again with the needless *u*). I was assigned a hotel room with four other male travelers from the group. Brian was assigned to a different room with a different group. He'd grown up with a family of ten brothers and sisters so, for Brian, rooming with four other people was the equivalent of a spa treatment. For me, as an only child, sharing a room with four other strangers was the stuff of nightmares. I was a trouper though, powering through it.

When I arrived at my room, the four additional occupants were already there. Luckily, the German terrorists were not part of this group. (They were with Brian. I prayed for his safety.) The television was on, turned to a soccer match. The four gentlemen were partially paying attention to the game, but mostly having a fast-paced conversation. They were speaking English, or trying to. Because they were all from various parts of Europe, I was having trouble understanding them. It sounded like they were bartering. I heard words such as "long dark hair" and "yellow blouse." It finally dawned on me: They were discussing the girls in our tour group. Specifically, they were calling dibs on certain ladies. A British guy called shotgun on Tabitha from Tasmania, making a crass comment about studying her map of Tassie; an Italian fellow wanted Kate, the holistic animal therapist, boasting about the animal therapy they would soon be practicing. The females' opinions in this matter were irrelevant.

The swagger and machismo of these guys was so exaggerated, it was obvious they would be spending most of their vacation with one another. I did not participate in the multinational talks, preferring to let things happen naturally. Brian and I had already agreed that in the event a female we liked showed interest in one of us, the other would graciously step aside. There was an entire two weeks for Cupid to sling his arrows. Actually one week for myself and Brian. The tour we signed up for was an exploration of the Australian coast and outback. In a week, we would be joining a different group in the desert. Still, one week for romance to take its course. Plenty of time.

We stopped at a koala reserve the next day, which was more like a koala bear commune. They were everywhere, in all the trees, plentiful as fruit. None of the koalas had any desire to drop down and strangle us. They were too busy being stoned out of their minds. The amicable ranger working at the reserve explained it was a common misconception that koalas get high from eating eucalyptus leaves. So they weren't stoned out of their minds. They just looked stoned out of their minds.

Our tour group formed three separate lines as we waited to pose for a picture while holding an adorable koala. When the ranger looked up at the trees and asked aloud, "Which one of you guys wants to come down for pictures?" all of the koalas turned away, refusing to make eye contact. Picture taking had become such a routine, they understood the ranger's question.

Three unlucky koalas were eventually plucked from the trees. I held one of them. My picture was taken and I quickly handed the puny koala over to the ranger without breaking it. A few minutes later, I walked back to the bus with my souvenir photo. I returned to the bus at the same time as Tabitha from Tasmania. She, too, had a photo with a koala. We smiled, said hello, and showed each other our photos. Tabitha gushed over mine. "Oh, you got a baby," she commented with the slightest hint of jealously. "The one they gave me was bigger."

I looked at Tabitha's photo. The koala she was holding was the size of a small man. It could have been her bodyguard. Now *I* was jealous. I wished I had posed with this guy. That would have made a great picture, especially if the koala was enjoying a beer. I mentioned this to Tabitha and she laughed. We got on the bus. I was about to take a seat next to her, but a girlfriend of hers moved in at the last second, cutting me off. Tabitha did not object so I let it go. I had made her laugh. That was groundwork. Progress. It was a Monday. By Wednesday we would hopefully be cuddling.

On Tuesday, we found ourselves on a typical Australian farm. A number of activities were offered before dinner was to be served in the dining hall. Strangely, Brian had chosen to fly in a WWII biplane. This meant he was going to be driven, solo, to a nearby regional airport where he would hop in an old airplane with a pilot and do loop-de-loops. It was a curious method of meeting girls, to remove himself entirely from the farm, but I trusted he knew what he was doing. I chose horseback riding. I am not a fan of horses. That is not to say I am horses' archenemy or vice versa, only that for the most part I have managed to avoid these thousand-pound animals in my daily life. However, I noticed Tabitha from Tasmania had signed up. I was willing to saddle up if it meant laying more groundwork. Plus, Kate the animal therapist would also be riding. If things didn't pan out with Tabitha, maybe they would with Kate.

The rancher leading the ride asked how much time I had spent on horseback. I explained my experience was limited to respectfully saying hello to ponies at petting zoos and that I should probably ride the gentlest, slowest horse on the farm. He put me on a horse named Raw. I didn't catch the names of the other horses, but if Raw was the gentlest, then the other horses must have had names like Bone Cruncher, Battle Axe, and Demon Seed.

Upon meeting Raw, I explained the situation to him, informing him my main purpose was to chat more with Tabitha and/or Kate. I'd really appreciate it if he kept things slow and steady. Raw gave me a look, wondering why I was making noises in the direction of his face. I climbed atop him and away we went. He kindly kept a leisurely pace. I was especially pleased with Raw's slower gait because I was riding on what I was told was an English saddle. An English saddle is a saddle without a horn, which is horseback-riding shoptalk for the handle a person needs to grab a hold of when he is in the process of falling off a horse. I had no need to hold on to the horn that wasn't there because Raw was behaving honorably.

We remained at the rear of the group. So did Tabitha, conveniently. Perhaps Raw understood after all. As we rode side by side, Tabitha began eagerly chatting. This was good. She told me how grateful she was to be seeing so much of Australia. It was lovely to get a look at her glorious country. She *needed* this vacation because of a recent most terrible experience she'd had in the Australian military. Curious, I asked if she wouldn't mind telling me what this recent most terrible experience was. Tabitha explained she had joined the military because she was interested in seeing various parts of the world and interacting with different cultures. During basic training her superiors continuously made her run—really fast— with heavy guns. They would not stop talking about killing people. It was horrible. That mean Australian military, with their heavy guns and constant running. Thank heavens she got out.

Her terrible experience gave me a chuckle. I commented that it was unfortunate the Australian military was so fixated on killing and guns. On the other hand, if a country's armed forces focused more on gingerbread recipes and bake sales, it would probably be more difficult to protect its citizens. After all, there was only so much damage one could do, throwing a cookie at someone. This was a lighthearted remark, similar to the one I made about wanting to pose with the giant koala guzzling a brewski. Given Tabitha's sociable persona, the way she enjoyed my koala comment, her willingness to refer to her map of Tassie—I thought she would laugh at my observation. But I saw right away I had crossed a line.

She stared at me, her anger building. "You're just like everybody else," she scornfully decreed. "Here I share something shocking about how the military expected me to shoot people and you make fun." The military expecting its soldiers to shoot people? Shocking? My unrestrained laughter deepened her rage. She admonished me, saying, "I've been through more painful experiences than you could ever imagine. You're scum." Tabitha figured out a way to make her horse go faster, trotting off in a huff. Cuddling would have to be postponed at least until Thursday. Or if Brian wanted her, he could have her.

Soon after Tabitha left me in the dust, Raw realized he was late for a meeting. Without warning, he took off the way horses take off at the Kentucky Derby. This was not a welcome development. I tried holding on to the edges of my useless English saddle as Raw raced past the other horses at light speed. The rancher called something out to me but there wasn't enough time for the sound waves of his voice to reach my eardrums since Raw was en route to the horizon.

In an effort to get him to slow down, I pulled on the leathery strings that were attached to the inside of his mouth. Whatever the technical term for these strings, in Raw's case pulling back made him go faster. I screamed for him to stop, yelling *whoa* in as many different intonations and languages as I could think of. But Raw had to see a man about a horse and was not interested in anything I said. It was a shame my trip was going to end abruptly with a broken back. In Australia, it's not the crocs or snakes or spiders you have to watch out for. It's the *horses*. My heart burst out of my chest as I held on to whatever I could.

Raw finally slowed down before coming to a complete stop. I immediately jumped off him and kissed the ground. Raw turned toward me. He seemed surprised I was still around. So was I. The rancher caught up to us. He asked if I was all right, wanting to know what had happened. I informed the rancher he would have to ask Raw. Whatever had set Raw off, he was calm now. The rancher suggested I get back on him and we'd return to the dining hall for dinner. This was like asking a person who had just escaped a lion's den to go ahead and crawl back into the den and we'll grab some grub in a bit. I told the rancher I couldn't get back on Raw due to my delayed New Year's resolution of not riding horses ever again for the rest of my life. And I stuck to it. I walked Raw the rest of the way, holding on to the leathery strings. It was a pleasant walk, mostly because I enjoyed being alive.

"Having trouble with your horse?" The soothing voice of Kate took me by surprise. In the terrifying excitement of being on a runaway horse I had forgotten about the other members of my group, even the pretty ones. I looked up at Kate, expertly straddling her horse as she approached. She was much more relaxed than when she'd spoken into the microphone on the bus. Kate gave me a comforting smile. She encouraged me to get back in the saddle, noting that my horse had only gone *a little* out of control. "You've got to show him who's in charge," she encouraged.

"He's in charge," I replied. "He's definitely in charge. There's no contest. I don't mind walking. In the United States, people take their horses for a walk all the time. It's pretty common."

Kate laughed at this. She stayed with me as the rest of the group rode ahead, including tempestuous Tabitha. After inadvertently offending Tabitha to her core, I decided to play it safe and let Kate do most of the talking. She had no problem carrying the conversation. I got the sense she was eager to share with someone, maybe because she was traveling alone. She told me she traveled alone quite a bit. It helped her clear her mind. Every so often I would say something like, "That's interesting," and she would take it from there. I didn't object. After my near-death experience riding Raw, I was in a quiet mood.

We returned to the stables, handing our horses off to the rancher. Kate and I were the last of the bunch. I wished Raw good riddance, whispering to him that he was a bastard. Raw appeared satisfied with himself. With the horses secured and the sun going down, we were expected at the dining hall for dinner. Kate remained with me, still talking about her life in Bermuda. She had covered various topics such as planting her own vegetable garden, her friendly neighbors, and was now on to describing the dog she had as a child, a dachshund named Button. As she paused to take a breath, I chimed in with, "Sounds like a tough dog."

We headed toward the dining hall. Through the windows, I could see our tour group gathered at various tables. The din of their chatter was audible in the distance. As we approached the dining hall entrance, Kate changed course. She walked away from the din-ing hall to a lit swimming pool, telling me she was an avid scuba diver. There was no acknowledgement of her new destination. She played it off naturally. I paused for a moment, glancing at the dining hall, and then decided to join her.

A waist-high chain-link fence enclosed the pool. Its gate was unlocked. Kate took her shoes off and dunked her feet in the luke-warm water as she sat down. I did the same. Kate obviously felt at home. I wasn't quite as relaxed because I didn't fully understand what was going on. Her spontaneous walk to the pool at dinnertime threw me. It was now dark out. The dim lights of the pool created an intimate atmosphere.

I wondered if skinny-dipping was in our future. If it was, it might prove problematic. For one thing, we didn't have towels. Dry-ing off would be a challenge. Plus, we were secluded but not com-pletely. Anyone walking out of the dining hall would get an eyeful. What would I say to someone who happened upon us? "Oh, hello. I've decided to swim nude in this pool with Kate. How are you enjoying your trip so far?" Last but not least, though Kate had not stopped talking since she started, I didn't really know her. Her unpredictable walking patterns and desire to share every unfiltered aspect of her life made me a little nervous. I hoped she wasn't going to take her clothes off and jump in. If Kate got in the pool wearing her birthday suit, I'd probably stand up and excuse myself, explain-ing, "You know what? I'm starting to get a little hungry. I'm going to go inside and eat some mashed potatoes." Leaving her there, naked in the water, would be unfortunate. Best if she just kept her clothes on, saving nudity for tomorrow or the next night. The feminine side of me needed to ease into things.

"What are you thinking?" asked Kate.

I told Kate she had a nice smile. She blushed, shook her head, and covered her face. Once again, I did not understand. Removing her hands, Kate looked at me and said, "People are talking about us right now." I found that highly unlikely. Most people didn't even know our names. In the grand scheme of things we weren't that late for dinner. The group probably hadn't even noticed our absence yet. Exhaling sharply, Kate stood up, deciding, "We better go inside, before all the food is gone."

There was a hush in the dining hall as we walked in. Everyone focused on us, certain that Kate and I had just fornicated. I saw Brian sitting at a table nearby with fellow travelers. He had returned from his WWII flight looking a bit pale. He gave me a subtle nod. I couldn't tell if it was a nod of approval or if he was nauseated. His table was fully occupied, as were most of the tables. Kate tenderly stroked my arm, pointing out two available seats at a table across the hall. The seats were beside the German terrorists. Of course those seats were available.

We served ourselves some food from the buffet trays and joined the bad guys. The Germans were staunchly anti-small talk, avoiding eye contact and tersely answering my questions. I gave up on them, hoping they wouldn't stick me with a shiv. Kate was amused by my attempt at being social. She leaned closer, whispering, "I think it would be nice to have dinner, just the two of us, away from this group. Maybe we can do that tomorrow night on Fraser Island."

I agreed, but was still unsure about what I had done to draw Kate in so quickly, other than ride a horse really fast and occasionally say "That's interesting" in response to tales of her homegrown tomatoes. She smiled at me, pleased. I noticed Tabitha from Tasmania at the table next to us. Our eyes met. She gave me a nasty look, still reeling from the way I had mocked her dismay at having to fire weapons in the army. It didn't matter. Tabitha's anger was moot. I was now in a relationship. Who was this Kate? She made me feel a little uneasy. Not as uneasy, however, as Brian, who I discovered puking his guts out in our assigned room. The plane ride had given him motion sickness. There wouldn't be any girls sharing a bed with him tonight, unless they liked vomit.

On Wednesday, we were on Fraser Island. Fraser Island is the largest sand island in the world. Everywhere we went there was sand. *Sand from the beach* sand. And, yet, vegetation was able to grow. There were forests, large freshwater lakes, creeks. Villages had even been established with hotels, general stores, restaurants. All on the sand. I'm not sure how this worked, but that's how it worked.

Kate and I had confirmed our plans to meet for a private dinner that night. During the day, she joined an optional whale-watching excursion. Brian decided to go whale watching too. Aware of my burgeoning romance with Kate, Brian promised to keep his hands off her—and also to let me know if she was cheating on me. It would have relieved me to discover she was also interested in someone else. I declined to go whale watching because, having done it before, I knew whale watching really meant *ocean* watching. It turned looking at water into a job. Occasionally, a whale would swim by. People would get to see it—a small portion of it—for a few seconds. In those few seconds, they would exclaim, "Look! There! Did you see it? It's gone." It mostly involved a lot of an uncertain pointing and monotonous staring. Pass.

I remained on land, choosing to go on an organized nature hike to one of the island's lakes. Before I left, I called my mother. She requested I call at least once during the trip to let her know I had not been eaten by anything. When she answered the phone I reported it was her son calling. "Everything's fine," I assured her. "Having a good time. There was some unexpected excitement yesterday."

My mother asked, "Does that mean you found a nice wool sweater?" I corrected her, telling her a horse named Raw provided the unexpected excitement. She gave me a retroactive, "Be careful," and then prodded me again about the sweater. I promised if I spotted one—which I hadn't yet—I'd provide it safe passage to America. Her obsession with Australian sweaters was a bit much.

Kate and Brian returned from whale watching along with a few other tour members. Brian did not look well. I asked him how the whale watching had gone. He told me he saw part of a tail for one second and then he got seasick. Also, Kate had remained loyal to me. He grabbed his stomach and said he was heading back to the lodge to lie down and maybe puke more. Brian had a unique method of attracting the ladies.

While the majority of the tour group gathered for dinner at the economy lodge where we were staying, Kate and I shared a meal at a nearby outdoor café. Kate was eager to tell me about her whale-watching experience. In the several hours at sea, she had seen a tail splash the water in the blink of an eye. I wondered if it was the same tail Brian saw. It was exhilarating, so she said. I paid attention to the best of my ability, but I was distracted by her familiarity. She reminded me of a spouse having just returned from work, wanting to share the events of her day. This was weird. Not necessarily a bad weird. It's just that after forty-eight hours, I still didn't feel like I knew her all that well. Sure, she had provided a countless number of facts about her grandmother's dishware and whatnot, but I still didn't *know* her. I tried to think of a diplomatic way of asking her to dial down the intensity to that of a vacation fling rather than holy matrimony, but couldn't come up with anything. As much as I was a fan of holy matrimony, something seemed off here. Kate gazed at me as if I were a rare quartz diamond, saying I was the first Carlos she had ever met. She asked, earnestly, if there were many other people named Carlos in Los Angeles. A wild dingo strolled through the café to make things more surreal.

After dinner, we walked to a nearby luxury hotel. Kate mentioned she was not particularly fond of her roommates and wasn't ready to go back to our economy lodge. I also preferred Kate's company over the band of European wannabe players who were busy drafting futile plans designed to get them into an imaginary girl's invisible pants. Kate and I wound up at the luxury hotel's bar. We ordered our drinks and went to the bar's upstairs lounge. No one was there but us. As I sipped on some hot tea, Kate talked about the wonders of Bermuda and how much I would enjoy them. She ended her spiel on behalf of the Bermuda Board of Tourism with a simple question. "Aren't you going to kiss me?" It was official. Kate liked me. I thought so.

"Yes," I replied. "I'm going to have a few more sips of tea. And then I'm going to kiss you." I had a few more sips of tea and then I kissed her. It was good, the kiss. I took her in my arms. She felt soft. While our passions escalated, an elderly couple joined us in the upstairs lounge. Kate and I broke apart as if a bucket of ice water had been thrown on us, which essentially it had. Having no sense of decency, the bothersome old people took a seat across from us, loudly voicing their dissatisfaction with the fish dinner they'd just eaten. We smiled, pretending to be happy to see them. I quietly made a bold offer to Kate. "I don't mean any disrespect. And I'm not suggesting we do anything more than what we were doing a few minutes ago. But for the sake of privacy and comfort, if you would like me to get us a room, I will." For the first time since I'd met her, Kate didn't say anything. She just nodded.

Our room was spectacular. It concerned me. Perhaps I had not properly understood the conversion rate between American and Australian currency. I crossed my fingers, hoping I would not receive a credit card bill for thousands of dollars mailed to me as a souvenir. Kate was in awe of our accommodations. She walked around the room, taking it in. A huge smile on her face, Kate gave me a tight embrace, commenting, "Isn't this nice?" I asked if her question was rhetorical. She responded by hugging me even tighter. I didn't feel like I was on a Rikki-Tikki-Tavi tour with buoyant twenty-somethings anymore. It seemed more as if I were celebrating my silver wedding anniversary. It wasn't like I'd imagined it would be.

Kate pulled away from me, a somewhat serious look in her eyes. She told me she didn't believe in sex before marriage. The way she said the word *marriage* didn't sound like she was saying it in the general sense. It sounded as if she was saying we would not have sex until after we got married. Kate sensed my concern, quickly adding, "I'm not making any wedding plans." She laughed nervously, which led me to believe she already had a dress picked out.

I was okay with Kate's declaration because I was not as animalistic as my European roommates. She was pretty. I enjoyed kissing her. It was nice to have such a spacious, comfortable room to ourselves. But I still only felt fifty percent comfortable around Kate and could not shake this. Sleeping together would have meant more to Kate than it did to me and she was already pretty fervent about things. If she had never been married, then by the transitive property of geometry, I deduced she was a virgin. Not a good idea, to be her first. Speaking of firsts, that was the first time I'd used geometry outside of high school. Shockingly, I was using it to talk myself out of going all the way with this girl.

Kate led me to the foot of the bed. We sat in silence. She gently caressed my hand, looking toward the floor. I looked at the floor as well, but didn't notice anything special. Only the carpet. Kate sighed. She said, "There's something you should know about me." I was surprised to hear she had left out a detail about her life; I thought she had covered everything. Taking another deep breath, Kate revealed, "I'm divorced." My initial thought was *so you're not a virgin* but I kept this to myself. I didn't say anything. She seemed a little disappointed. "I just dropped a bombshell on you. How does that make you feel?"

Her divorced status was not a bombshell. The revelation affected me as much as if she had said she used to have bangs. Judging by Kate's dramatic confession, it was obviously a big deal to her. That she expected it to be a big deal to me as well showed that she was a little farther along emotionally in our two-day relationship. I liked Kate, but not to the point where she could drop a bombshell on me. Unless she said something like, "Carlos, I'm half leprechaun." But she hadn't said that. She was simply divorced.

Kate continued staring at me, still waiting to hear my view of her failed marriage. It was a sensitive subject and I treated it as such. I responded, "I don't really have any strong feelings one way or another. I'm just registering that information right now. Thank you for telling me." Kate remained quiet. She hugged me again. We kissed, moving farther onto the bed. It was a long, memorable night—one that did not break Kate's policy, but pushed its limits. The night was vastly more enjoyable than if had I bunked with the European horndogs and sickly Brian.

Early Thursday morning, still in bed, Kate asked if I would consider moving to Bermuda. It was not a hypothetical question. She felt Los Angeles was a corrupt, morally depraved city filled with shallow inhabitants and that I would find life in Bermuda to be more tranquil and fulfilling. I defended Los Angeles, telling her it got a bad rap. For example, my dentist—Dr. Edmond Chin—was a fine fellow. And Grace, who regularly cut my hair, did so with the warmth and affection of an aunt. There were plenty of decent folk in the greater metropolitan Los Angeles region.

Kate sat up. In a calm but determined tone, she declared, "I need to know where this is going." I waited for her to continue, expecting to hear something like, "I realize I'm moving at light speed here. But, hey, the heart wants what the heart wants. Whaddaya gonna do?" Kate never said this or anything remotely similar. She just waited for me to tell her where things were going. It seemed as if I was finally getting what I wanted. Someone as ready and eager and willing to make a commitment as I was. But I didn't want it. Not with her, not like this. This felt forced. Kate wasn't crazy, I don't think. I hypothesized she was lonely and my willingness to listen appealed to her immensely. At any rate, I did not feel threatened or alarmed by her behavior.

Perhaps this was stupid. Perhaps I should have bolted from the room, telling her, "You know what? I just remembered I need to take my vitamins. They're back at the lodge. I'll see you up there. And, by the way, Carlos is my nickname. My real name is Rodrigo Pimento. And I actually live in New Brunswick, New Jersey." For whatever reason, Kate did not scare me. Maybe because I was on the other side of the world, she lived on the other side of the continent, and this leg of the tour would be over shortly. Kate was still staring, still waiting for me to tell her about our future. I explained that while I enjoyed the time we had spent together, I wasn't ready to uproot my life and join her in Bermuda. I did appreciate the invitation though.

She was not angry. Nor did she appear hurt. Kate seemed re-signed. She told me that she also enjoyed the time we'd spent together, but felt it would be best if we did not communicate for the remain-der of the trip. Our relationship had run its course. We'd lasted about as long as an adult may fly, a little bit longer. Kate got dressed, primped herself, and left. She asked that I wait at least ten minutes before returning to the economy lodge, to protect her reputation. I did wait ten minutes, though I doubted anyone assumed Kate and I stayed in separate rooms simply because we returned to the lodge ten minutes apart.

Thursday was devoted to the Great Barrier Reef. Much of the day consisted of riding a boat out to the reef. I thought the reef was one giant reef, located within swimming distance of an Australian beach. There are actually three thousand reefs. We only had time to visit one of them that Thursday. The boat trip from the mainland to the reef felt like it took about thirty-seven hours, though I could be wrong. Kate spent her time on the boat avoiding me, true to her word. She avoided me in such a way as to remind me that she was avoiding me, always staying within sight. Not too close, not too far. Just enough for me to be aware. She was like a floater in my eye. For much of the trip she sat beside Brian, who looked healthy for a change. Predictably, she did most of the talking. Brian looked concerned.

When Kate moved on to other travelers, Brian took a seat beside me, saying, "That girl really likes you. How come?" I told him I didn't know. Brian informed me Kate had spoken exclusively about me the whole time she was sitting with him. He offered his body-guard services if I wanted them. I thanked Brian, but told him they would not be necessary. We finally arrived at a pontoon near one of the reefs that made up the Great Barrier Reef. I bought a T-shirt in a souvenir shop on the pontoon and got on the boat to begin the long journey back. During the return trip, Kate dutifully remained in my peripheral vision at all times.

Kate and I got back together on Friday. She took a seat next to me on the bus as we rode to the city of Cairns, deciding it was best to enjoy what little time we had together rather than squander it. Kate was sorry for avoiding me the day before and asked how I'd spent my day, as if she had not been shadowing me. She looked slightly hurt when I told her the day on the reef had been enjoyable. I quickly followed this with, "But I'm glad we're talking again." She smiled faintly. Reunited and it felt so . . . okay. There was a hair too much drama in this relationship.

That night our tour group was treated to a comedic vampire dinner theater production meant to capture the spirit and essence of Australia. One of the vampires made a joke about a brand of car I'd never heard of. All the local Australian audience members laughed heartily while I struggled to understand. First of all, why was a vampire driving? If so, then the vampire would have to stop for gas and I just didn't see that happening. Kate wasn't laughing either. She spent most of the show looking at me.

Our tour group returned to the budget hotel. I sat next to Brian on the bus. Once again, he looked under the weather. I asked what was wrong with him. This time the culprit was bad risotto from the vampire restaurant. I offered help. Brian said he would be okay; he just needed to lie down. He got off the bus and made his way back to his room. If a play were written about the night he spent in that room, it would be entitled *The Diarrhea Monologues*. I thought I played it cool with the women, but Brian brought it down to a whole new level.

Kate asked if I would walk her to her room. We headed to her room but, not surprisingly, Kate changed directions and we ended up at the hotel's pool. Maybe there was something about pools that drew Kate in like a tractor beam. At any rate, we were sitting on the edge of another pool. I couldn't help but think of how we had done this when we first met. Things were so exciting back then, so full of promise and wonder—three days earlier. We were at the end of the road now. I would be joining a new tour group in the morning, exploring Australia's outback.

"I want to know something, and I want you to be honest." Kate sounded forlorn when she said this. "Is there any chance at all you might consider moving to Bermuda?"

Somehow I felt guilty saying, "I don't think so, Kate."

"There has to be at least a slight chance. Your mind should always be open to possibilities," she protested. I acknowledged that anything was indeed possible, but it was highly unlikely I would ever become a resident of Bermuda. She brightened upon hearing this and asked specifically, mathematically, what I felt the chances were. I quietly told her they were astronomical. She wanted me to be more specific.

With hesitation, I informed her, "The chances of me living in Bermuda are like one in ten trillion."

Kate nodded, registering my statement. "So there's a chance," she responded. I immediately thought of the timeless classic film *Dumb and Dumber* in which master thespian James Carrey has a similar reaction after hearing his chances with the woman he loves are one in a million. That film was a comedy. Kate was currently acting out the dramatic version.

Slowly shaking my head, I informed her there wasn't really a chance. I suggested we appreciate the time we had together and look back on it fondly. After a few quiet moments, she moved closer and kissed me passionately. Then she smiled, said it was nice to have met me, and went to her room. I got the feeling she would be latching on to someone else during her next vacation. No doubt they would be sitting on the edge of a pool once or twice.

In the morning, a recuperated Brian and I boarded a plane and headed to the outback. Only two other people from our original tour joined us for the new trip—the German terrorists. Brian and I did not speak to them or sit near them on the plane because we didn't want to be potentially assaulted. The new outback tourist group reminded me of the one I had just left behind. There were as many women as there were men, from various parts of the world, mostly Canada and Europe, intent on having a good time. They had been traveling together for a week already. In traveling time, a week is like a year—boy, didn't I know it. Consequently, this new group had already formed their allegiances. They showed no interest in either Brian or myself. There was hardly a basic hello or even nod of the head in recognition of our existence. I thought perhaps it was because we'd arrived with the Germans. Maybe this tour group considered us guilty by association. The Germans kept to themselves, undaunted by the group's cold shoulder. Brian and I also kept to ourselves, by default. Nobody liked us. It made me kind of miss Kate. Kind of.

At sunset our group was driven by bus to Uluru, the Eiffel Tower of Australia's outback. Uluru is a red sandstone rock formation in the desert the size of several city blocks. As I took photographs of Uluru I spotted a curious sign, which read something along the lines of: *Uluru is considered a sacred landmark in the Aboriginal culture. The Aborigines would prefer that no one hike on Uluru. But if you would like to go for a hike, the trail begins here.* I did not climb Uluru because I'm not a jerk. As the sun went down, our group gathered to watch Uluru magically change colors against the orange hue of the waning sun.

Our tour guide, an Ozzie named Bob with a goatee, passed around plastic champagne glasses. He then proceeded to fill everyone's glasses with champagne. It was a tradition, at least on this tour, to toast the Uluru sunset. I didn't normally drink, because I never acquired a taste for alcohol, because alcohol tastes horrible. As a result, on the rare occasions I did drink, I held my liquor like a nun. Still, I was on the other side of the planet, staring at a giant red rock with a bunch of inhospitable strangers. I wasn't going to be doing any driving—at least I hoped not. If everyone else got so drunk it fell upon me to drive the tour bus back, getting to our hotel would take hours, perhaps days, even though it was ten minutes away. No, I would not be driving. What better time to pound one down then? I gladly held my champagne glass out as Bob poured some poison into it. Champagne, above all, was my kryptonite. One sip is all it took. I was flying. After three sips, look out. Brian stood beside me, enjoying his champagne. He stayed close, since we were all we had in this treacherous land. But then Brian unexpectedly turned to me and said, "I'm going to go talk to that Italian girl." Perhaps it was the alcohol. At any rate, he left, finally about to make a move on someone.

As I stood there on my own, admiring both Ulurus, I suddenly noticed a woman from the group beside me. She introduced herself as Helga or Jamie—I didn't know what her name was. She had an accent from some place and said she lived in a city that ended in *vania* or *aria* or something. Alison or whatever she was called asked me what I thought of my new tour group. I looked at her and retorted, "Your group sucks, Marcia." She was a bit taken aback by my estimation of the group. To clarify, I expanded by saying, "I don't feel welcomed at all. You guys haven't made any effort to be friendly." The girl asked if I had met Mira. "Probably not," I answered. "I haven't met anybody." She held up her index finger, gesturing for me to wait. She then left momentarily, returning with a Nordic blond woman named Mira, from Sweden. Mira looked like a 1930s screen goddess.

The first girl turned to Mira and told her, "He doesn't think we're friendly." Mira took over from there, immediately making out with me. Mira, I would remember. Our tour guide rounded us back onto the bus. As we rode to our hotel, the bus driver began blasting disco music. People danced in the aisles. This was literally a party bus. Brian was somewhere in the mix, hopefully doing the *lambada* with an Italian girl. I danced as well, an occurrence as rare as me drinking champagne. The dancing was easy, since my main dance move consisted of continuing to make out with Mira. There was a guy from Canada dancing in the aisle on the other side of me. I noticed him and the Canadian maple leaf stitched onto his shirt when I came up for air from necking with Mira. (In Australia, Canadians went out of their way to identify themselves as proud Canadians, smothering their suitcases and clothes and toiletries with all things Canadian, lest anyone mistake them for ugly Americans.) I asked the Canadian if Mira had made out with every guy on the bus, cognizant enough to realize I might be kissing a petri dish. The Canadian told me, no, she was not a tramp. I thanked him and went back to making out with Mira.

We arrived back at our desert hotel where the dancing continued in an open patio area. Mira poured me another drink, which I consumed when I was not busy kissing her. I was wearing a fedora I had bought at the airport before flying to the outback. Mira took the hat and placed it on her head. She looked good. Really good. With a lascivious smile, she led me off the dance floor to a nearby desert trail just off the grounds of the hotel. As we continued walking along the trail, the music in the patio area became faint. We followed the trail with the help of some faded moonlight. Either I was about to have one of my kidneys harvested or Mira and I were going to get to know each other a lot better, at least physically. I continued following Mira, just in case.

We arrived at a desert-viewing lookout point. Presumably a person could see things here during the day. In the moonlight, all I could see was a modest wooden bench in the dirt. I took a seat on the bench and Mira took a seat on me, followed by more kissing. I was still drunk, but my buzz was starting to wear off. I couldn't help but feel like in a way I was cheating on Kate. But I wasn't. No, I was not cheating on Kate. This was fine, I kept telling myself. The contrast was stark between Mira and Kate. While Kate hardly ever stopped talking, Mira rarely said a word. Rather than going on and on about the time she saw a whale for half a second, Mira silently attempted to suffocate me with her ginormous breasts. This sort of thing never happened to me, spontaneously sucking face with European film stars in the Australian desert.

"And then?" At first I didn't hear Mira because she spoke so softly. But she repeated her question, "And then?" I understood the words, but didn't quite grasp their connotation. She was asking the way a teacher might quiz her student. "And then?"

I attempted to pass her test, answering, "And then . . . I'm going to kiss you here." I kissed one of her erogenous zones.

She was quiet for a bit and then, "And then?" I had to come up with another move, which I did. Every few minutes, yet another move was required. I am not the greatest at improvisation, especially sexual improv, but I did my best under pressure. Mira unexpectedly upped the ante by sliding off the bench and lying down in the dirt. In the dirt! She looked up at me and asked her favorite question.

A number of thoughts ran through my mind, none of which involved doing the nasty with Mira. Perhaps if I had been rip-roaring drunk. But I was not. As I gazed at Mira lying in the dirt, I thought, "I don't even know this person's last name. Her clothes are getting filthy. She's going to be upset about that tomorrow." I also half expected Kate to emerge from the darkness in tears, asking how I could do this to her. This was improbable, since Kate was continuing her tour along the coast. But still, in the back of my mind . . .

Puff adders were also a concern. As I considered lying beside, or on top of, Mira in the desert, I thought of all the snakes Australia had to offer. For some reason, the puff adder jumped to the forefront of my mind. I wasn't even sure if puff adders lived in Australia, but they sounded mean and vicious. I'd hate to be rolling around with Mira, only to get my neck punctured by a puff adder. (Later I would find out puff adders live in Africa, so my concerns were misguided. In Australia, there is the less intimidating death adder.)

"And then?"

And then I got on the ground and continued making out with Mira. The ground wasn't very comfortable. I tried to use Mira as a buffer between me and the dirt in an effort to keep my clothes as clean as possible. There are probably some men who would have gladly scored a home run with Mira, without using or even thinking of protection, and then later boasted about it over a beer with their *Monday Night Football* buddies. I am not one of them. As attractive as Mira was, the possibility of contracting an STD or unintentionally fathering a child was not appealing. Fortunately, I was not drunk enough for either of those two possibilities. And hopefully never would be. I knew full well that bad things could happen when people get drunk.

Once again, Mira asked, "And then?" The only move left I could think of within the realm of my self-imposed boundaries was to suck on her elbow. This seemed to confuse her as well as wake her from her sexually charged stupor. She sat up, covered in dirt. Brushing off the only spot on her clothes that was clean, Mira rose to her feet. So did I. We walked back to the hotel. The dancing had ended; the music was no longer playing. Mira had a bit of trouble remembering which room was hers, but she finally found it. I walked her to the door. Not much for words, she went inside without looking back at me or saying good night. I found my room a few minutes later. At this hotel, I was bunking with Brian and two other strangers, whom I woke up by loudly knocking over three suitcases and a trash can before locating my bed in the dark.

Brian was combing his hair when I awoke in the morning. I felt a little groggy, but not too bad. When I noticed Brian, I asked him if he had any luck with that Italian girl. "Not really," he said. "I was walking over to her, with my cup of champagne, and as I got about five feet away she said 'Whoa' like she was afraid I was going to bump into her. So then I left her alone. I talked to this dude from Canada. He's pretty cool. His name is Kyle." Brian and I were having very different experiences in Australia. At least he didn't have diarrhea. That was an improvement. As Brian put on the finishing touches, he commented, "I saw you with that girl. You seemed to be having a good time. I was surprised. She doesn't really seem like your type. See you out there." Brian left the room, heading to breakfast. I slowly got up. It took a few seconds for Brian's last comment, about the girl not being my type, to sink in. What did that mean?

It meant she didn't look like 1930s screen goddess at all. I ran into Mira at the dining hall. We faced each other over the pancakes tray. She looked strikingly different in the sober light of day. Mira looked so different, my first inclination was to say aloud, "Ugh." Mira was short and stocky, like a medium-sized freezer, with folds and cankles. The perils of intoxication. I did not say "Ugh." Instead I said, "Good morning." Mira had a similar reaction to mine. Judging by the expression on her face, I looked like a primate to her. We avoided each other for the remainder of the tour and we were both okay with that.

There were no further desert trysts. The group did become a little more sociable, but no new lifelong friendships were forged. Nevertheless, Brian and I had an interesting time in the outback. We fed some camels, took a helicopter ride over a group of impressive large-domed rock formations known as Kata Tjuta. Also, I saw a lizard the size of my leg. I was glad it hadn't presented itself while I was sucking on Mira's elbow.

Our epic trip to Australia was winding down, with only one more full day in Sydney ahead of us. On our final morning in the desert, as Brian and I got a taxi to take us to the airport, the German terrorists ran out and asked if they could share our cab. They were also headed back to Sydney. We agreed, though not without hesitation. It seemed this had been their plan all along—to ambush us at the very end of the group tour. They hopped in the cab. Brian and I remained on alert, ready for them to whip out their guns. Surprisingly, the Germans wanted to chat. They reintroduced themselves as Detlef and Ralph. Ralph explained they were in town for an international gay dance competition and had decided to take a tour afterward. Detlef was competing; Ralph was supporting. They were married. Detlef, it turned out, was the international gay dance champion. Ralph was the doting husband. And my assumptions about them had been way off. We arrived at the airport. Ralph wished us safe travels, noting that Brian and I made a wonderful couple. Clearly, Ralph had not been paying attention.

We spent the last few hours in Australia shopping like responsible tourists. Brian and I visited a Sydney tourist trap known as The Rocks, which featured one store after another. Brian bought enough souvenirs to open up his own gift shop upon returning to America. Never one for shopping, I mostly walked around. I saw a kangaroo scrotum skin pouch for loose change, however I did not see any of the mythical Australian wool sweaters my mother dreamed about wearing. My mother probably would not have liked the kangaroo pouch, so I did not buy her one.

As I continued to amble through the collection of shops, I came upon a vision that took my breath away. I saw a woman, an Indian woman—from India—working in one of the stores. She looked to be about my age. Her face was a work of art. I was not drunk. She was undeniably exquisite. She was looking down, doing some kind of detailed work with her hands. I went into the store, if for nothing else than to get a closer look at her. When I walked in, she greeted me with a gracious smile. It made me sad to run into this person during the final few hours of my vacation. Not that I would have had the courage to do anything if there had been more time, but it would have been nice to have the option to wimp out.

She was painting a small button. I wanted to marry her. She asked me where I was from. I told her I was from California and wanted to ask if she ever thought of moving to California. But I remembered how this turned me off when Kate asked if I would relocate to Bermuda, so I refrained. Instead I asked what she was painting on the button. She was painting a tiny koala, and doing a fine job of it. Genuinely curious, I asked her what the button was for. She flashed an amused smile, gestured around her, and said, "These."

For the first time, I noticed I was in an Australian wool sweater store. I was surrounded. The place was Sweaterlandia. There were more sweaters in one location than I had seen in my entire life. "Oh no!" I exclaimed. The sweater I ended up buying for my mother cost me a pretty penny. A very pretty one.

We were going to stop in Bora Bora *again* on the way back, but both Brian and I decided it was best to endure the long voyage home, so we changed our flight and headed directly to Los Angeles. Two honeymoons was overkill. I thought about our epic trip on the airplane, feeling a bit of sympathy for Brian. He went all that way and had nary a fling to speak of. Brian pointed out he had received one of the sexiest lap dances in the history of mankind. That was something. As for the civilian girls, why he hadn't landed so much as a kiss would remain one of the greatest unsolved mysteries of his life. I assumed it had something to do with all that vomiting and diarrhea. Plus, his choosing to isolate himself on WWII planes or march the opposite direction just because a girl said *Whoa*. That might have been a factor. Whatever the reason, Brian declared visiting Australia had still been an amazing experience and he would not trade it for anything. As far as girls were concerned, he was in charge of his own destiny—just as I was in charge of mine—and he would have to find his own way.

I considered Australia a learning experience. It put what and who I was looking for into perspective. For all my impatience to get married, to meet my wife, I realized it wasn't so much that I wanted to get *married* after all. If that had been the case, I would've been packing my bags for Bermuda to share my life with Kate. It wasn't the getting married part I was interested in. It wasn't the institution. It was the *who* of it all. It was finding the *right* person. Not just any person, not a dog therapist in Bermuda or a Swedish girl built like a freezer. Someone who was a happy medium between hypersensitive Kate, who was ready to get engaged after saying hello, and the stocky Mira who enjoyed drunkenly rolling around in dirt. Neither of those were for me, especially not the one with the cankles. Gross, the cankles were gross. Australia helped me determine who I *was not* looking for and that was helpful. The only problem was, the more I thought about who I *was* looking for, the clearer it became: I had no idea.

MY SECOND PROM

Late one Friday night in June, I arrived home and discovered the following unexpected monotone voice mail message: "Hi, Carlos. This is Beth Mango. The reason I'm calling is I would like you to take me to my prom tomorrow night. Thank you." I had many issues with Beth Mango's message. Not the least of which, I was twenty-nine years old.

The moment I heard Beth Mango's message, my heart sank. If Beth had phoned when I was in my early twenties, I would have told her I needed to wash my hair and called it a day. But now in my late twenties, on the cusp of thirty, I had experienced personal growth. *Personal growth* sounds as if I had a boil on my chin, but it was far worse. I now had a modicum of maturity. I was able to put myself in another person's shoes. Remembering my own foibles as a high school student, my troubles securing a prom date in particular, I understood Beth's plight. I knew how she felt. If Beth was calling *me*, the night before, she was truly scraping the bottom of the bottom of the barrel. I had to have been her last scrape. Her only hope. Her Obi-Wan Kenobi. I felt a pit in my stomach. Because I knew I was going to have to take Beth Mango to her prom. Being mature sucked balls.

Beth Mango was a friend of the family. More accurately, the family was aware of her existence. Her mother used to work with my mother. I barely knew Beth. She was an odd girl, eleven years younger than me, who resembled actor Gary Busey in his early years and, as far as I could tell, possessed the same personality traits as a bag of cement. On the rare occasions I would come face-to-face with her, I would say hello, ask how she was doing. She would look at the floor, mumble that she was fine, and we would wait until our next meeting the following year to do it all over again.

To be fair, the tree did not fall far from the apple. As a whole, the Mangos were an unusual bunch. The usually rumpled mother spoke seventeen decibels louder than what is necessary to be heard by the human ear and occasionally would display hints of a fiery temper while addressing her husband. The husband had a curious juvenile streak, which he would display when least expected, or appropriate. Besides Beth, there were two younger daughters. They were copies of Beth, and presumably had names.

The last time I saw them, the Mangos stopped by for a visit while I too was visiting my parents. As he walked into my parents' house, Mr. Mango spotted a black rubber rat on the floor. The rat belonged to my parents' constantly amped wiry Welsh terrier, Max. It was Max's favorite toy. Max quickly ran over to claim his treasure, fearing the first thing these new visitors would naturally want to do upon their arrival was swoop in, bite down on his beloved rat, and whisk it away.

Max was right. When Mr. Mango spotted Max heading toward the rat, Mr. Mango immediately got down on all fours, took the slobbery rat into his own mouth before Max could get to it, and began lurching toward the distressed Max with taunting growls. Max angrily barked at the thief.

As my parents and I watched this spectacle in disbelief, I thought out loud, "That rat has spent a lot of time inside of Max's mouth." Mr. Mango responded by growling a little louder. I don't remember my specific reply to his growls, but I believe it was something like, "Wow."

An annoyed Mrs. Mango vociferously instructed her husband, "Honey! Say hello first!" The two younger daughters laughed uncontrollably at their father's antics.

In case anyone was confused by the current situation, Beth began to narrate, using alternating points of view. "It's a big mouse and it's trapped in his mouth! Mmm . . . I love it!" That was the last time I'd seen Beth Mango, about a year earlier.

Now Beth was calling, asking me to escort her to prom. Only one scheming mastermind could be behind such a nefarious plot: my mother. A few months earlier, I had traveled with my mother to Mexico City, to attend my cousin Claudia's *Quinceañera*. In Latin America, the *Quinceañera* is a major event commemorating a girl's fifteenth birthday. During this event, the girl goes to church and the priest gives her a speech. She then dances a waltz in a banquet hall, at which point she is officially transformed into a woman.

While I sat in the banquet hall watching Claudia and her girlfriends basking in her new womanhood, my mother pointed out one of Claudia's friends sitting at a table across the large hall from us. I thought my mother was referring to a friend of Claudia's named

Victoria, an aspiring model/lady of the night who was fifteen going on twenty-five. It surprised me that my mother would want me to notice her. Victoria was a girl best ignored.

My mother corrected me. She wanted me to notice another girl at the table, a behemoth named Maria. My mother informed me while all the other girls at the table had gotten up numerous times to dance with the boys in attendance, poor Maria had been sitting at her table the entire evening. I acknowledged this information by nodding my head and remarking, "That's not surprising."

The way my mother was looking at me, it was obvious she expected me to walk across the banquet hall and ask the extra-large girl to dance. It was more likely I would walk across the hall and perform a pirouette atop the girls' table. (This is to say it was highly unlikely I was going to ask the girl to dance.) My mother kept imploring me, kept telling me how kind it would be to dance with Maria-zilla, begging me to please do this simple thing.

There are three things I detest in life: eating eggs, wrapping a present, and dancing. I only dance against my will, when in a party bus on the other side of the planet, with the full moon positioned just so. My dance style is an homage to the way Rain Man moves when he's agitated. The concept of moving my body around in all sorts of herky-jerky directions to acknowledge music is being played has never appealed to me. To do this with a female who could easily tackle me was even less appealing. But my mother was relentless. Finally, to make her stop, I got up and did walk across that banquet hall over to Maria's table.

All the teenage girls seated at the table fixed their eyes upon me with blushing smiles as I approached. The aspiring model/call girl was also still sitting there. She was the only one who looked away as

I got closer, a queen unwilling to make eye contact with one of her subjects.

Undoubtedly, every girl at that table assumed I was there to ask the aspiring model/jailbait to dance. With a friendly wave to the group, I turned my attention to Maria, the big one. I introduced myself and commented (in Spanish), "I couldn't help but notice you haven't danced tonight."

"No, I haven't," she confirmed.

"Would you like to dance?" I asked. Shock and awe rumbled across the table.

With a pleasant smile, Maria decisively responded, "No, I would not."

It took a few seconds for my brain to compute I had been rejected. When I realized this, I gave Maria a nod and responded, "Okay," quickly leaving before she changed her mind. It did sting a little. But only a little. My mother was convinced I asked Maria for the time, rather than to dance. No matter how many times I insisted otherwise, she did not believe me.

Once again, I faced the prospect of dancing with somebody I barely wanted to shake hands with. And not just a dance—a night of dancing, at a prom. There was no chance Beth Mango would reject me as her prom date, considering she was the one who asked in the first place. As I suspected, my mother had indeed had a hand in this conspiracy. Before Beth made the call to me, Beth's mother contacted my mother, explaining that Beth's prom was taking place the following night and Beth was in need of a date. The Mangos wondered if I would be willing to do the honors.

Instead of dousing this proposal immediately, as she should have, my mother said, "Oh, that would be wonderful. Here's Carlos's number . . ." No doubt my mother felt this would more than make up for the time I failed to dance with Maria at my cousin's *Quinceañera*.

I returned Beth's call the next morning, the day of her prom. As the phone rang, I savored my last few moments of freedom. Beth answered like an automaton. I cleared my throat, forcing the words out of my mouth with the enthusiasm of an exhausted coal miner heading back to work. "Hi. Beth. It's Carlos. I got your message. Um . . . I can't . . ." Part of me wanted to stop there, but I forged on, muttering, "I can't tell you . . . how much . . . I would love to take you to your prom. I really can't." I shook my head, cursing the skies above. What had I just done? I expected Beth to cry tears of joy, to thank me profusely as she jumped up and down in celebration. But she reacted to the news as if I had just told her the washing machine she was expecting would arrive later that afternoon between noon and five p.m.

"Okay, be here at six," she advised without emotion. I explained that with such short notice, I probably wouldn't be able to rent a tuxedo in time. This was not a problem. Her father had a tuxedo in the closet. Oh, happy day, I could wear his. And that is how, at the ripe old age of twenty-nine, I found myself preparing for my second prom.

Beth lived about an hour and a half from me. On the way there, I stopped at a florist and purchased a corsage. The lady behind the counter launched a full-scale investigation when I told her I needed a thing to put on a girl's wrist. She interrogated me. Did my date have a favorite flower? I had no idea. What color dress was my date going to be wearing? I didn't know. What was the event we would be attending? I hesitated, and then responded, "I'd rather not say."

I cannot accurately describe the utter happiness I was greeted with when I arrived at Beth Mango's house. Her parents were amazed someone actually showed up. Both of them gave me bear hugs. They mentioned what an exciting day it was in the Mango household. After all, Beth was the first in the family to go to a prom. They spoke of prom as if it were Harvard.

Before I changed into Mr. Mango's tuxedo, which I was told "should" work since Mr. Mango and I were "about" the same build, they asked me to wait a few minutes because Beth was almost ready to make her entrance. I sat on the couch, across from Beth's sisters. Her sisters gazed at me in wonder, the way I suspect the Mayans looked upon the arriving conquistadores. I swore an oath to myself that when the time came, I would most certainly not accompany either of these two girls to their proms.

"Oh, here she comes," Mrs. Mango gushed as Beth walked down the hall into the living room, wearing a frumpy white gown that appeared to be somebody's secondhand tacky wedding dress. "Isn't she beautiful?" Mrs. Mango asked, thrilled by her daughter's appearance. Beth was not quite as thrilled. In her defense, I don't think she had ever been thrilled about anything in her life.

Assuming the question about Beth's beauty was rhetorical, I said nothing. But I did get off the couch for Beth. She looked at me blankly and said, "Hi," with a perfect pitch of indifference. I presented the corsage. For some reason I had difficulty placing it on her wrist. It seemed more as if I was checking her pulse than decorating her with a flower. Beth was alive.

It was now time for me to try on the father's tuxedo. Mr. Mango handed me a garment bag and escorted me to the bathroom. As I closed the door, I could hear the family whispering in hushed tones. They seemed to be talking about me. I couldn't clearly make out what was being said, other than someone warning someone else, "No—don't. You're going to scare him."

When I unzipped the garment bag, I exhaled sharply as if being kicked in the gut. I knew the tux I was looking at wasn't a joke, considering the source. Had it been, it would have been a cruel joke (though a great one). The tux smelled like musty mothballs. It was a washed-out baby blue number with some sort of coffee stain, I hoped, around the left shoulder area. To complete my humiliation, it had ruffles and possibly bell-bottoms. Either they were bell-bottoms or the fabric had been stretched and loosened after years of inexplicable wear and tear. It was the kind of outfit one would lend to someone who needed it for a costume party, or to an enemy. For a moment I thought about returning to the living room and asking Mr. Mango, "Seriously?" But I already knew the answer to this question. Mr. Mango probably thought I was lucky to be wearing such a spiffy getup. It pained me to put the tuxedo on. When I did, I tried avoiding my reflection in the mirror. Mr. Mango's tuxedo kind of fit, but not really. He was a little smaller than me. Things were a little tighter than they should have been. Still, if the year had been 1978, I would have looked dyn-o-mite!

Mrs. Mango greeted me with as much enthusiasm as she had her daughter when I made my entrance. Wanting to see how the shirt fit, she asked me to take off the jacket. I did. Then she asked me to turn around. I did. Then she observed, "Ooh, the pants fit nicely. Do you work out?" I quickly turned around, put the jacket back on, and offered a laugh as uncomfortable as my tight outfit. Beth and I posed for a few casual prom pictures, with Beth placing her cold, clammy hand on my arm as Mrs. Mango snapped photos, gathering proof her daughter had netted a date should anyone question it, which they probably would.

Before we hit the main event, it was announced we would have prom dinner. This was a pre-prom tradition I had forgotten in my effort to mentally block the evening out. Beth's sisters desperately wanted to join us for dinner, but Mr. Mango explained this special night belonged to Beth. The only ones who would be attending prom dinner would be Beth, me, and Beth's parents. Next thing I knew, I was riding in a minivan with Beth and her parents, on our way to prom dinner. The dinner setting for my own prom, the previous decade, had been elegant and romantic; the Marine Room overlooked the Pacific Ocean and provided an ambience one would expect for a senior prom. For prom dinner with Beth and her family, we went to Coco's. For those unfamiliar with Coco's, it's like Denny's. Those unfamiliar with Denny's are Communists.

I will never forget walking into Coco's in my absurd tuxedo, with my prom date, and her parents. It felt as if I had lost a bet. A young, attractive hostess greeted us. She studied my ensemble, and I'm fairly certain had to keep herself from laughing. As the hostess led us to our booth, I felt all eyes in the restaurant upon me. I regretted it was June and not October. Halloween would have made things a lot easier. I ordered the fish 'n' chips dinner. Service was slow, allowing plenty of time for a potential ulcer to develop.

Nothing against Coco's, but it was no Marine Room. Sitting in the booth with the Mangos brought me back to my first prom dinner as an eighteen-year-old. I thought of that night. How dramatic it had been. I pined so desperately for Isabelle Cambria. It had crushed me to see her with another guy at prom. I could still remember how that felt. As Beth Mango contemplated whether she was going to order coconut or banana cream pie for dessert, my thoughts drifted to Isabelle. I hadn't spoken to her in eleven years. *Eleven years.* What had become of her? I hoped she was happy. Hopefully she had found love and was raising a family. What if she walked into Coco's at this moment with her family? I struggled mightily to dismiss this thought before it became a reality. What if she saw me like this? I'd have to get up in my clownish tuxedo, shake hands with her husband, meet the children. She would ask me what I was up to these days. And I'd tell her with an uncomfortable laugh, "Still going to prom." That could not happen. I was determined to keep to myself and stay under the radar to the best of my ability.

Our waitress rushed by. Mrs. Mango pounded on the table. Then she pointed at me, shouting at the waitress loud enough for everyone in the restaurant to hear, "Can you hurry up and bring his fish 'n' chips? They have a prom to go to!" I wanted to melt into the floor under the table, like the Wicked Witch of Any Direction. Or if a house had fallen on us at this moment, that would have been good too.

As I drove to prom, alone in my car with Beth, I missed being at Coco's. I'm not the world's greatest conversationalist, but compared to Beth I could host my own talk show. I tried to pry information out of her, for the sake of courtesy. I asked her about her school, about the friends we would see at prom. She told me school was "all right." And then, in an apparent effort to brief me on the friends I would meet, she started reciting names. "Liz. Kathryn. Diana. Mary. Heather." I thought she was finished, but about a minute later she threw in, "Rachel." Despite my efforts, we mostly sat in silence. At one point, Beth did initiate conversation. At one point, out of nowhere, she did say, "I'm starting work at Del Taco on Monday."

We finally arrived at some fancy hotel where prom was being held. I mistakenly drove into the valet parking lane and got stuck there even though I had intended to go directly to the self-parking lot and stash the car as far away as possible. Instead my neon blue Toyota Corolla was in plain sight, sandwiched in between a pair of stretch limos overloaded with obnoxious high school seniors. A valet parking attendant approached. I got out of the car, took the claim ticket and thanked him as I tried to pretend I wasn't wearing far and away the most ridiculous tuxedo of the evening, and perhaps of all time. The attendant, like the girl at Coco's, stifled his laughter. I was beginning to grow accustomed to this kind of reaction.

We entered the lobby of the hotel. Beth made eye contact with a stylish teenage girl who nodded her head in recognition. Either that or the girl had a nervous tic. It was hard to tell. At any rate, the moment quickly passed. Beth informed me she had to go to the bathroom. I waited for her outside the women's restroom as teenager after teenager, all dressed to the nines, paraded by on their way to the ballroom. The various reactions I elicited from the students as they walked past me were a combination of confusion, amusement, and condescension. Sometimes one person would go through all three emotional stages. A few students took pictures of me. I think they thought I was an unfamiliar new teacher, some sort of mascot, or possibly a magician. Most of the dudes were giants who towered above me. If any of them chose to make fun of Beth, it would be up to Beth to defend her own honor. Beth returned from the bathroom, and I was actually relieved to see her.

The ballroom of the hotel was a much more inviting location, on account of it was darker, thereby making anonymity easier. Beth and I sat at a table, just the two of us, saying nothing. My watch seemed to be broken because every time I looked at it only about a minute had passed. I asked Beth if she wanted to find some of her friends and say hello. She told me she'd already found her friends, referring to the girl with the possible nervous tic who had nodded her head at Beth when we'd first arrived.

Looking around the ballroom, at all the dressed-up high school seniors partying and having a good time, I couldn't help but feel bad for Beth. Our quiet table showed just how much of an outcast she was. The past four years of high school must have been an emotional boot camp for her. No doubt she had been routinely ridiculed; no doubt people were ridiculing her in this very ballroom. The fact that she had arrived tonight, escorted by a date, was itself a triumph. I would not have shown that much strength when I was a high school senior. There's no way I would have attended prom under Beth's circumstances. I would have spent prom night hiding under my bed, letting it pass like a hurricane. If I were able to tell the high school senior version of myself I'd be doing this, the high school senior would have fainted.

But here I was. Here *we* were, at a prom, all dressed up (kind of), the music blasting. With supreme confidence, I took Beth by the hand, led her to the dance floor, and as AC/DC wailed about being shaken all night long, we shook it. Whereas I danced like Rain Man, Beth danced like Bride of Rain Man. It didn't matter. We let loose. We escaped through dance and in the process we ended up owning that prom. Beth had a blast. I know she did, because she smiled.

After boogying to a countless number of songs, I was sweating buckets. My hair was thoroughly disheveled, the ill-fitting tux in disarray. I was a wreck. Suddenly Beth proclaimed, "Time to get our prom pictures taken." I followed her off the floor, to the area where prom pictures were being captured. We passed several tables. I hastily grabbed napkins from each, trying to towel all the sweat off my face.

Still out of breath from dancing, sweat dripping down my temples, I oh so gently held Beth by the waist and grimaced for the camera.

The photographer looked at me and sarcastically remarked, "Looks like somebody's been held back a grade or two."

Without dropping my forced smile, I responded, "Take the picture."

Prom night eventually came to an end. I drove Beth back to her house, quickly changed into my civilian clothes and said good-bye. She thanked me, genuinely. I gave her an instant, completely asexual kiss on the cheek, and headed up the freeway to my world, where I belonged. No one would ever have to know about my good deed. It was done. Beth would always be able to answer, "Yes," whenever anyone asked if she went to her prom. And I probably wouldn't even see her for at least another year.

I saw her the following month. She was at a Fourth of July party, attended by friends and family. Beth was kind enough to have brought me our prom pictures, bless her heart. Without looking at them, I quickly and discreetly asked Beth to hand them to my mother. Mistake. My mother loved the pictures. She loves any picture with me in a tuxedo, even if my hair is messed up, forehead sweaty, and wardrobe laugh-out-loud-able. She looked through each picture carefully, and happily, to my dismay. These were not meant to be viewed in public. As my mother thoroughly vetted the pictures, a guy named Marc walked by. He was from the neighborhood, a casual friend of mine, and more so of my parents. Marc noticed the pictures. He approached my mother, asking out of curiosity what she was looking at. My mother proudly informed him, "Carlos's prom pictures!"

Marc studied the pictures a little more closely. He tilted his head in confusion, and commented to my mother, "These look recent." Obviously, Marc was a keen observer of things. Yes, they were recent. So recent, I still hadn't gotten a haircut since they had been taken. I survived the experience. Hopefully, I was even a better person for it. My prom date with Beth Mango was one for the karma jar. The next round of dates would *have* to be as easy and relaxing and comfortable as going to Beth's prom was not. Hadn't I earned it? Definitely. I looked forward to meeting whoever was around the corner. Without question, she was going to be a keeper. How could she not be?

THE H WORD

The time had come to find a soul mate. Enough was enough. I was thirty years old and now more than ever ready to share my life. Up to this point, my romantic history consisted of hopeless infatuations, short-lived relationships (if that was the right word), and the occasional prom date. There were also uneventful regular dates interspersed throughout that went nowhere so fast, atoms were split by the mutual indifference. It all amounted to a whole lot of emptiness. I still didn't know exactly *who* I was looking for, besides the basics—a full set of teeth, not too hairy—but I did know I wanted something meaningful, passionate, and lasting. My past experiences had taught me that most people were on a different wavelength. The key was finding somebody tuned to the same frequency. I'd know who that person was when I found her.

Pinpointing my soul mate's exact location was a challenge due in large part to my inherently antisocial tendencies along with the demands of my work schedule. I was still making my way up the Hollywood food chain. (Progress had been made, but I wasn't a mogul.) Meeting new people was half the battle. If only there were somewhere I could see a list of single women, a place where those women posted pictures of themselves and maybe wrote a few details about their lives, the kinds of qualities they were seeking in a companion. Then it dawned on me. Mail-order brides! Perhaps that was the answer. I decided it would be too much of a hassle returning a bride if things didn't work out. The postage alone was probably through the roof. Instead, I gave Internet dating a try.

I resisted Internet dating for a good long while. Something about it didn't seem natural. I didn't like the idea of finding my soul mate the same place somebody could become addicted to porn, learn how to build homemade bombs, or catch a virus just by clicking on *Here's those pictures you asked for.* But the opportunity to meet hundreds, if not thousands, of available women who might be on the same frequency led me to traverse the perilous netherworld of the Internet. I am not permitted to mention the dating Web site I joined. (It starts with an M and rhymes with Snatch.com.) Upon joining, I was asked to create a screen name for myself. I came up with: ChickenWhisperer. The name was an homage to my beloved feathered friends who helped me get through sixth grade. It also served as a reminder to go forth in my search for a mate the same way a chicken would—with self-assurance and tenacity.

Meeting someone through this site proved to be a bit of a challenge at first. I wrote to a number of women, I'm guessing about five or six hundred. I'd send messages such as "Hi, SexySoCalGirl26, this is ChickenWhisperer. We seem to have a lot in common. I like to have fun and laugh all the time too! Tell me about that dog in your pictures. The one wearing the sunglasses and baseball cap. He looks like a real character."

Most of the women I contacted ignored me. But at last, a kind response arrived, from BeachVixen78. She informed me she'd love to meet for a drink sometime. We did, later that week. I had a lemonade. Her actual name was Trinity. She was an attractive girl, with brown eyes, milky skin, and long brunette hair. Trinity asked how many women I had met through the Web site. I told her she was my first. She mentioned she met with pretty much every guy who wrote to her.

A few nights later, I took her to dinner at a fancy hotel on the beach in Santa Monica. From where we sat, I could see the Santa Monica pier festively lit up. I remarked that the pier looked nice. With a coy smile, Trinity blushed, stroked her hair, and responded, "Thank you."

For a moment, I thought of clarifying my words, "No, no. The pier." I kept quiet, allowing the accidental compliment to make me seem smoother than I actually am.

Three dates later, in her apartment, we had what is commonly referred to as sexual intercourse. I can't say I was falling in love with her—nor she with me—but certainly she was charismatic enough to get intimate with. And intimate we got. Not to be too graphic, but I did a little traveling—taking a lengthy trip downtown. Her airport had a narrow, well-maintained landing strip, wink wink. Afterward, as we were resting in her bed, I stared at her ceiling—not a euphemism, I was actually staring at her ceiling—and marveled at the power of the Internet. The Internet was amazing! Why hadn't I tried this before? Trinity snuggled closer, and whispered, "I have to tell you something . . . I have . . . the H Word."

Two H words immediately came to mind: HIV and herpes. And so I suddenly found myself silently praying, *"Please, God, let it be herpes. God, if You give me herpes, I will be the happiest man on Earth. I will be Your servant. I will help fight childhood obesity. I'll donate my car to somebody who has restless legs syndrome. Whatever You want."*

I calmly turned to her and asked which H word she was referring to. She sighed heavily and stated, "I'm only going to say this once," followed by a dramatic pause. Finally, she blurted out, "Herpes!" Then she squealed and hid under the sheets like a little kid, even though she was thirty years old. As she remained burrowed beneath the sheets, I stared at her ceiling, and marveled at the power of the Internet. For only $39.99 a month, I could catch herpes. The Internet was evil. Trinity eventually came out from hiding and explained as dryly as if she was doing my taxes, "I probably didn't give it to you, but if I did, you'll find out within the next two weeks."

I turned to her and said, "I probably won't burn your house down, but if I do, you'll find out within the next two weeks." Sensing I was upset, she told me if I wanted to leave, she would understand. She continued speaking, though I can't be certain of what she said, because I was in my car on my way home.

The next twenty-four hours were spent online, researching herpes. I learned a lot of things. For one, even though, yes, I had used protection, I was not out of the woods. One of the main ingredients in transmitting herpes is simple skin-on-skin contact—no visible symptoms required. As easy as getting into any community college! And here was an added bonus I discovered through my research: It was entirely possible for her genital herpes to break out on my nongenital mouth. What an exciting two weeks I had in store for me!

While I was on the computer, I received an e-mail from Trinity.

It occurred to her she should apologize. She said if I was no longer interested in a physical relationship, she hoped at the very least we could remain "good friends." She wanted to be friends because she really enjoyed my "sense of humor, easygoing personality, and *infectious* smile."

I politely wrote back, thanking her for the message and letting Trinity know I would have a difficult time considering her a "good friend." Good friends give each other a ride to the airport. Also, I recommended she change her screen name from BeachVixen78 to HerpesGirlSimplex2. It wasn't so much that she had herpes. People get herpes, that's life. Heck, maybe even I had it thanks to her! It was how and, more specifically, *when* she decided to divulge this information that rubbed me the wrong way, in a manner of speaking.

The following two weeks, I was on herpes watch. Every little itch, twitch, shiver, tic, tinge, twinge, tingle, bristle, shudder, flutter, and pinch made me nervous. I would freeze and ask myself, *what's that?* As fate would have it, those two weeks were spent in Washington, DC, visiting my parents, who had moved there about a year earlier from California. Every so often my mother would quizzically ask, "Carlos, are you all right? You look a little stressed." I told her nothing.

A week after I got back from Washington, DC, I saw my doctor—a tall, slim, good-humored Trekkie in his late fifties named Dr. Kovac, who had a life-sized cardboard cutout of Mr. Spock in his office. He planned to retire someday and move back to his home state of Kansas, where he intended to build a spaceship on the farmland he purchased. The spaceship wouldn't be functional. It wouldn't be for space travel, just for enjoying a beer and watching a football game inside. I never expected Internet dating would lead me to my doctor's office, but if there's one thing Trinity taught me, it's that life is full of surprises. Dr. Kovac walked into the examination room with a striking young blond understudy or whatever it was he called her. He smiled and said what he always said whenever he first saw me, "Good to see you. I know one thing we won't be doing today."

I nodded in agreement, as I always did. "Right. Not until I'm forty." He was referring to a prostate exam. The specific reason he enjoyed referring to this was because he enjoyed joking about the time another patient of his, in for such an exam, grew alarmed after Dr. Kovac put on a latex glove. The patient balked, telling Dr. Kovac he thought the exam was going to be digital. Dr. Kovac displayed his index finger and proclaimed, "You're right. This is the digit." It was a story I had heard before, but clearly his present associate had not. She laughed with approval. He introduced her as Lauren. Lauren firmly shook my hand. I noticed she wasn't wearing a ring, which was surprising—not only that someone as good-looking as her wasn't wearing a ring, but the fact that I remembered to peek at her ring finger. Before we got to the specific purpose of my visit, Dr. Kovac explained Lauren would do a general checkup. He left me alone with her, saying he would return shortly.

Lauren instructed me to take my T-shirt off, something I was more than happy to do, although this meant I would have to suck in my gut the entire time. As she methodically placed the stethoscope on my chest and listened to me breathe, I had an epiphany. Perhaps meeting Herpes Girl was destiny. She was the instrument that brought me directly to Lauren, who dutifully continued to check my vital signs. If I hadn't have met Herpes Girl, I never would have encountered Lauren. Lauren was quite possibly, *quite probably*, the girl for me.

"Try to relax," she said as she pressed the stethoscope against my back. I assured her I *was* relaxed. Perhaps the thought that I would soon have to tell her I was potentially contaminated was making me a little tense, but I did my best to ignore it.

I decided to engage Lauren in a little small talk, asking her, "Have you seen any good movies lately?"

"Yes, but I can't date you." Apparently, Lauren was not the girl I was looking for after all. Where she seemed at ease and ready to laugh around Dr. Kovac, she was straightforward and painfully blunt to her patients, at least to this patient. She was like a Vulcan. Maybe that was why the Trekkie Dr. Kovac had chosen her.

I gave her a casual fake laugh and told her I wasn't looking for a date, only making conversation. Then, to disprove my point, I added, "Although I don't think it would be the worst thing in the world to go out with you."

Lauren stared at me without emotion. She asked, "Would you like a rectal exam before I get Dr. Kovac?"

"Yes, but I can't date you," I replied.

Without cracking so much as a half smile, Lauren told me she would be right back with Dr. Kovac. The two of them returned within minutes. "What brings you by today?" Dr. Kovac wondered. My eyes darted to Lauren momentarily. In that moment, my hopes for getting to know her better were dashed. I told Dr. Kovac and the Vulcan my story about Herpes Girl. They listened intently. It made me feel like I was presenting some sort of fireside radio play.

When I finished, it was Lauren who spoke first, with concern. "You should always use condoms." I told her I did. She told me there were condoms on the market that covered the entire area—not just "the shaft," which sounded like a car part the way she said it in her clinical, unsexy tone.

Then Dr. Kovac chimed in. "You want to know what the problem is with full-body condoms? You can't breathe." Lauren laughed enthusiastically. Everybody was having a good time. How wonderful that we could get together like this. If I only I had more brushes with herpes. No doubt, if Dr. Kovac knew this was what I was thinking, he would have commented that Brushes with Herpes would be a good Native American name for me. He looked at me with a serious expression and confessed, "Since people are telling you things after it's too late, I should probably come clean and let you know I don't have my medical license. But I'm hoping for next year." Then he crossed his fingers and laughed uproariously. "But seriously, folks," he went on, "I do have a license. I'm just joshing you."

The one-liners came to an end and Dr. Kovac got down to business. He ordered tests for every STD under the sun—including herpes I, oral herpes. Herpes I isn't really a true STD; most of the world population has it. Anyone who doesn't have it is kind of a loser. Of course, my testing included herpes II, the bad kind. I must admit, when I went down to the lab with my papers and a lab technician asked what I needed to be tested for, it made me feel a little proud when I said, "*Everything.*" I couldn't help but feel like a stud. The results for my tests came back days later. No STDs at all. Not only did I not have herpes II, I didn't even have herpes I. Not having herpes I was a little disappointing. I figured I'd made out with enough women to have caught that long ago.

In spite of my less than auspicious start to Internet dating, I was now doubly determined to give it a chance. Not catching the bad herpes (and finding out I didn't even have the good herpes) was like a new lease. I could go forth into the world without worrying about taking time out of an intimate moment to delicately ask a girl,

"How do you feel about catching herpes?" Of course, I'd use caution in my future endeavors. I wouldn't do anything with anyone without first ascertaining they weren't contagious. But I wouldn't shy away from anyone either. It was a brand-new day. A day in which I would accept all invitations. Though I planned on continuing to meet girls through the computer, I wouldn't rely solely on that. I'd meet them through however many sources were at my disposal. It was a numbers game. The more women I met, the more likely I'd meet The One. I didn't care how many freaks there were along the way. However many it took. This new, improved course of full-on intensive dating was going to be like a second job. ChickenWhisperer was getting out there more.

FRIEND OF A FRIEND OF A FRIEND

Slowly but surely, responses to messages I sent out to single women on the Internet began trickling in. The average seemed to be for every five hundred messages sent out, one would come back. At least that's what it seemed like. Though it was hard work, I remained undeterred. I was going on one or two Internet dates a month. What I learned from most of the Internet dates—aside from the odds being fifty-fifty the girl actually looked like her picture—was that they were very similar to going out on dates with people I met in the real world, in that the Internet dates were shallow and draining. They felt less like dates and more like conversation practice. That wasn't such a bad thing, as I was the first to admit my conversation skills could use a bit of polishing. (I once saw my expressionless mailman and asked him, "How are you doing? Are you sad?" Flustered, he told me he wasn't and wondered why I asked. I was just making conversation. Lesson learned.) While it remained entirely possible the right woman could show up through an Internet date, I held true to my oath and remained open to all opportunities. One opportunity unexpectedly presented itself in my apartment building.

There was a sixty-something-year-old man who lived on the floor above me. I did not know his name even though we had been in the same building for years. We mostly saw each other in the elevator. He was a good-natured man, always smiling. While he was not without his quirks, I preferred sharing an elevator with him over some of the other residents. Another nameless man—overweight, tall, and imposing, with shaggy gray hair—once walked into the elevator, looked at me, and matter-of-factly asked, "Are you circumcised?" This guy was worse at conducting small talk than I was.

I brushed his ridiculous question off with an equally ridiculous answer. "You bet. I get circumcised every morning."

The good-natured man in his sixties mostly made innocuous comments about the weather or the preponderance of junk mail he was receiving. These weren't the most riveting topics, but far better than discussing whether or not I had foreskin.

One time the good-natured man did ask me a personal, albeit inoffensive, question. He wondered if I was still dating a "parade of ladies." Apparently he was keeping tabs on me from a distance.

I chuckled, telling him, "You bet. Why? Do you know someone?"

The good-natured man knew a woman who knew a woman who was single and looking. "You're a fine young fellow," appraised the good-natured man. "I told my friend about you. I told her the next time I saw you I'd find out if you'd be interested in going out with her friend." Basically, I was being asked by a man whose name I had never learned if I would like to go on a date with the anonymous friend of his anonymous friend. Remembering my newfound philosophy, I told him I'd be happy to. Mr. Good Nature was pleased. "Perfect," he said. "I'll leave her phone number taped to your door. What apartment do you live in?"

A few days later, I found a piece of paper taped to my door with the woman's phone number. Her name was Crystal. My upstairs neighbor wrote a quick note to go with Crystal's number. *Don't know much about her. I hear she's attractive and friendly. I'm going to step aside. Best of luck! Norm.* So the guy was Norm. That was one positive that came out of this situation. Now I knew Norm's name. I would do my best to remember it.

Later that night, I called Crystal. Someone who sounded like a nine-year-old girl answered the phone. When I heard her voice, it occurred to me I didn't know how old Crystal was—I had assumed she was around my age. I asked if I could speak with Crystal, hoping the nine-year-old would not respond with, "Speaking." Fortunately, the little person very formally asked, "Who shall I say is calling?" After identifying myself, I heard, "One moment please," as Crystal's secretary put me on hold.

Next came the withered voice of an old woman, asking, "Hello?" This one sounded like she was a hundred and nine. My first inclination was to hang up as fast as humanly possible. I'm sure she was a wonderful person, but centenarians were not in my dating pool.

Before I responded, I heard a third woman call out in the background, "Grandma, it's for me." The third woman took the phone, greeting me right away. "Hi, this is Crystal." Her octaves were much more within my ballpark.

Crystal sounded pleasant, but distracted. She apologized for any confusion, telling me she had been expecting my call and looked forward to going out. In a bit of a hurry, Crystal gave me her address, instructing me to pick her up for dinner that Friday night at seven o'clock. She would be waiting on the sidewalk in front of her house. With that, the conversation ended. Crystal was obviously someone who cut to the chase. I liked that about her. Also, I especially liked that she lived ten minutes away. This was a *huge* plus. In Los Angeles, if someone lives on the other side of town, they might as well be a leper. Plus, Crystal had a nice voice. There was actually potential here.

If the rest of Crystal matched her voice, I planned on taking her to dinner at Alonzo's, a cozy, romantic Italian restaurant in my neighborhood. Alonzo's was named after the restaurant's owner, Alonzo. He was a seemingly gruff man with buzzed white hair on the sides of his otherwise bald head who always wore a chef's uniform without the silly hat. The first time I walked into his restaurant, Alonzo gave me a stern look, ready to kick me in the shins should I say something he did not approve of. He asked if he could help me. I told him I was interested in eating, hoping I didn't sound unintentionally sarcastic. After careful consideration, Alonzo showed me to a table. The food was delicious. I returned many times. Alonzo and I were now friends. Whenever he saw me, he would tell me a hackneyed joke and I would wait for the appropriate moment to provide fake laughter. If I went to the restaurant with a young lady, he would sing my praises to her. Which is why I planned on bringing Crystal to Alonzo's. Unless Crystal's voice did not match the rest of her. Then we would go to McDonaldo's.

Crystal lived in a single-story home located on a busy four-lane street cutting across the city. Traffic was typically congested on this street. From my car, I spotted Crystal waiting on the sidewalk. She was holding her purse protectively in front of her. I was still a little too far away to get a look at her face in the dark of night. Based on what I *could* see, so far so good. She had shoulder-length brunette hair, tight-fitting jeans, black boots that came up to her knees, and a puffy pink jacket. Since I had called Crystal a few moments earlier, she knew to look for my beast of a car. (A woman on her cell phone smashed into the back of my midsized sedan a few years back. It was traumatic, but I was okay. I subsequently bought an SUV for revenge.) When traffic permitted me to cruise up to Crystal's house, she got in the car before it came to a complete stop, as if escaping in a getaway vehicle. Crystal greeted me with a friendly hello. She looked a little younger than me. Her smile was inviting. We would definitely be dining at Alonzo's.

"I'm starving," reported Crystal. "I hope you've decided where we're going."

As we drove away from her busy street, I asked, "Are you Crystal?" It was an attempt at humor.

My attempt succeeded. But laughter suddenly turned to concern. She faced me, holding on to the door handle. "Wait a minute. Are you Carlos?" I almost told her I was someone else, again aiming for humor. But this might have genuinely frightened her. Instilling fear was probably not the best way to go. Crystal visibly relaxed when I confirmed I was Carlos. If she wanted to double-check, I offered to show her my driver's license and also noted that I knew her name in advance. She was satisfied. "You scared me for a second. I was going to jump out of your car."

"That's never good," I said. "When the date jumps out of the car, that's not a good sign." On a roll, I scored another laugh. She asked me if I ever had a date jump out of my car before. Feeling brash, I went for the hat trick. I told her, "Not very often. Less than five times this year." Boom! Hat trick. She was still laughing as I pointed out how quickly Crystal climbed into my car without asking questions. "There were other SUVs on the street. You could have easily got into the wrong one. We probably should have come up with a safe word."

"A safe word?" She did not understand.

"A code word. To identify ourselves. To make sure that we were both who we hoped we were. Like maybe when you opened the door, we should have agreed ahead of time that I would say *zonkey*." I don't know why my brain chose this word, other than hoping for a fourth burst of laughter. The word was initially met by silence. Maybe Crystal had a bad experience with a zonkey.

Crystal asked, "What's a zonkey?" I explained a zonkey was a half zebra, half donkey, surprised to still be on this subject. There was more silence, followed by, "That's weird."

"Yes, it is weird. You don't see zonkeys around here very often." Perhaps *I* was the one being referred to as weird. Crystal's silence was diluting the lighthearted mood set by her earlier laughter.

Changing subjects, Crystal wondered, "How do you know Susan?"

"Who's Susan?" It was my turn to be confused.

"Oh, that's right. You don't know Susan. You know Susan's friend Norm."

"Never heard of Norm. Don't know any Norms." All these names Crystal was bandying about. She thought for sure I knew Norm. Then I remembered. "Oh, *Norm*." The guy in the elevator who lived on the floor above me. The matchmaker. "Right. Norm. He's cool. You can always count on Norm." I had never had to count on Norm for anything. But he was probably dependable.

We parked about a block away from Alonzo's. As we walked to the restaurant, I saw a familiar man heading toward us. He was another man whose name I did not know and probably never would. For convenience, I thought of him as Jerry. In his fifties, Jerry was an eccentric sort who I often saw walking through the neighborhood. I never spoke to Jerry. Jerry never spoke to anyone, except the voices in his head. He was always carrying on lengthy conversations with no one in particular. Based solely on his aimless chatter, it was easy to mistake Jerry for a transient. But he was well-groomed, clean-shaven, with his hair carefully combed at all times. And he wore expensive clothes. Sometimes he wore suits. On other occasions he would wear slacks and a sweater, with either a bathrobe or trench coat as an extra layer. He was wearing a light brown trench coat as he walked toward us. I alerted Crystal that Jerry talked to himself. "It's fine, just act natural," I advised.

Jerry walked by, looking straight ahead. As usual, he was deep in conversation, talking to some unknown entity. They were currently discussing stockings. "It's the white stockings. When they wear the white stockings, they're sending a message . . ." He continued walking at a brisk pace. His conversation trailed off before I was able to hear what the message was behind white stockings. Hopefully it wasn't important.

Crystal laughed. She wanted to know if Jerry and I were friends. I answered in the affirmative. "Yes, he's the one who set you and me up."

"For real?" Crystal's eyes widened. I clarified that I was joking. Her eyes went back to their normal size. "I can't tell when you're joking and when you're being serious." She wasn't the only one.

I offered a solution. "How about . . . whenever I'm joking, at the end I'll say *waka waka waka?*" Crystal gave me a blank stare. I told her I was joking.

Alonzo greeted me with a firm handshake and then warmly kissed Crystal on both sides of her face, rocking it European style. He welcomed her to the restaurant, telling Crystal what a great guy I was. We were seated at a table near the front window. Alonzo smiled at Crystal, saying, "I'd offer you a glass of wine, but I don't think Carlos will join you. That's the one thing that's wrong with him. Never trust a guy who doesn't drink." He shook his head in disappointment.

Crystal looked at me in dismay. "You don't drink wine?"

"Maybe he does tonight, with a pretty lady like you," suggested Alonzo. I politely shook my head. Alonzo shrugged his shoulders. "All right, I'll bring water." He left the table, but once he was behind Crystal, he sent me a flurry of gestures, communicating: *have some wine, loosen up, you're with a nice girl, things will go better, what's wrong with you?* I shook my head again, ever so slightly.

Crystal wanted to know why I didn't drink wine. I explained that I didn't drink alcohol because I didn't want to go to Hell. Her eyebrows furrowed until I threw in, "Waka waka waka." She chuckled. "I'm more of a hot chocolate, apple juice kind of a guy. It tastes better. And tea. I like tea." Crystal said she loved wine. I nodded, telling her, "You're not alone. A lot of humans enjoy wine." She looked perplexed. I realized the way I phrased things, a lot of *humans*, made me sound as if I was from another planet. Hoping to ease her anxiety, I quickly added, "I'm human too. I didn't mean to make it sound like I'm not human. I totally am. Earth is my home planet." If I was intending to sound human, I wasn't doing a very good job of it.

Crystal started to laugh. "You're strange," she concluded. But a good strange it seemed, judging by her laughter.

Over dinner, Crystal and I got to know each other a little better. I told her about the pet chickens I used to have, that I was valedictorian of my high school, and that I had lived alone my entire adult life. Crystal shared that she lived at home with her nine-year-old daughter—along with her parents, her uncle, and her grandmother. She had not been on a date in ten years, and also she felt uncomfortable around "the gays." It was a lot of information to register over lasagna Bolognese.

I wanted to delve deeper into each of her statements, so I chose to begin with the daughter part. "So that receptionist who first answered your phone, the one who put me on hold, that was your daughter?"

"Yes. My daughter is the best thing that ever happened to me in my life. Even if she was an accident."

"That's sweet," I responded.

Crystal took another sip of her wine. She had ordered a glass after all, to Alonzo's delight. I stuck with water. "My daughter's birthday is coming up. Next month. She told me all she wants for her birthday is a daddy."

"Oh, is that all?" It sounded like Crystal was starting to get a little tipsy. Either that or I was being tested. She wanted to see if I was going to sprint out of the restaurant upon hearing that her daughter hoped to wake up the morning of her birthday to find a man wrapped in a ribbon wearing a T-shirt with DADDY written on it. This didn't scare me. Someone having a daughter wasn't a deal breaker. After all, in the unlikely event Crystal and I fell in love, maybe we could find someone else to play the part of her daughter's daddy. Specifically, maybe the daughter's dad could be her dad. I asked Crystal where the father was. "In prison," she said, drinking more wine.

"I've got a joke for you." Alonzo approached the table, ready to dazzle us with his comedy stylings. I wanted to tell Alonzo jokes were not necessary, as Crystal was already saying a bunch of hilarious things. Listening to Alonzo's so-called jokes was always the most challenging part of eating at his restaurant. Not only was his material not funny, it was confusing. I don't know if it was the content or the delivery or what, but I always had trouble pinpointing the actual punch lines. I would listen intently, waiting for him to stop talking. That would be my cue for hollow laughter. As Alonzo began the exposition of his joke, I affixed a plastic smile on my face. He told Crystal and me about a lawyer who came home early for lunch and someone else's boots were under the bed, so on and so forth, until Alonzo finally stopped talking. I laughed. He looked at me in surprise. "Have you heard this one?" He wasn't finished with the joke; he had just stopped to take a breath.

Realizing my mistake, I covered with, "No, I haven't heard it. But it's funny already." Alonzo continued. Boots under the bed and the lawyer's wife was holding a broom upside down and the lawyer warned he was going to sue her for embezzlement. His joke was like a math problem. There was another long pause. Alonzo had finished. I laughed again, this time correctly, though not sincerely. "Another good one," I praised. I liked Dr. Kovac's jokes better: *What does a suspicious mole look like? It's wearing sunglasses.* That joke I could understand.

Alonzo turned toward Crystal, patting her on the back. "Is Carlos treating you all right? You having fun? Food is good?" Crystal answered yes on all counts. Alonzo gave me a nod of approval. He left to socialize with his other customers.

I had another question for Crystal. "Did I hear you correctly? Did you say you haven't been on a date in ten years?" She had not. "Wow. That's a long time. I've had dry spells. But none that lasted a decade."

Crystal revealed that after she got pregnant—which was after the first time she had sex—she took a break from dating to raise her baby. Plus, she spent a great deal of time fighting with her parents, not to mention the "fuckface father" of her angelic child. The fighting had subsided lately, what with the father behind bars for an undisclosed crime and her parents initiating a truce for the sake of their granddaughter. "My parents think I'm a slut. I've told them a million times to look *slut* up in the dictionary. A slut has sex more than once. And you don't have to worry about my daughter's father—he's not getting out for a long, long time. Anyway, my friends have been telling me I need to meet new people, start dating again. So here we are." Holy moly, here we were.

"Um . . ." I wasn't quite sure what to say. "Have you gone out with anyone else recently? Do you have other dates lined up? I'm just curious. I mean, it's been so long for you. I think you should probably go out with tons of guys. Well, not tons, but you know. When people are shopping for a house, they don't buy the first house they see. I don't think."

Crystal finished her wine. She smiled at me and said, "I'm not shopping for a house. Not yet. And, no, I don't have a ton of dates lined up. It's difficult. Because everyone is gay these days." She excused herself and went to the ladies' room, while I tried to make sense of her last comment.

Alonzo came back to the table in Crystal's absence. "Carlos, what's happening with this girl?" I told him there wasn't enough time to brief him. "Do you like her?" I didn't think we had much of a future. Alonzo told me not to think. "Just relax. Let things happen naturally." Not the greatest advice. After all, letting things happen naturally is how Crystal came to be known as the town slut by her understanding parents.

After Alonzo's, Crystal wanted to have a latte at her favorite coffeehouse nearby. Neither of us had finished our meals. Alonzo neatly wrapped them in take-out boxes. Because I didn't want the food to sit in my car for a long period of time, I asked Crystal if she wouldn't mind stopping at my building before going to the coffeehouse so I could leave our food in the refrigerator. I told her she could stay in the car and I would run up to my apartment. That way she could protect her virtue. (Although it was kind of too late now, wasn't it?) Crystal said she didn't mind stopping at my building, and was also fine with going upstairs.

As we drove to my building, I asked her about everyone being gay. What did she mean exactly? "I mean everyone's gay. Ricky Martin. Everybody." I wondered if she had a problem with gay people. "Not really," she responded. "I just don't want to be around them."

"How many gay people do you know?"

"I don't know any." This was hard to believe. Not only because of general statistics, but because in her case those statistics were compounded by the fact that she was a hairdresser.

"I'm pretty sure you know somebody who is gay."

"Oh, I don't think so," she proclaimed. Ironically, it was a gay man who'd had a hand in introducing us. Norm, from upstairs, was gay. This was pure speculation on my part based on strong indications. There were a number of times when the elevator doors opened and I saw Norm dressed from head to toe as a woman, complete with a sophisticated, stylish makeup job. He would still greet me with his ever-present smile and make comments about our perfect weather. Only his voice was higher-pitched. He was now Norma. That Norm enjoyed dressing in drag did not automatically signify he was gay. What really led me to this assumption was the time the elevator doors opened and I discovered him with a well-dressed conservative man. Norma was all decked out in a cocktail gown. He and his happy date were holding hands until the doors opened. I noticed them swiftly let go of each other as I stepped into the elevator. It made me feel a little bad, them not holding hands on my account. It didn't matter to me if someone was gay—I had other things to think about, like paying my bills and doing laundry.

I parked in my building's garage. While Crystal and I waited for the elevator, I prayed it would arrive with Norma. What a thrill it would be to introduce him/her, explaining that he/she was the one who had told me about Crystal. Unfortunately, no one was in the elevator. When we got into my apartment, I went straight to the kitchen and put our leftovers in the fridge. Crystal walked around on a self-guided tour. "It's so peaceful and quiet," she remarked, looking around the apartment as if it was some kind of wonderland. I asked if she was ready to go to the coffeehouse. She took a seat on my couch, saying, "I'm actually pretty comfortable. I could stay here if you want. Got anything to drink?"

I poured Crystal a glass of wine. Even though I didn't drink, I kept wine in the apartment for people who did. I sat beside Crystal, nestled on the couch. This was an unexpected turn of events. I wasn't positive, but it suddenly seemed as if a make-out session was in the works. "What's in that album?" Crystal was looking at a photo album I kept under the coffee table. I told her they were pictures from a trip I took to Australia. Crystal wanted to see them.

As I reached for the album, she moved a little closer. We casually looked through the pictures of my Australian adventure. I was about to turn the page when she planted her index finger on one picture in particular, asking, "Why do you have a purse?" It was a legitimate question, with a legitimate explanation. In the picture, I was standing in an Australian rain forest, wearing a purse. Before I left for Oz, my mother gave me a black camera bag. My camera fit perfectly inside. I thought nothing of it. It wasn't until nearly the end of my trip that I realized the alleged "camera bag" was actually a woman's small purse. Consequently, I unwittingly traveled through much of Australia towing a purse and had the photographic evidence to prove it. Norm would have been proud. Crystal could not stop laughing. She was in tears. Every time she spotted another picture with me and my purse, she would bust a gut all over again.

Then Crystal saw a picture of me and a young woman. My arm was around this woman. We looked very much like a couple. Crystal quieted down. She wanted to know who the woman was. I didn't want to get into a whole big long story about how the woman was named Kate from Bermuda and she wanted me to move in with her after we spent the night in a hotel room on Fraser Island, etc., etc. There was no point in sharing this with Crystal. I simply said, "That was a girl I met from Bermuda. She was nice."

I studied the picture, Kate's expression. She seemed to be looking at me, questioning, "How could you be with someone else right now?" In some ways, Crystal reminded me of Kate. When I met Kate she basically said hello and asked me to live with her in Bermuda in the same breath. Crystal wasn't asking me to move in—*yet*—but she *was* pointing out that I was her first date in ten years and her daughter wanted a daddy big-time. Was there something about me that attracted these types? Was it a result of me letting them do most of the talking? Perhaps these girls mistook my silence for interest. It probably would be a good idea to start talking more. Interrupting Crystal several times might go a long way. The problem was I was starting to get tired, and was in no mood to be chatty. Maybe dating girls with heavy baggage that they were ready to immediately unload on my front door reflected a deeper psychological issue. Maybe it pointed to a repressed desire on my part to care for someone who needed more nurturing and patience than the average girl. Or maybe meeting these types of women was just bad luck.

I turned the page of my Australian photo album. It nearly slipped off my lap. In grabbing it, I ended up scooting closer to Crystal. She immediately turned toward me with a seductive look. I thought, *"Oh my goodness, we're definitely going to make out."* We continued gazing at each other. I courteously asked how she was doing. She was fine. Next, I courteously informed Crystal I was going to kiss her. I was going to kiss her on the cheek, for starters. When I slowly leaned in, Crystal engulfed me. She kissed me, my lips, like someone who had not kissed anyone in ten years. I had to hold on tight to keep up, as if I was careening through roaring rapids. It was kind of exhilarating. I couldn't help but think what a good neighbor Norm was.

Crystal suddenly pulled away from me, concerned. I asked her what was wrong. She wanted to know if I was gay. I didn't understand the question. Crystal said, "You had a purse in Australia." I told her, again, I didn't know it was a purse. She was quiet, thinking. Then Crystal prodded, "How come you don't have a girlfriend or a wife?"

"Because I haven't met the right woman. Not because I'm gay." It was strange to be explaining myself. Kissing her seemed to be ample evidence. I must not have been doing a good job. She stared at me, still suspicious. "I'm not gay," I repeated. "Look." To allay her concerns, I gently squeezed her boobs. Up to this moment, I had not slid into second base, but this seemed to be the appropriate time. Crystal did not protest—on the contrary. I told her I enjoyed feeling her up, which I did, and complimented her form. In Crystal's mind, these actions proved I was heterosexual. We went back to making out as if there was no tomorrow.

I had known the woman for about an hour. This was a record. In North America, it generally took me at least four to six weeks of courting a female before there was any physical contact. Sometimes it took years. Our couch session was fun to be sure, but I essentially knew next to nothing about Crystal. I knew that the father of her child had committed a heinous undisclosed crime and that Crystal operated under the fallacy that she didn't know any gay people, even though according to her they were everywhere at all times. Still, on a purely superficial physical level, it was a pleasurable experience.

Crystal pulled away from me, concerned about something else. Reading my mind, she pointed out that we hardly knew each other. She looked at me and said, "You could be crazy." I assured her I was not crazy, though for future reference I suggested she determine such matters *before* entering someone's apartment. She voiced another slightly ill-timed worry. "What if you have sexually transmitted diseases?" I nearly threw the question right back at her, but felt confident she was disease-free considering she was just coming off a ten-year drought. When I told Crystal I didn't have any STDs she asked, "I'm supposed to just take your word for it?" Actually, she didn't have to. As fate would have it, the results of the recent STD screening ordered by the inimitable Dr. Kovac were on my kitchen counter. Crystal wanted to see my papers.

I brought my test results over from the counter. We took a time-out so Crystal could vet them thoroughly. "Where's syphilis? I don't see syphilis." Syphilis was on the second page, but she still didn't see it. "Where?" She was getting a little upset. I showed her. Negative results for syphilis were about a third of the way down on the second page. Until she saw it with her own eyes, she was convinced my body was teeming with syphilis bacteria. It reminded me of when someone is at a restaurant and doesn't believe the restaurant serves salmon until they see it on the menu firsthand, regardless of whether or not a friend has promised there is definitely a grilled salmon special.

Convinced I was not a carrier, Crystal wanted to know why I had been tested in the first place. I didn't really feel like telling her it was because an Internet girl had attempted to give me herpes. Instead I calmly informed her the tests were part of a physical I had recently completed. Satisfied, Crystal continued kissing me. She pulled away a third time after things started to get more intense. "It's too much. You better take me home, before I have another baby." I was more than happy to take her home. Crystal sighed contentedly in the car and told me she was going to sing because she liked singing. Suddenly she began belting out a number I was not familiar with. The out-of-tune tune featured lyrics such as *mighty kingdom* and *power and the glory* and *guiding light*. I was starting to conclude this woman was not the best match for me.

Crystal asked me to pull over a few houses down from her own. She said if I dropped her off in front of her house, the entire family would be staring through the windows and would ask her more questions than she already knew they were going to ask. I stopped the car, as requested. Crystal gazed at me with a smile. She thanked me for the evening and lamented that what we had done was morally wrong. "We shouldn't have kissed like that. We can be friends for a while and then maybe we can be more than friends. We'll see." I nodded, telling her that was reasonable. Crystal leaned closer. "One more time because we already have tonight." She gave me a deeply lustful kiss good-bye. She had already sinned. Our kiss was just another sin on the pile. I watched her walk back to her house and never saw her again.

A couple of days after my dinner with Crystal, I ran into Norm in the elevator. He was dressed as Norm and appeared happy to see me. Norm made a few brief comments about how hot it had been lately and the stack of bills in his hand, and then asked, "Did you go out with my friend's friend?" I told Norm I had, reporting that she was nice, but we did not make an ideal pair. Still smiling, Norm shrugged and said, "Oh well," as he walked out of the elevator. Oh well. That was fine for Norm to say. He could go upstairs and put on a nice dress and all was right with the world. But I was disheartened, as much as I tried not to be. Every time I went out with a new person, the evening began with the quiet yet profound anticipation that this new girl might be *the* girl. And every time I came home with the wind out of my sails, I felt rudderless. I needed to buck up, remind myself that this was a marathon not a sprint.

After my date with Crystal, I felt some tweaking might be in order. My new approach of going out with *any* girl also single and looking was admirable, but not necessarily practical. It might be a good idea to find out a thing or two about them before agreeing to meet. For example, learning beforehand that a girl entertains herself by breaking out into spontaneous excruciating gospel while in the car would save us both a lot of time. A referral would be useful too. It would be good to have someone I trusted tell me things other than just *she's cute.* Perhaps I might start requiring people who set me up to provide me with a document outlining the girl's family history, past relationships, and taste in music.

Also, on most of the dates I went on—including the one with Crystal—I took the girl out to dinner. This guaranteed we were stuck together for a significant amount of time, not to mention that my wallet would be lighter at the end of the evening. A new policy was in order. No more dinners. One tea and out. Unless I fell for her. Then *after* tea we'd have dinner and after dinner we'd get married. Not necessarily *right* after. But for starters: one tea and *hasta la* bye-bye. Teas allowed for quick escapes. I felt good about my new revamped dating procedures, eager to put them into practice. Though my spirit had been slightly bruised, I was still gung ho about meeting women. After all, I was only looking for one.

BLIND DATE

It was a lazy Sunday. After firing off a few halfhearted Internet dating messages to girls who would probably not respond, I began aimlessly surfing the Web. Somehow, for some reason, my computer led me to a list of top ten things a person can do naked. Intrigued, I decided to examine this list a little more closely. Besides the obvious, the activities one could do in a birthday suit included skydiving, skinny-dipping, running across the field during a professional sporting event, and naked yoga. While streaking past the fifty-yard line was enticing, it was the naked yoga that really piqued my interest. I had been considering yoga. There was a studio near my apartment building. I often saw beautiful people blissfully strolling out of it. If I were to become a yogi this would probably be the studio I would attend. But I was willing to keep my options open. I clicked on the naked yoga link provided and found there was a yoga class regularly held in Los Angeles in which the students practiced au naturel. The class was attended exclusively by men and the men, per the Web site, were predominantly gay. But straight men were welcome! I didn't go. I did, however, read the Web site's frequently asked questions, of which I had many.

I assumed the questions would range from, "How much do the classes cost?" to "Should I bring a towel?" However, the most frequently asked question, when it came to yoga at this particular studio, was, "What should I do if I get a boner?" The answer was simple. "Be proud of it." This is what I was reading when the phone rang.

It was my mother. "What are you doing?" she asked. I told her I was looking at a Web site for a yoga studio where the people practiced naked. She gasped in shock. "Naked! You mean without any clothes?" I clarified that, yes, that's what I meant—I meant *literally* naked, not emotionally. Since I had just read the most frequently asked question and found it amusing, I decided to share it with her. My mother's response took me by surprise. "What's a boner?" she innocently inquired. She had now lived in the United States longer than in Mexico. Despite her English being ninety-nine percent proficient, every now and then she'd encounter an unfamiliar word among the one percent. *Boner* was one of them. The new word of the day. Hoping against hope, I asked if she was serious. "Yes," she replied, "I've never heard that word. What is it?"

Not wanting to answer at all, I answered as delicately as possible. "A boner is what happens when a man gets excited."

"Ohhhhh," uttered my mother in recognition.

Since we had gotten to this point, I thought it only fair to share the Web site's answer. I first asked my mother what *she* thought the Web site advised in the event of a boner. After careful deliberation, my mother replied, "Ummm . . . leave it on the floor and we'll clean it up later."

At this point I decided the best course of action would be to pretend our conversation never took place. I hit the reset button, asking my mother, "How are you doing? Are you calling me for something specific?"

Thankfully, my mother swiftly changed directions with me. "There's a girl I want you to meet," she reported. Earlier, I had told her in passing about my efforts to go out on more dates. She translated this as me asking her to moonlight as my pimp. That was not my intent, but I didn't stop her. It wasn't the first time she had attempted to play matchmaker. But since I had expressly stated I wanted to meet as many women as possible, she was putting in extra pimp hours. In the past, she'd set me up on blind dates with a young lady who was a friend of a friend from her sewing group or her exercise class or with the sister of her dental hygienist. Of course, I'd never forget her role in my second prom. I was still trying to figure out a way to get her back for that. If my mother sensed an opportunity, she seized it.

I'd go out with these women, just in case, and then later I would ask my mother what she was thinking. They were either boring or humorless or, in one case, an Amazon woman nearly two feet taller than me. (A deal breaker to be sure.) Upon discovering I was not interested in a second date, my mother would respond, "What's the problem? She's nice." I'd remind my mother that of the top five qualities I was looking for in a woman—*nice* was not one of them. My mother would say, in all seriousness, "It's such a shame you're not going to marry that girl." And so it went. The vast majority of dates set up by my mother were for the most part dull, though there was one blind date unlike any other. My mother once set me up on a blind date with a girl who was actually blind.

Her name was Erika. She was a friend of a woman named Susanna, who my mother knew from the Viking Club. The Viking Club sounds like a club for badasses but is actually a group of people who are passionate about sewing. Apparently Viking is the Harley-Davidson of sewing machines. At one of these Viking Club meetings, Susanna asked my mother if I was still single, and if I was, would I be interested in meeting Erika? Erika was a wonderful girl who had just moved to the San Diego area from Monterrey, Mexico, to study international relations at the University of California, San Diego. She was on her own and having a difficult time meeting new people, especially the kind of people she could go on dates with. That's where I came in. According to Susanna, Erika was smart, pretty, funny, friendly . . . and blind. She had been blind her entire life. Susanna wondered if I would be willing to go out with a blind girl. "I don't know," responded my mother. "I'll ask."

When I called Erika, she answered right away. Her voice was bright and cheery. Anyone speaking to her over the phone would never guess she was blind. I'm not sure what I was expecting, perhaps the sound of her crashing into things as she walked around her apartment. But there was none of that. I did hear a rambunctious dog barking in the background. Erika shouted, "Be quiet, Helen!" and the dog, Helen, hushed up. We spoke for a few minutes. Erika gave me her address. We decided the following Saturday night I would drive down from Los Angeles and we would have dinner. This meant that the first date I went on after enacting a new policy of no dinners was one in which I agreed to drive one hundred miles from Los Angeles to San Diego so that I could have dinner. I had to make an exception. She was blind. Erika told me she looked forward to meeting me. I replied, "See you later," instantly regretting my choice of words.

By the time I got to San Diego that Saturday night, it was dark outside. The lights were off in Erika's apartment. I assumed she was not home. This annoyed me. We had plans, I drove all the way from Los Angeles, and the girl wasn't even there. What a jerk! Then it occurred to me. Erika wasn't the kind of girl who was into lights. I knocked on the door. A dog immediately began barking. Soon after, the lights went on. The door opened. I was greeted by a well-dressed, smiling young woman with long, curly reddish hair and the most beautiful green eyes. Erika stared directly at me with those eyes. Her stare was so deep and intense, she was effectively gazing into my soul. I thought maybe she could see, at least a little.

"Can you see me?" I asked, with hesitation. Erika's smile widened and her eyes drifted upward.

"No. I'm blind," she explained. I told her she had just been looking right at me. She declared, "Lucky shot." I was invited inside, where I met her dog, Helen—named after Helen Keller. Helen was a black Labrador who was overjoyed to meet me. She jumped all over me, licked me, brought me her toys and a piece of rawhide. Erika had to calm her down. I think the dog was happy mostly because the lights were on. The dog wasn't blind.

I took a seat on the couch beside Erika, with Helen settled at Erika's feet. We exchanged pleasantries and then I asked Erika, "Would you like to touch my face?" I asked this out of courtesy, based on the blind people I had seen in the movies.

Erika chuckled. She shook her head and replied, "I don't need to touch your face." Once it was determined there would be no face touching, we decided to head out for dinner. As we got ready to go, Erika grabbed a harness and slipped it onto Helen. The moment Helen was in the harness, she became a completely different dog.

She didn't want anything to do with me anymore. Helen was focused, on a mission, like the Terminator. Only like a nice Terminator. The kind of Terminator who would help little old ladies, or a blind person, cross the street.

Helen rested on the floor of the front seat of my car, in between Erika's feet. We drove to the Gaslamp Quarter in downtown San Diego, a popular entertainment district with numerous restaurants. It took a while for us to find parking. We circled around the block a few times. At one point, Helen sat up from the floor, looked out the window and loudly, impatiently, sighed. Despite the fact that we were different species, I understood. I told Helen we would find parking as soon as we could. She accepted this and went back to the floor. Erika passed the time cracking dirty jokes. Jokes that would make a Spanish sailor blush. "What did you just say?" I asked, needing to double-check. With a sly smile, Erika assured me I had heard correctly. I suspect part of the reason she so freely told these jokes was because she knew if I shared them with others, no one would believe they came from a sweet blind girl and I would be chastised for being so vulgar. After all, blind girls didn't talk that way. Oh, but they did. When she wasn't busy telling R-rated jokes, Erika's vocabulary was peppered with the kind of colorful words that would have earned her detention in high school. It was great.

Eventually we found parking and the three of us walked to a Thai restaurant. As we headed down the crowded sidewalk toward the restaurant, we received various, yet distinct looks from our fellow pedestrians. Helen was treated to tons of anonymous affection, as if she were a popular theme park mascot. Erika would kindly ask people not to pet Helen because Helen was working. People would kindly ignore Erika's request and attempt to cuddle with Helen. It didn't matter that people ignored Erika. Because Helen ignored people. She wanted none of their loving caresses, dismissively shaking them off. Her body language made it clear their touch was nothing more than a nuisance. If she could speak, she would have said, "I ain't got time for affection," while chomping on a cigar. As I watched Helen in action, I felt proud, thinking of how she had been climbing all over me earlier in Erika's apartment. I wanted to tell people that I *knew* Helen. We were friends.

The looks directed at Erika were strikingly different from those Helen received. It would take a moment for some people to process a blind woman was headed in their direction. Once they did realize this, many suddenly appeared to have been afflicted with rigor mortis while uncomfortably shifting their gaze to the sidewalk. On a few occasions, people would move away in an exaggerated manner, as if Erika were a wide load who required the entire sidewalk to get by. They appeared to do this out of misguided sympathy rather than sheer stupidity, though stupidity could not be discounted. Some people would somberly shake their heads, thinking, *poor woman—so brave to go out in public like that.* These looks of sympathy started to annoy me. I wanted to tell the people who were not so discreetly shaking their heads, "No, no. It's fine. I've been hanging out with her. She's cool. You should hear her joke about a hooker in a bagel shop. She isn't looking for sympathy; she just wants some food." Erika's face was affixed with a knowing, pleasant smile, seemingly aware of and accustomed to other people's stares.

If Erika was used to the reactions she elicited while out in public, I was not. People were looking at me in a whole new light, one that took a little while for me to identify. I was getting these weird smiles. Smiles that made me feel like maybe my fly was open or I had a dime stuck to my forehead or something. I finally realized Erika was significantly upping my street cred as a good person. Especially when she took my arm to navigate through particularly populated sections of the sidewalk. Where people shook their heads at Erika, I would get nods. *Good for you* nods. *You're such a saint for being with a blind girl* nods. Again, I wanted to comment, "Seriously. She's normal. We're just going to get Thai food. Pad See-Ew." Since there wasn't time to set people straight, I decided to embrace their approval. I walked down the sidewalk with a bit of a strut, nodding right back at them, my expression conveying, "That's right. I'm a sweetheart. What are you going to do about it?"

When we arrived at the Thai restaurant, we were greeted by a teenage hostess who squealed at the sight of Helen, stating, "You can't. There's no dogs allowed in here." The way this hostess was shaken up, one would've thought Helen was a snake or a mouse or a great white shark. Helen, true to form, ignored the hostess. I was willing to give this uninformed hostess the benefit of the doubt, generously assuming that as a child she must have mercilessly been attacked by a band of rogue Seeing Eye dogs. Erika was in no mood to cut her this kind of slack. She directed a controlled laserlike fury at the hostess, using many of her more unladylike phrases to explain the law, the consequences of not letting us in, both personal and professional. By the time Erika was done, the hostess had long forgotten about Helen and was now terrified of Erika—terrified that Erika would follow her home and haunt her in her dreams. We were shown to our seats.

"I hate it when people don't want to let Helen in. Maybe I was a little rough on that girl, though," Erika concluded as we sat at the table, with Helen calmly lying underneath.

"You were awesome," I praised. "Like Dirty Harry."

"Dirty Harry?" she wondered. She was very bright, spoke English and Spanish perfectly as well as a bit of French, but somehow *Dirty Harry* had gotten by Erika the way *boner* had gotten by my mom. When I explained Dirty Harry was a San Francisco cop played by Clint Eastwood who shot bad guys using the most powerful handgun in the world, Erika concurred with a pleased smile. "Yes, I'm like Dirty Harry."

A friendly waitress brought us menus. It seemed the waitress was too busy to notice Erika's special circumstances, which was ideal. With the initial tension of our arrival a thing of the past, I read Erika the menu. In full disclosure, I skipped a few items. Some of the entrees didn't sound very appetizing. After the menu reading and our orders were placed (Pad Thai and Pad See-Ew—which is still delicious even though it includes the word *Ew*), Erika asked what I was wearing. For a split second, I forgot. As I looked down at my wardrobe so I could begin describing it, I heard Erika comment, "You have to look?" She could tell what I was doing by my pause. At another point during our conversation Erika displayed her heightened senses by suddenly observing, "That's a big truck." I didn't know what she was talking about until a few moments later, when I looked out the restaurant window and saw an enormous truck drive by.

Throughout dinner, Erika continued to brandish her uncouth sense of humor. Since she was kidding around so much, and in such an edgy way, I thought I'd try my hand at a twisted joke. I told her, "I'm going to use the men's room. If I'm not back in an hour, call a taxi." The part about using the men's room was true. The part about call a taxi was obviously a joke. But to Erika it was obviously not. Her expression instantly turned pale, concerned, a bit frightened.

For the first time since I had met her, she seemed genuinely vulnerable, which was saying something. It was saying that I felt like a horrible person. I took her hand and did my best to comfort her, apologizing profusely and promising it was an awful, misguided joke. She calmed down, a little. I considered not going to the bathroom. But I really had to go. Part of me thought it might be worth the sacrifice to go number one while sitting across from Erika so she wouldn't have to be left alone. But given her special powers, she would undoubtedly smell urine right away. Plus, Helen was napping on the floor at my feet. Helen was my friend. You don't do that to friends. I excused myself, rushed to the men's room, and peed as fast as I could.

When I returned, I saw Erika sitting on the edge of her seat, listening. "I'm back," I announced. She visibly relaxed. The rest of the evening continued without a hitch. Erika told me of her studies, her family back home, her desire to travel the world. She especially wanted to visit Paris. I thought this was interesting because given her situation if she ever did go to Paris, she would essentially have to take people's word for it. She patiently informed me there were many ways to experience Paris, and the world for that matter. Erika could envision Paris through its sounds, its food, the people, the energy. Through her mind's eye she could envision everything the world had to offer.

Dinner came to an end. I drove Erika back to her apartment. Helen's harness was removed and she was once again happy-go-lucky. I told Erika I was going to give her a kiss on the cheek and then I did. We did not become an item. Our chemistry was not of the romantic kind. We both knew it. But we did become friends, which was fortunate because she kept me posted on all things eventful—such as her trip to Paris and how she moved to Vancouver to live with her new boyfriend. I was happy for her.

Meeting Erika was worth the drive to San Diego and having yet another dinner date (I promised myself that all future first dates would be *tea and out*). Erika helped put things in perspective. On those few occasions I found myself getting down over silliness such as terrible traffic or even more pressing issues like the pace of my rise in Hollywood or—the most serious issue of all—my inability to find love, I'd remember Erika. I'd think of what Erika would tell me. She'd probably say, "You can friggin' *see*, idiot!" Only she'd use a different F word. Maybe I was overly concerned about how and *when* my dream girl was going to show up. I wouldn't stop looking, but I'd try to stay relaxed about it. Her arrival was up to her. She would show up when she showed up. When I got back to my apartment from San Diego, I checked my computer to see if any Internet dating responses had arrived. There were none. Even so, I slept soundly that night.

SAY AGAIN?

The amount of responses I received through Internet dating was dwindling. They were never the greatest to begin with. Just when it seemed I had perhaps reached the end of the road, a message arrived from VenusBlossom. It was as if I was playing the slots, on my last penny, and suddenly I hit three pineapples allowing me to continue a little bit longer. VenusBlossom's earthly name was Claire. Claire apologized for the delay in getting back to me and, if I was still interested, asked for my phone number. If and when we spoke, she would decide if she'd like to meet in person. It seemed she assumed I would undoubtedly want to meet her. To refresh my memory, I reviewed Claire's profile on the dating Web site. She was cute, but her picture consisted of *only* her face—in black and white. I had gone on enough vacuous Internet dates to know that type of photo meant *proceed with extreme caution—suspect may be older and heavier than she appears.* Despite my concerns, I gave Claire my number, reminding myself that if she wanted to meet in person, under no circumstances were we going to dinner. Tea and out.

A few days later, I received a very strange call. When I answered the phone I heard a mature woman with a businesslike tone inform me she was a TTY operator, whatever that was, and that Claire was placing a call. "Do you accept the call?" asked the woman.

I had no idea what she was talking about. The woman's introductory statement was so foreign, for a moment I didn't even remember who Claire was. Some woman was calling to inform me that some other woman named Claire was calling? "What is this?" I wondered aloud. Without offering any additional information, the woman stated again that Claire was attempting to contact me. Would I accept the call? "Is this like a collect call? Are you asking me if I accept the charges?"

"No, sir. There are no charges involved. Do you accept?"

By now I remembered who Claire was, but that confused me even more. Flustered, I continued to question the woman on the other end of the line. "I don't get it. Why are you telling me that Claire is calling? Why isn't Claire calling herself?"

The woman dryly responded, "I can't talk to you, sir."

"You *are* talking to me, ma'am. Why isn't *Claire* talking to me? Is she in prison?"

"I can't engage in conversation with you, sir. You can either accept the call or not." Her voice was tinged with a hint of irritation. Cautiously curious, I accepted the call and waited to find out what was behind Door Number Two.

The same woman who seconds earlier said she could not engage me in conversation began engaging me in conversation. "Hi, Carlos," she said in her cold, monotonous tone. "It's Claire. I said I would call. I'm calling. How's it going?"

I began to formulate a theory of what might be happening, but still required clarification. I asked my new nonfriend, "Wait a minute . . . so . . . Claire is typing and you're reading what Claire is typing?"

This time I heard a definite sigh. "I can't engage in conversation with you, sir."

"Can you at least answer *yes* or *no*?"

"No," she replied.

"Does that mean *no, you're not reading what Claire is typing* or *no, you can't answer yes or no*?" We were quickly becoming enemies, she and I.

Suddenly the irritating woman apathetically asked, "Are you having a nice day?"

I put two and two together, deciding to answer this question to find out if I was correct. "It's been a pleasant day. How about you?"

There was a pause. And then: "My day has been great. Thanks. I bought a fabulous new pair of shoes."

Claire was clearly typing and the other one was clearly reading Claire's words with the passion of a toadstool. But that still did not answer my big question. "Why are we communicating like this, Claire? Do you live in a bubble?"

"I'm deaf. This is how I communicate over the phone."

And also, apparently, that's how she informed people she was deaf. "Wow," I remarked, "I feel like a dickhead." Then I felt like even more of a dickhead because I realized the operator now had to write the word *dickhead*. I decided to break protocol once more and address the woman as she transcribed my latest statement. "Sorry for making you write that word. I'm a little unprepared here."

The familiar mantra began, "Sir, I can't—"

"I know, I know."

The operator read Claire's latest statement. "Don't feel bad, Carlos. I thought what you just said about living in a bubble was funny."

I now had a handle on things. "Basically this is similar to instant messaging on the computer, right? Only instead of you reading my words directly there's a woman, who doesn't like me, sitting in a dark room somewhere acting as our go-between."

"That's right," I heard with a bit of hostility.

"Well, why don't we cut out the middlewoman and hop on the computer? Let's instant message the old-fashioned way."

Through the operator, Claire answered, "Sounds kosher to me." We said our momentary good-byes. Before I hung up I told the operator to enjoy the rest of her weekend, out of spite.

Communicating with Claire on the computer was a lot easier. I mentioned my contentious relationship with the operator. Claire informed me some operators were better than others. The last phone conversation she had was with a friend. At one point the operator wrote that her friend was *snoring* when the friend was actually *sneezing*. These operators could really change the context of a discussion. Phone sex and arguments could really be distorted if an operator typed the wrong word. I traded a few more sentences with Claire. Despite my determination to only have tea on first dates, we made *dinner* plans for the following Friday. I had to make an exception. She was deaf.

"You're kidding," quipped my friend Joann Socrates (no relation). Joann was a tough broad of Greek descent from New Jersey who had been in a number of fistfights, mostly with men. She was beautiful, if you like Greek goddesses, but brawlers aren't my type and anyway she was married, so there was that too. I knew Joann through a short film we'd collaborated on. She had been the lead actress. I was happy to have her as a friend, if for no other reason than she might protect me from muggers. When Joann heard I was going to have dinner with a deaf girl, she could hardly believe her ears. "Didn't you just go out with a blind girl?"

"Yes, I did," I confirmed. "She was super cool. Erika."

"Do you have a thing for disabilities? Because I know a girl who limps."

"No, I do not. It just happened to work out that way. Crazy coincidence. I didn't even know this girl was deaf. She didn't tell me."

My statement confounded Joann. "What do you mean she didn't tell you? What did you think? That she was ignoring you all night?"

"I haven't met her in person yet. We're having dinner on Friday. She's an Internet girl. We've only talked on the phone."

Joann's confusion grew. "How did you talk on the phone with a deaf girl? Like this?" She began rhythmically tapping the wooden table where we were sitting with her fist. While Joann's version of Morse code was amusing, I explained there was an operator on the phone with us, reading what Claire typed. Morse code would have taken hours to get through. For starters, I'd need to learn it. Joann wondered how Claire and I were going to be able to talk in person. Claire had explained she was an excellent lip-reader, and even though she couldn't hear, she could speak. I certainly hoped that was the case. Now having all the facts, Joann made her prediction. "This date is going to be a disaster."

The designated Friday night arrived. Claire and I had agreed to meet at a popular 1950s-style diner in a soulless tourist trap known as Universal Citywalk, a place that required a down payment for parking. I would visit this location whenever I felt like getting depressed or sitting in traffic for hours. Citywalk was on the other side of town, though it might as well have been on the other side of the country. It was convenient for Claire because she lived nearby and could take the subway. I'd heard of a Los Angeles subway system but thought it was an urban legend. According to Claire, it existed.

I was the first to arrive at the diner. The diner was loud, blasting music from all eras through its sound system. I realized it wouldn't matter to Claire. It was a little more nerve-racking than usual, waiting for my date to appear. She did, a few minutes later, looking like her picture. Claire smiled at me and said something. The moment I heard her speak, I knew I was in trouble. Unfortunately, but not surprisingly, she sounded like a deaf person. That is, completely unintelligible. In a bit of a panic, I nodded my head and replied, "Yes," hoping that was the right answer. Claire's expression turned glum. She said something else. A few moments later it registered, as if on a seven-second delay. She said she was sorry; she was apologizing for something. Then her first words sank in. She had asked if I had been waiting long. And I had amicably confirmed, yes, I had. "Oh—no. No, no, no. *I'm* sorry. I haven't been waiting long at all. I just got here." Claire looked at me in confusion. I could see *she* was in trouble. She was an excellent lip-reader, as long as she wasn't reading the lips of people named Carlos.

And so began the longest hour of one of the longest dates I've ever been on. With great effort and concentration we caught about every other sentence. We couldn't take our eyes off each other, not because we were crazy about each other, but because it was our only chance at comprehending what the other one was trying to say. Everybody in the restaurant probably thought we were the most intense couple ever to share a meal. I could understand Claire better if I focused on her mouth. She discerned my words more effectively if I spoke slowly, with overemphasized enunciation. Our waitress walked up just as I was telling Claire, "I grewwww . . . upppp . . . innnn. . . . Sannnn . . . Di-egooooo." To the waitress's credit, she said nothing.

Even though we were giving things our all, we were still often at a loss. Since we were having such difficulty, I almost suggested we text each other on our cell phones but that would have been too ridiculous. Eventually we took to writing comments on napkins. It was like instant messaging the *old* old-fashioned way. Due to our limitations, our words were simple. We asked each other questions such as: *When is your birthday? Do you like animals?*

When our meals arrived, Claire and I gave up all together, eating quietly across from each other with an occasional pained smile. As we ate, "Jane Says" by Jane's Addiction began to play on the restaurant's sound system. I had a knee-jerk reaction to it, exclaiming, "This is one of my favorite songs!"

It was the one utterance of mine Claire was able to understand perfectly. She strained, tilting her head toward the ceiling, struggling to hear the slightest note. Then she looked at me and shook her head with eyes that telegraphed, "In case you didn't notice—I'm deaf, jackass."

I missed the phone operator. It would have been nice had she been sitting in the booth with us, guiding us. I wondered how she was doing, wishing I could give her a hug and lean my head on her shoulder. Communicating with Claire was so tiring, I excused myself to go to the restroom—so I could *rest*. Somehow, we soldiered through the evening. I accompanied Claire to the edge of Citywalk. We gave each other the standard hug. She said it was nice to meet me, I think.

On the drive home I magnanimously decided going out with Claire was worth a second try. Maybe I would better understand her the more time we spent together. I was willing to give us a chance. When I got home, there was an e-mail from Claire waiting for me. Claire's message was straightforward: "You're a good guy, but not the guy for me." She dropped me like a hot rock. Probably for the best. I would have broken her heart.

Another fruitless Internet date was in the till. It had been nearly a year since I first joined the dating Web site. Along the way, I'd become a member of other dating sites as well. The home pages looked different but the girls were the same, literally. They did not change their profile pictures. I didn't have the nerve to write to the same girls across several different singles sites. Unless maybe I posted a photo of me in a fake mustache so they would think I was a different person from one Web site to another. That would be too much effort. (Where does one buy fake mustaches?) Sooner or later the girls would figure it out. It occurred to me that if things had gotten to the point where I was recognizing many of the same women across different sites and rarely spotting a new face, perhaps the time had come to give Internet dating a rest. I wasn't quitting, just going on hiatus. It had been a valiant effort. There was no shame in taking a break. There were other avenues. If all went well, I'd never have to log on to an Internet dating Web site again. I could get along fine without the Internet. After all, Neanderthals were able to find mates without a broadband connection. If a Neanderthal could do it, so could I.

DUMMY

The phone rang, as it did from time to time. On this particular occasion, Dominic was calling. Dominic was a friend of my father from their Navy days who now lived in New York. I didn't talk to him very often, but I knew him. Like any good New Yorker, he cut right to the chase. "Carlos, I've got a girl for you. She's posed for *Playboy*. You intere—?"

"Yes," I interrupted. He had me at *Playboy*. It wasn't that I was a horndog. It was that I was a heterosexual male, and when presented with an opportunity to go out with a *Playboy* Playmate, all single heterosexual men and many married heterosexual men will say yes. I had no choice. I *had* to do this. For all the guys who could only dream of such possibilities. It was like having a chance to ride in the space shuttle or win a Super Bowl. It was something I could one day tell my grandchildren about.

Once I was officially on board, Dominic gave me her stats. Her name was Amber. She was twenty-three, from Long Island, the daughter of a man Dominic went to school with. Amber had just moved out to Hollywood in hopes of becoming an actress. She didn't know very many people. My two previous dates had been with girls who were blind and deaf, respectively. I was excited to go out with Amber not only because of her résumé, but because she could see *and* hear. Amber's name didn't ring a bell, as I was not an aficionado of *Playboy*. I had, however, encountered the publication a few times on the road of life and each time I couldn't help but notice that the women in the magazine were incredibly attractive. You never saw a Playmate with a double chin or pooch. It was as if some-body was paid to exclusively photograph gorgeous girls.

When Amber answered the phone, I assumed she answered in a red teddy. I wondered what month she was, but refrained from asking. Nor did I ask what she was wearing. I did ask how long she'd been in California, and how did she like it so far? Disheartened, she answered, "It's fine, I guess. Taking a while to get a movie part." She had been in Los Angeles an entire month. Since I didn't know her, I thought she was being facetious. I played along, advising her to give things at least one more month.

Normally, I didn't pay attention to such things—I didn't care—but during the course of our conversation, I couldn't help but notice she did not ask me a single question. Not one question about myself, or anything else. I would ask her a question. She would provide a short answer. Then I would ask another question, as if I were inter-viewing her for her centerfold bio. Occasionally, I would add a state-ment rather than another question in response to something she said. I'd chime in with, "Blue is my favorite color too—dark blue though, not light blue," or, "You're right. That's definitely one thing

California has going for it. A lot easier to get tan here." Part of me wanted to continue asking questions until she couldn't take it anymore, to discover what her threshold was out of *curiosity*—a quality she quite strikingly lacked. But I didn't want to ruin things.

In a timely manner, I got around to asking if she'd like to go out. She said, "Okay." Once again breaking my vow only to have tea on first dates, I suggested to Amber we spend the day at Knott's Berry Farm, a popular amusement park about an hour down the freeway. I had to make an exception. She was a bunny.

Amber vetoed my idea right away, saying, "I don't want to go to a farm. I don't like cows. Their nipples are gross." After I explained Knott's Berry Farm was a place with rides and games and food, she changed her anti–cow nipple tune. "All right. Let's do that."

When Amber opened the door to her apartment the following Saturday, my first thought was *this woman has not posed for* Playboy. She was definitely attractive. But she didn't look glossy, or airbrushed. She looked normal. As normal as a person could look who was dressed like an Atlantic City escort, or at least how I imagined Atlantic City escorts dressed (I'd never been). Her gold, shimmering, revealing dress and matching high heels were definitely head turners. She gave me a light hug and a half smile, telling me she was ready to go. I gazed at her heels, politely asking, "Are you sure you want to wear those shoes? We might be walking a lot." She said they would be no problem. Suddenly, being seen with a *Playboy* Playmate didn't seem like such a good thing after all. Since she wasn't going to change her outfit, I thought maybe I should change mine and dress like a pimp. That way people would hopefully think we were trying to be funny. Ultimately, I didn't feel like stopping at a thrift store to buy a feathered fedora, oversized sunglasses, and a fake fur

coat. At least I'd had the good fortune of planning a date well outside the city limits. Being seen with her by a friend or acquaintance
would have been mortifying.

We got to know each other a little better on the long ride down
the freeway. For the record, it should be stated that Amber's comments and actions in no way reflect those of any other woman who
has appeared in *Playboy*. I'm sure most, if not all, of the other women
are sexy Einsteins, undoubtedly much more intelligent than Amber.
Nor does Amber represent anyone else who happens to be from any
islands near New York City that are really long. America's greatest
poet, Walt Whitman, was born on Long Island. And though Mr.
Whitman was not available to accompany us on the ride to Knott's
Berry Farm, I'm sure if he had been sitting in the back, listening to
Amber, he would have exclaimed, "Holy shit! You're such a moron.
Let me out of this car." And the fact that Amber was blond—utterly
meaningless. I've known many a smart blonde, including my very
first girlfriend, Yvonne, who in the fifth grade was able to recite the
capital of each state in record time. If Amber were asked on the spot
to name the capital of Montana, she definitely would not have come
up with Helena, or known that it had been Montana's capital since
1875. Yvonne would have smoked Amber.

As we hit a bit of traffic, I asked Amber if she'd had a chance to
explore much of California outside of Los Angeles. "No," she said,
adding, "There isn't really much in California that's interesting." I
was impressed by her high standards—apparently if something was
going to spark an interest in her (coloring) book, it had to be far
more appealing than, say, Hearst Castle or San Francisco.

"What about Yosemite?" I questioned.

"What's Yosemite?" I got the impression she asked this not out of a sincere desire to find out what this strange Yosemite place was, but more because we were stuck in traffic and it gave her something to do. I took a moment to hide my surprise and then explained that Yosemite was one of the most beautiful national parks in the country, in the world. She followed up with, "How long does it take to get there?" I told her from Los Angeles it was about a five- or six-hour drive. There was momentarily silence as she formulated her next thought. "Why would anyone drive five or six hours just to go to a park?"

To amuse myself, I told her, "Well, the swing sets are *amazing*." No laughter on her end, or response. I was starting to get a headache. "I hear you've done some modeling," I commented, in an attempt to steer the conversation toward a subject she might know something about.

She proudly stated, "I was in *Playboy*. In one picture." That explained it. She was *not* a Playmate, *not* a centerfold. She told me she had appeared in a pictorial featuring the Girls of Ernie's Pizzeria or something like that. "It's a picture of me lying on my stomach, on a heart-shaped bed. They made my ass look really artistic. I'll show it to you later."

This got my attention. "Are you going to show me your ass, or the picture of your ass?"

My question elicited a sudden mousey yet boisterous laugh from her, as if she were being tickled. It was a bit startling, and definitely irritating. I was immediately thankful she hadn't thought any of my earlier attempts at humor were funny, and hoped never to hear that laugh again. "The picture, you pervert," she clarified. She continued talking about the photo shoot and modeling in general. It brightened her mood. Talk of modeling turned to talk of her passion for acting, which led to the subject of living in Los Angeles. She soured again.

"Everybody in Los Angeles is just so fake," she declared while looking directly at the person driving the car who lived in Los Angeles. "I don't belong here. I feel like that fuckin' girl who slept in the beds."

The synapses in my brain went into overdrive, working hard to identify *that fuckin' girl who slept in the beds*. I hesitantly asked, "Do you mean Goldilocks?"

"Yeah, that one," she contemptuously confirmed. I was strangely proud of myself for getting the answer right. As I continued to pat myself on the back, Amber spoke of her struggles to meet anyone who could help her in the film industry.

It reminded me of who I had seen the prior week, walking past my apartment building. As I was pulling out of the garage, I had to stop in the driveway to let Ron Howard walk by. *The* Ron Howard. He was just walking, in no particular hurry, like a regular person. I mentioned this to Amber. She asked me the inevitable question, "Who's Ron Howard?"

If one were to travel to a Buddhist monastery in Nepal and report to a monk that Ron Howard had been spotted ambling along a Los Angeles sidewalk, it would be understandable if the monk wondered who Ron Howard was, though the monk would probably know. But an actress not knowing Ron Howard? That's like a Catholic asking, *"Who's the Pope?"*

Skipping the highlights of his acting career, I informed Amber, "Ron Howard is a movie director. He's directed a ton of blockbusters, like *The Da Vinci Code*."

"I hated that movie. Tom Hanks's hair was—" We said *the worst* together. It bothered me a little that I was able to finish Amber's sentence. Then again, Tom Hanks's hair was pretty bad. Amber perked up once again, asking, "So Ron Howard goes for walks in your neighborhood?"

I told Amber I had only seen him the one time—I didn't think he walked past my building on a regular basis. "Maybe I should walk up and down the street in front of your building." If Amber walked up and down my street in her current outfit, she would have no doubt been arrested. Amber asked what Ron Howard looked like so she would know whom to approach. I described Ron Howard in great detail, praying she would randomly ask him, or someone who looked like him, to *please* make her an actress. Hopefully I would be close enough to film this encounter and put it on the Internet.

After what felt like a three-day journey, we arrived at Knott's Berry Farm. The parking lot was packed. We found a spot some distance from the entrance. As we walked to the ticket booths, we ended up behind a family of four also heading toward the entrance. It was the mom and the dad along with their teenage daughter and younger son. The son looked to be no more than nine years old. We continued walking behind this family when suddenly the boy smacked his sister on the behind—a pretty forceful spanking. His sister was not happy about this. But it was the funniest thing Amber had ever seen in her life, judging by the explosion of superannoying laughter that made me want to stab myself in the eye.

"Quit it, Tommy!" the sister angrily commanded. But Tommy, fueled by Amber's overly enthusiastic laughter, spanked his sister again. Amber laughed again, as if seeing the kid spank his sister for the first time. This motivated Tommy to give his sister a third spanking. Amber laughed again, as if seeing the kid spank his sister for the first time. The spanking went on for several more rounds. Amber's laughter never waned. Each time was just as hilarious to her as the first. I had only previously seen this kind of unwavering laughter in babies, when they are engaged in a high-stakes game of peekaboo.

I commented to Amber, "You'd think after the seventeenth time, it would get old." Tommy spanked his sister again. Amber roared with her nails-on-the-chalkboard laughter.

The sister whipped around, glared at her brother, warning him, "Do it one more time, I will knock you out." No one could doubt her sincerity. This made *me* laugh. Not an obnoxious sidesplitting guffaw. More like a reserved chuckle. It would have been great to see the sister clock her nuisance of a brother. Tommy got the message though. He stopped, to my slight and Amber's sizable disappointment. She had to catch her breath from all the laughter.

I bought our tickets and we entered Knott's Berry Farm. My plan was to jump on the enormous wooden roller coaster. I looked forward to its high speeds, its death-defying drops that would clear my head and make me forget about the person I was with. As I turned to Amber, about to mention which ride we should go on first, she disclosed, "Just so you know, I don't like fast rides."

This was the kind of information that would have been best made public a little sooner. Perhaps she could have mentioned it during our initial phone conversation when I first proposed we visit a farm. Or as we were walking to the park entrance. Or as I was about to buy our tickets. I thought of telling her we should separate and meet up near the exit in six hours. If she wasn't willing to stay six hours, I was willing to give her cab fare for the ride home. But I internalized a groan, touched by a better angel. At least Amber shared her fear of roller coasters the moment we walked in, as opposed to waiting forever in line and her saying, just as it was our turn, "I'm not getting on this." That would have truly sucked.

"Okay, so we won't go on any fast rides," I assured her, thereby ruling out the majority of worthwhile attractions at Knott's. There was a popular mining train, located in the center of the park, the Calico Mine Ride. This ride had been there since the Paleolithic Era and moved slightly faster than an old tortoise. Still, it had its appeal. People sat sideways in an open cart as the minitrain gently trudged through a gold mine, offering glimpses of hardworking animatronic miners who moved with the agility of mannequins. A friendly conductor offered an audio guide through a horribly muffled sound system reminiscent of many a fast-food drive-thru speaker in which patrons had to yell back, *I said I'd like two tacos and a hamburger!* I calmly explained all of this to Amber.

Amber studied her map and found the ride, along with its description, which she slowly read aloud, *"Descend into the dark depths of Knott's very own gold mine to the infamous Calico Glory Hole."* That sounded unnecessarily, overtly sexual. Amber was too concerned about the ride's potential speeds to notice. "It could be a fast ride," she said with suspicion.

"You just told me you don't like fast rides. I don't really know you. I wouldn't do that to you." Amber obviously wasn't convinced. I recommended we walk to the ride so she could see for herself just how slow it was. We saw the train traveling in super–slow motion, carrying numerous small children as it made its way into the mine tunnel.

Amber watched it disappear, remarking, "It could go fast once it gets inside." I was quick to point out the little kids happily on board and promised, from the bottom of my heart, the train did not travel any faster than what we'd just witnessed. She got in line with me, anxious. It was a long line, moving about the same speed as the train itself. We were the only couple. Everyone else consisted of families with groups of little people who had just learned to tie their shoes. Every few minutes, Amber would take a deep breath, like someone about to bungee jump. I would remind her that she was okay, that everything was going to be okay.

Half an hour later, it was our turn. The train pulled up with its current occupants. Among them was a pint-sized ponytailed girl, laughing and smiling, having a wonderful time with her parents. My promises to Amber apparently meaningless, Amber turned to the scruffy teenage boy in miner's attire operating the train and asked, "Does this ride go fast?"

I stood behind Amber, gesturing to the teenage miner to please, *please* not kid around. "Oh yeaaaah," he replied, adamantly nodding his head. Amber became hysterical, ranting about how cruel I had been attempting to get her on a roller coaster. The teenage miner, feeling guilty, did his best to calm her down, admitting it was only a joke. But he, too, was now not to be trusted. I pointed to the happy little ponytailed girl getting off the train with her parents, noting that there is no little ponytailed girl in the world who would get off a ninety-mile-an-hour roller coaster laughing and smiling. Besides, as Amber could see, there were no seat belts on the train. What kind of roller coaster would permit anyone, let alone children, to ride without a seat belt? Bodies would be flying everywhere. The train would return half empty. It would be on the news.

Amber announced, "I'm not getting on this." She then followed the little girl and her family out the exit. The teenage miner sheepishly shrugged his shoulders. I eyed him with disapproval and reluctantly followed my date.

When I caught up to Amber she informed me she would not be getting on *any* rides because she simply did not trust me. She said this without hostility, merely stating a fact. Amber and I went for a walk through Knott's Berry Farm, the way Ron Howard went for walks through my neighborhood—without a good reason for being there. We said nothing. Me, because I was in no mood for talking. Her, because her general policy was not to speak unless the subject was herself. Eventually we made our way to Camp Snoopy, an area of the park designated for children. At Camp Snoopy there were an array of attractions featuring Charlie Brown and the Peanuts gang designed for the very young. Even these rides we did not go on because they were either too small or, per Amber, "too scary."

Our walk continued into the carnival game section of the park, the section where people could attempt to knock bottles down with baseballs or have water cannon races or some such thing. Finally, something Amber could participate in without fear of being killed. She strolled over to a ring toss booth. There were a number of glass bottles laid out on a table. Most of them were clear bottles, though some were blue, some were green, and one was red. People were tossing rings at these bottles. If a ring landed on a blue or green bottle, they received a modest prize. If it landed on the one red bottle, they would receive the grand prize.

I paid four dollars and Amber was given four rings. She casually tossed the first ring and it promptly landed around the neck of the red *grand prize* bottle, causing Amber to clap uncontrollably and laugh with glee, exclaiming, "Oh my God! Oh my God!" over and over again. The grand prize was a giant stuffed Snoopy about my size. Because Snoopy was so big, the man running the booth offered to hold him there for us until we were ready to leave the park.

"We'll take it now," I told him. I had been ready to leave the park ever since we got there. *Now* seemed as good a time as ever to head back up the freeway. The man hoisted Snoopy over to me.

Snoopy was so big, I could not fully wrap my arms around him. It was like carrying my dad. Though we agreed it was time to go, Amber led me on a few detours, suddenly deciding she wanted to see more of the park. If I was worried before about Amber's attire possibly attracting attention, I no longer needed to be concerned. Snoopy ensured that everybody focused on us as if we were celebrities. I did my best to ignore the stares, but still managed to catch a glimpse of a few people wondering with a mixture of amusement and confusion, *why is he carrying a giant dog for that hooker?*

All bad things come to an end, which meant eventually we made it back to the car. I put Snoopy in the backseat and the three of us drove to Los Angeles. We hit more traffic, predictably, and kept conversation to a minimum. As we sat quietly, I eyed Snoopy in the rearview mirror. He was smirking. Snoopy knew what I was just beginning to figure out. Of the three beings in my car, only one of us was a genuine dunce. Me. I was so taken by the notion of going out with someone who had posed for *Playboy*, I naturally assumed embarking on a road trip and spending an entire day with her would be nothing short of fantastic. I thought only of her physical attributes, willfully ignoring the red flags she was so blatantly raising during our first phone conversation. *I* was the dummy. Amber was dumb, no question, but she was just being herself.

We arrived at Amber's apartment building. I carried Snoopy upstairs, planted him on her couch, and silently wished him luck. As I turned to say good-bye, Amber asked, "Would you like to see the picture of my ass?" So as to not make the entire day a waste, I quickly took a look at the picture. It was okay. With a forced smile, I gave Amber a quick hug and left, knowing full well I'd never see her ass again.

What an incredible succession of dates. I had gone out with a blind girl, then a deaf girl, and finally a dumb girl. Blind, deaf, and dumb. What were the odds? I probably should have driven to Vegas to continue my roll, but I wanted to go to sleep. Though the three characteristics—*blind, deaf, and dumb*—are commonly lumped together, I learned firsthand that they are most assuredly separate and *not* equal. Erika refused to let her blindness keep her from leading a rich, full, and vibrant life. My deaf date was so independently undaunted by being deaf she didn't think it was even worth mentioning upon our first introduction. Amber was planning to stop people on the sidewalk to ask if they were Ron Howard. Determining who possessed the greatest limitation was a no-brainer.

The past three dates required a bit of reflection and retooling. Though ultimately unsuccessful, they offered insight into how I could improve my search, how I could make it more practical and efficient. Each of those dates took up a great deal of time. One thing I absolutely *had* to do was begin enforcing my *one tea and out* policy—a policy I had not adhered to since I first conceived of it. I also needed to traverse less distances. Half of my time was spent on travel alone. If I could somehow manage to stay within a five-mile radius, that would be superb. It was a challenge, but I'd do my best. Finally, I needed to keep my chin up. Yes, I was still a bachelor, but if there was one thing the past three dates illustrated, it was that I had much to be thankful for. I had all of my faculties, I knew what Yosemite was, and I was in the process of efficiently revamping my dating strategies. Things could only get better.

NOT MAKING OUT

In my ongoing and ever-expanding search for a soul mate, I decided to give speed dating a try. Speed dating sounded right up my alley. With speed dating, I would go to a restaurant-bar, sit down at a table with a girl, date her for three minutes, then move on to the next table and date the next girl for another three minutes. At that rate, by the time I finished my *one* tea, I'd have dated a multitude of women! I was probably saving around forty-five thousand dollars not taking any of these women to dinner. Why hadn't I done this before? No matter, I was doing it now. I imagined the way it worked was as the guy approached the table, the girl decided whether or not she would like to sleep with him. In all probability, the guy had decided long before he got to the restaurant. *Most* guys had already decided. I enjoyed physical contact as much as the next fellow but I was hoping to find something more— something that went beyond mere physical pleasure. To make this clear, I wore my nice green cashmere sweater.

The event took place at a restaurant on the west side of Los Angeles, a promising short drive from my neighborhood. When I arrived I was greeted by a young, tan hostess whom I immediately wanted to have a long-term relationship with—one that lasted at least six minutes. She flashed a friendly smile, asking if I was a party of one. I told her, "I'm here to date people." The hostess laughed and directed me upstairs, wishing me luck. Hopefully her twin sister would be in the speed-dating pool.

Upstairs, a forty-something spinster with a whistle around her neck, dressed for a White House state dinner, welcomed me. She introduced herself as Florence. Florence handed me a speed-dating care package, consisting of a numbered name tag I was supposed to stick onto my sweater, an official speed-dating pen (it was a normal blue pen), and an official speed-dating pamphlet where I could jot down the names of all the wonderful women I was about to fall in love with. Florence said we would get started momentarily, suggesting I relax at the bar. The energy of the room reminded me of a junior high school dance. Most of the men were there alone and kept to themselves. The women arrived in packs. They were excitedly chatting with one another. Many of them were laughing far too loud for their laughter to be genuine. I guessed they were masking a deep-seated pain with their laughter, a pain that stemmed from having to go speed dating.

A few minutes after my arrival, Florence asked everyone to sit at a table across from a member of the opposite sex. Once we took our seats, she blew her whistle with the zeal of a high school gym coach. The games began. My first speed date took place with a girl named Dana. After writing each other's name down on our official speed-dating pamphlets with our official speed dating pens, Dana asked, "Have you done this before?" This would prove to be the most popular question of the evening. Dana spoke to me as if she thought I was a hypersensitive three-year-old. The interesting thing about Dana was that she wasn't interesting. We struggled to come up with conversation topics before our three minutes were up. I was relieved when Florence blew her football coach whistle, ending things. With an overly pleasant smile, Dana shook my hand and commented, "It was nice to meet you." Then she added, "Really," in case I didn't believe her, which I didn't because her condescending tone made it sound as if she were saying, "We're going to have to let you go." Dana and I didn't click. No harm, no foul. Nobody got hurt. One date down, twenty-nine to go.

I was tired by the fifth date. By the tenth date, I was exhausted. Besides, "Have you done this before?" other popular questions were, "What do you do? Where did you grow up? What's your favorite kind of food?" I'd humbly tell them I was an aspiring filmmaker, I grew up in San Diego County, and I enjoyed eating spinach. When I finally sat down for my thirtieth and final speed date, I felt like my head was in a vise. The last girl I speed dated, whoever she was, looked as if she felt the same way. Most of the women blended together. Rather than thirty speed dates, it seemed more like one ultralong date in which I was asked over and over if I had done this before. When it was done, I looked at my pamphlet and saw that I had put five of the women down as a yes, though I was foggy on who they were.

There were a handful of women who stood out, but not necessarily in a good way. One was Charlene, a former high school cheerleader. Charlene informed me she hoped to travel to China in hopes of spreading Christmas cheer throughout the country. "Christmas in China!" she exclaimed. When I asked if she really thought this was possible, she responded, "Hell yeah!" Then she gasped and covered her mouth in shame at having just uttered the word *hell*. I put Charlene down as a no mostly because Charlene was going to be too busy converting over a billion Chinese people. This was a lofty task. I would just get in the way.

Another memorable moment took place with a young lady named Jesse. Things were going fine until I made the mistake of asking if she had a dog. Jesse freaked out when she heard this question. Her eyes widened, her breath quickened. "How did you know that?" she demanded. She even lifted the napkins on our table to see if somehow the information that she had a dog had been posted underneath. It was not posted. I didn't know she had a dog. I was just making conversation. Jesse calmed down, a little, when I explained myself. Luckily, I did not ask if she had eaten lunch earlier in the day. She would have screamed, "Have you been following me?"

Out of the thirty women I met that night, thirty of them never wanted to see me again. At first I thought it was a technical issue because the results were sent online. There must have been something wrong with my computer. I thought of taking it into the shop, telling the computer wizards, "Nobody wants to go out with me. Fix this." But the computer was working fine in all other areas. I had most likely been truly rejected across the board. All thirty? How was that possible? I didn't have movie star looks, but I wasn't the Elephant Man. Even the Elephant Man would have gotten a least one yes if he had tried speed dating, because people are into all sorts of things.

Attempting to rationalize these thirty rejections, I thought of something my platonic friend Joann Socrates had told me. Out of curiosity, I once asked her, "In the course of a day, how many women do you think see me and consider me attractive?"

Joann earnestly responded, "Seventy percent." So a C minus is what she was giving me, but that was another matter. If she was right, if seventy percent of the women who encountered me throughout the day thought I was sexy, then thirty percent did not. Meaning, out of a hundred women, thirty of them would not be interested in me. It appeared I had met those thirty women during my night of speed dating. If Joann was correct, then statistically the next seventy women I met while speed dating would put me down as a yes. I had no choice; I had to go back.

My second go-round of speed dating took place at a different restaurant-bar. Florence was there again, in her uniform ball gown with a whistle around her neck. She remembered me and seemed to speak in a kinder, gentler tone. Perhaps she knew what a reject I was. I did not wear my green cashmere sweater, in case that was the problem. This time I went with a long-sleeved dark blue shirt. And I had nice shoes on. Oxfords, I think they were called, but who knew really? They were the professional black shoes I wore on special occasions. At the first speed-dating gala, I'd worn tennis shoes. I was being myself. That obviously wasn't a good idea.

This night, the most distinct person I crossed paths with was not one of the women I dated, but rather the man who was just in front of me on the speed-dating mule train. He was tall and lanky, dressed in all white—not renowned author Mark Twain all white, closer to renowned cannibal Hannibal Lecter all white. He appeared to have a sheen of sweat covering his skin. His hair had a thick layer of gel in it. I was glad Hannibal was just ahead of me in the chain. Following him probably made me all the more desirable, especially with my nice shoes.

Hannibal proved to be a canary in the coal mine of sorts. If the whistle was blown and I went to the next table, only to find Hannibal still talking to my next date, she was possibly a keeper. If I walked to the next table and Hannibal was long gone, there was little potential. At one point, we were sitting at tables next to each other. As my date asked, "Have you done this before?" I could not help but notice Hannibal tell his date he was going to check his messages. The girl forlornly doodled on her official speed-dating pamphlet with her official speed-dating pen while Hannibal took out his cell phone and really did check his messages for the remaining one minute and thirty seconds left in their date. Classy. I was definitely going to clean up, following this guy. Every girl there was going to put me down as a yes.

Speed dating ended a lot quicker this time. It was not as grueling because there were fewer people. I met fifteen women all together. There were three I would have liked to see again. With Hannibal as my opening act, I was confident all three would want to go out with me. I ended up leaving at the same time as Hannibal, though I didn't intend to. As we glanced inside the restaurant at all the civilians having dinner, laughing and talking and smiling, I pointed out, "That's how normal people socialize in the real world."

Hannibal nodded, though he didn't seem to catch my drift. He asked me if I put Barbara down as a yes. I didn't remember Barbara. "She was the lawyer," he told me. That didn't help. It seemed like most of them were lawyers. "She had the giant gazongas," Hannibal went on. I assumed he meant breasts, but I didn't remember meeting anyone whose breasts leaped out at me. Having no desire to continue speaking with him, I told Hannibal I probably did not put Barbara down as a yes since I didn't remember her. Hannibal stated in no uncertain terms, "I put her down as a yes. She was my top pick.

I'm going home right now and entering her as a yes in the system."
I wished him luck. My well-wishes appeared to threaten him. There
was a flash of concern in his eyes. He hurried off to access the system
before I did.

Out of the fifteen women I met my second time around, fifteen
of them never wanted to see me again. How was this possible? Was
it because I had walked out with Hannibal? Did the girls assume
we were buddies? A tag team? They couldn't possibly think that. I was
so much more put together. We didn't really start talking until we
got outside and no one could see us. Hannibal couldn't have been
the reason. Whatever the cause, I was now O for forty-five at speed
dating. I gave it some thought and decided to go for a hundred. That
number seemed easily attainable. After all, with the first forty-five I
wasn't even trying to get rejected. Now, the next time a girl asked
what my favorite kind of food was, I'd politely tell her, "Fried puppy,
you're a bitch."

"Have you done this before?" Same speed-dating question, different speed-dating day. This time I wore a gray sweater with a
white-collared shirt, blue corduroy slacks, and the fancy shoes. I was
not a jerk to anyone during my third attempt at speed dating; I did
not allow my initial hostility toward being O for forty-five get the
best of me. I was going to do this, damn it. Florence and her whistle
greeted me with pronounced sympathy. When she saw me arrive,
she said something about the third time being the charm and gave
me a thumbs-up. She was obviously aware of my record.

The third time did seem to be the charm. I had gotten through
four blah dates when I met Jasmine. Jasmine had come to this alone.
She looked like she did not want to be there. My kind of girl. She had
short reddish-brown hair, doe eyes, and a smattering of freckles

stylishly spread across her face. I sat down. We introduced ourselves. Her voice was nearly a whisper. Once we wrote our names down, Jasmine asked the required question. "Have you done this before?"

"Yes, I have. I've done this twice. I met forty-five women all together. And all forty-five of them rejected me."

Jasmine laughed, in spite of herself. "You should not tell people that," she advised.

Looking at Jasmine, I was reminded of being a member of Key Club in high school. Key Club was a social group that helped the community. One of the helpful things Key Club members did for the community was visit old people who had been unceremoniously dumped in a local nursing home by their families. The nursing home was dreadful. It smelled of urine. The minds of its aged inhabitants had long slipped away. They were children, unaware of their surroundings or even themselves. I remember trying to help an old woman in the dining hall open a plastic packet of crackers. She was attempting to eat the crackers, plastic wrapper and all. When I took the crackers from her and began to unwrap the plastic, she put her hand into my mouth. Her entire hand. I did not enjoy that.

My fellow Key Club members and I would go room to room, saying hello to everyone. The conversations were rarely lucid, but the old folk seemed pleased nonetheless that they had company. At the end of one of the hallways, we walked into a room and were stunned by what we found. The room was like no other. It was comfortable, charmingly decorated. It was warm and welcoming, like a beloved grandmother's house. The woman in this room was also warm and welcoming. She was nicely dressed. Her hair was dyed red, done up. She looked to be in her eighties, perfectly healthy, both mentally and physically. When we arrived, she offered us oatmeal cookies. We did not understand what she was doing in this place; we wanted to take her home—to rescue her. Unfortunately, none of our parents would have let us keep her. One thing was for sure. She did not belong.

"Let's get out of here," I suggested to Jasmine as I sat across from her at the speed-dating table.

Jasmine seemed to give escape serious consideration. "We've only been on five dates. Shouldn't we meet everyone?"

"It's only going to get worse. I've done this. I'm a veteran. I know what I'm talking about. By the end of the night, you're going to need a week to recharge your soul. You're going to need to go to Bora Bora to replenish."

She laughed and asked, "Have you been?" When I told her I'd been there twice, her eyes lit up. "What's it like?" she asked. I spoke of Bora Bora's captivating beauty, its turquoise waters and golden sunshine. Jasmine took in a deep breath as if wishing she were there at this very moment. "Sounds romantic."

I confirmed it was. "Of course it would have been more romantic had I gone with someone other than my parents the first time, and my friend Brian the second."

Jasmine laughed again, shaking her head. "You should not be telling me these things. You should be trying to impress me."

"I was valedictorian of my high school. Does that count?" Florence blew her whistle at the end of my sentence. Three minutes with Jasmine felt like two minutes. For the first time in the countless number of times I had heard Florence's whistle (fifty), I regretted having to move on. I remained seated across from Jasmine, as the next guy showed up. Suddenly, I was the jerk who wouldn't leave. Leaning closer to Jasmine, I whispered, "Even though I'm seeing other people, I'd like to go out with you again." She nodded and smiled as I left.

None of the other speed dates compared to Jasmine. I waited for things to be over so I could hopefully talk to her more. Florence finally blew the last whistle. Once the speed dating had officially ended, Jasmine was swarmed by guys seeking to extend their time with her. I am terrible at fighting for attention. Most of the men surrounding Jasmine were taller than me. Had I gone over there, I would have come across as the runt, the little boy battling for whatever paltry scraps were left behind. I began to walk out of the restaurant, hoping Jasmine would be the first speed dater in history to put me down as a yes. Then maybe we could have a longer conversation. But what was this? What inspired, unexpected, but happily accepted stroke of good fortune was taking place? Jasmine left the men and their dangling tongues to join me. We walked out of the restaurant together. *Booyah.*

"I feel so drained. You were right," sighed Jasmine. "How could you possibly do that three times?"

"Well, I kind of had to. I'm a Navy SEAL, in training. They make us go speed dating. It strengthens our ability to withstand torture." Another laugh from Jasmine. It was refreshing not to have to tell her I was kidding. I walked her to her car. Trying not to sound too nervous, I revealed that I had put her down as a yes on my pamphlet, suggesting that if she also put me down as a yes then we should exchange phone numbers. It would save the time of having to log on to a computer. Besides, I didn't trust my computer when it came to speed dating. Jasmine hesitated. I thought the house of cards was about to come tumbling down. But she gave me her number. As I walked back to my car, I threw my official speed-dating pamphlet away, not interested in whether any other girls had put me down as a yes. I assumed they all did. It didn't matter. Too late, ladies.

I took Jasmine to a popular hilltop restaurant overlooking the entire city of Los Angeles. It was a clear night. The view was incredible. Jasmine and I both had tea. I was finally just having tea on a date, but with Jasmine I didn't mind how much time I spent. I'd picked this spot not only because it was near where Jasmine lived, but because of its romantic veranda. The veranda was an inspiration point. People who did not make out on this veranda were fined. At least they should have been.

Things were going well. I tried not to get too excited. After we finished our tea, I suggested we admire the view on the veranda. Jasmine hesitated, again, but agreed. The veranda was secluded, reachable by stairs. It was covered by tall trees and landscaped shrubs with the restaurant's entrance above it, along with arriving cars and valets who tended to them. Below the veranda was the City of Angels. We stood side by side, taking in the luminous skyline. Jasmine mentioned she was cold. That was good news. I gave her a chivalrous hug to help warm her up. She gladly accepted it. My right hand, as if having a mind of its own, slowly made its way to her left buttock. The moment I touched her there she asked, "Carlos, may I communicate something to you?" It was like I'd pressed a button. I wondered if she would say something else if I pressed her right buttock.

Unfortunately, in one form or another, I had heard other women ask if they could *communicate* something to me before. Since we had our clothes on, I wasn't too concerned about what Jasmine needed to impart. I told her, yes, she might communicate something, hoping she had recently won the lottery. She hadn't. Instead Jasmine informed me her heart had been broken not long ago. She thought she was ready to get back out there, which is why she tried speed dating. But she realized she was not emotionally available. My hand was still on her ass. I asked if I should remove it. She told me it was fine to keep it there; she just wanted me to be aware of where she was emotionally. I thanked her for telling me and put my other hand on her other butt cheek, half expecting her to say, "Carlos, may I express something of relevance to you?" She didn't say anything. Despite her broken heart, she was fine with her ass being grabbed.

Since things were proceeding, I went in for the kiss. Jasmine backed away, telling me, "I'm not ready for that. Sorry. It's too intimate." My knowledge of prostitutes was limited to the film *Pretty Woman*, starring Julia Roberts. In that film, Julia Roberts plays a hooker with a heart of gold. One of her rules was no kissing on the mouth because it was too intimate. A little voice inside my head encouraged me to ask Jasmine if she was a prostitute, or at the very least ask if she had seen *Pretty Woman*. I didn't. It would have spoiled the mood. Jasmine was probably not a prostitute, and even if she was—prostitutes are people too.

The closest I ever came to hiring a prostitute was after a Thanksgiving in which I ended up with an overwhelming amount of leftovers. For some reason, I thought of searching through the phone book for escorts to see if anyone would be willing to come over and help me eat the turkey in my fridge. I imagined a hooker with a heart of gold asking me what I desired. No doubt she would think I was talking in code when I said, "I'd like you to help me eat the rest of the turkey." It would probably take half an hour to convince her I *really* wanted her to eat some turkey, and maybe help finish drinking the milk before it expired. It was more trouble than it was probably worth, and so I allowed this fleeting thought to vanish.

Still embracing me, Jasmine clarified our situation, seductively whispering in my ear, "We can do anything you want, except kiss." *Anything you want* covered a lot of ground. I was tempted to find out exactly what she meant, but in the end realized I would have felt self-conscious engaging in soft and/or hard-core sex acts while valets were on the job just above us. Jasmine and I began heavy petting. We caressed and tastefully touched each other. But no kissing. Still, our lips were practically touching—our *eyeballs* were practically touching.

I stared into Jasmine's pupils, telling her, "You're so pretty and so close. I really want to kiss you." She said nothing, staring deeply into *my* pupils. "I'm going to kiss you." Still nothing from Jasmine. Just her stare. I slowly, respectfully, began leaning toward her, reaching for a kiss. She slowly backed away. I followed her. She veered left, then right, then left again. The entire time I matched her movements, inches from her face. The two of us ended up in a super-weird snake charmer kind of dance. It was like we were practicing erotic tai chi.

Occasionally, someone else would walk by on the veranda. We would stop until they were gone and then go back to not kissing. In a way, it was more sensual. All things being equal though, I would have preferred tongue. Jasmine moved away from me once and for all, gathering herself. It was time to go. I dropped her off at her apartment building. She caressed my face with a sad expression, telling me she enjoyed the evening and I was a nice guy, which was the equivalent of throwing me into an active volcano as part of a ritual sacrifice. It came as no surprise then, that she did not return my subsequent calls or texts. Not one for bothering people who don't wish to be bothered, I erased her number from my phone. *C'est la vie.* Weirdness aside, meeting Jasmine was a valuable experience. She further clarified what I was looking for in a girl. This has been such a difficult question to answer for so long. What was I looking for?

A vision of the perfect girl was slowly coming into focus. She was somebody whose father didn't want to blow me away with his shotgun just because I didn't go to his church. She wouldn't abandon me in the produce section by the strawberries, but did dream of visiting the South Pacific with her lover. She wasn't ready to move in with me the moment we made eye contact, nor was she the kind to let random strangers suck on her elbow in the desert sands. She didn't have herpes, or if she did—she'd tell me about it over a nice, quiet dinner rather than under the hot, sweaty sheets afterward. This was negotiable, her having herpes, but preferably she didn't have it or any of its cousins. She wasn't homophobic or dumb, which were one and the same. And when we kissed, our lips touched. When I met someone who fit into all of those categories, my search would finally be over and I could take a nap.

PRISONER OF THE COUCH

We had been sitting on the couch in my apartment for nearly three hours. Annette was still talking, as she had been ever since she sat down. I smiled at her, wondering how this was going to end. More important, *when* was this going to end? It was a battle of attrition. A casual observer might erroneously assume Annette and I were competing against each other to see who could sit on the couch longer. Whoever got off the couch first, lost. The winner would receive a million dollars and a two-week stay in Hawaii. If only.

This had all started a week earlier, thanks to my mother. She was at it again. A coworker of my mother mentioned a cousin Annette who lived in Los Angeles. Annette was single and looking. That was all my mother needed to hear before donning her pimp cap. Annette? Single? Oh really? My mother reminded her coworker she had a son in Los Angeles who was also single. Perhaps the two of them should meet. Contact information was exchanged and before I knew it, I was sitting in a local bar waiting for Annette.

Annette selected the location. I was the first to arrive. We had traded a handful of e-mails earlier, which included our pictures. On the whole, she looked ordinary. Not a beauty queen, not a sideshow freak. None of the pictures she sent revealed much of a backdrop or what activities Annette might have been participating in when they were taken. They offered no insight into Annette's personality, other than a uniformly bland smile that suggested she was either a covert CIA operative or boring. Since my mother was involved, I lowered my expectations way below sea level. Yes, my mother was instrumental in my meeting the inspirational sight-impaired Erika. But Erika was the exception, not the norm. Most of the time my mother set me up with girls who made cardboard seem exciting and were about as attractive. On the off off *off* chance Annette might have something, I agreed to sit down with her for drinks.

Annette arrived at the bar about ten minutes after I did. Sometimes when two people first come face-to-face, there is an instant connection. An excitement at having encountered someone on the same wavelength. A desire to discover every intimate detail about that person. This was not one of those times. It was another mom date. Annette looked just like her pictures. Part of me was slightly disappointed. (I was hoping she just wasn't photogenic.) She was dressed in a pantsuit, having driven directly to the bar from work. Her job involved selling office supplies or something to that effect. It was difficult to hear on account of the drunken slobs surrounding us who were yelling at one another the way drunken slobs do. I'm sure I looked very prim and proper with my teacup and kettle. Annette commented she would have suggested another location had

I informed her I didn't drink. I told her not to worry about it, that the bar was delightful, as I took another sip of my mint tea and she a swig of her draft beer.

We stayed at the bar for about an hour. Besides the fact that she hawked executive pens, I also learned that Annette went to the gym every morning. She liked exercising but did not enjoy the way men constantly hit on her. Men were pigs, so said Annette. She couldn't believe they actually thought they'd get somewhere by constantly hitting on her. Men were constantly hitting on her, Annette reiterated a few minutes later. The more she said it, the less I believed it.

When it was time to go, Annette wanted to know if I'd parked far away. I had not. She asked if I wouldn't mind giving her a ride to her car because she had parked quite a distance from the bar. We walked to my tank of a car, engaging in more uninspired small talk. She suddenly grabbed my arm, concerned about something. "Oh jeez. Look at this guy." A man wearing a trench coat and slippers was heading toward us. He was talking loudly to himself.

"That's Jerry," I informed her.

"You know him?"

"Yeah, we play racquetball."

"Really?" Annette was stunned.

"No, not really. I don't know him, but I see him around. I'm just guessing his name is Jerry. He's not going to do anything." Jerry passed us, rambling about the benefits of Thai massage. According to him, it was a great stress reliever. Also, he had an appointment with the Secretary of State on Thursday.

Annette and I approached my car. I clicked the button on my key, unlocking most of the doors. Before Annette got in, I explained that the driver's-side door lock was not working. It had been acting funky for a few days, refusing to unlock under any circumstances. I was going to have to climb into the driver's seat from the back, so I advised Annette not to be alarmed.

With Annette in the front passenger seat, I opened the back door on my side of the car. Climbing into the front was like maneuvering through an obstacle course. There was a lot of bending and twisting and a great deal of unintentional proximity to Annette. I apologized as I brushed against Annette, finally settling down into the driver's seat. Skeptical, Annette asked, "Is this really your car?"

I assured her the car was mine. It had been showing its age lately. A few weeks earlier, the right horn button broke on the steering wheel. A spring had come loose. The only problem with this spring coming loose was that it caused the horn to randomly honk. And not just a friendly *toot toot*. More like an enraged *kill them all!* ear-popping repeated blast. Soon after the horn button initially broke, I ended up stopped near a freeway onramp at night behind one other car.

There were two lanes heading toward the on-ramp. We were both on the outside lane. A posted sign clearly specified right turns onto the ramp were prohibited during red lights. So we were idle, waiting for the light to change. That is when my car decided to start honking as if I wanted to annihilate the driver in front of me along with any other living creature on the planet. I immediately raised both of my hands to show the driver it was not me, it was my Benedict Arnold car. But it was dark out, so I was not visible beyond my bright headlights. The raucous honking was made all the more preposterous by the fact that if I really wanted to get onto the freeway, I could have easily driven around the car in front of me into the open lane. I believe what protected me that night was my appearing to be insane to the point of frightening whoever the driver was in front of me. The light turned green and I sped past the other car, on my way home, with the obnoxious horn honking most of the way.

Annette laughed upon hearing about the horn. It was the first time she'd laughed since we met. She wanted to know if the horn was going to go off as I gave her a ride to her car. I told her we were safe, since I had ripped out all the other springs and covered what remained with masking tape.

We arrived at her car without incident. I got out to give Annette a proper hug good-bye instead of a cold one-armed car pat. She embraced me tightly, which I did not expect, saying we should get together again sometime soon. This was also unexpected. It seemed we had ended with a whimper, just as we had begun, and once we both told each other, "It was nice to meet you," I assumed we would part ways forever. Annette asked if I was free the following weekend. I told her I was and we agreed to get together again. Maybe that elusive spark would be ignited during our second outing. Maybe.

Maybe not. For our second date, if that's what it was, Annette met me at my apartment. From there we went to dinner at a seafood restaurant. I ate mahi mahi and Annette ate whatever she ate. After dinner we went back to my place. It surprised me that Annette returned to the apartment. I thought this time for sure she would leave in order for us to resume our lives. There wasn't any chemistry between us. No rapport, no clever banter, not a trace of sexual energy. We were simply in each other's presence. Occasionally, we would have to get out of the other person's way.

In the apartment, I offered Annette something to drink. She declined. I then took a seat on the far end of the couch. Had I known how long I was going to be sitting in this particular spot I would have brought along emergency supplies. Snacks, water, a blanket perhaps. A video camera would have been useful. I could have set it up beside me to film myself giving private testimonials throughout the night, whispering such reports as, "It's Hour Three and she's still here. She's still talking. There is no sign of when she will exit the apartment." Sadly, I was not aware that I was about to become a prisoner of the couch. When I took a seat, I looked at the time on my cable box. It was a little after nine. I hoped to be necking with Annette by nine thirty. If I could be asleep by eleven, that would be ideal. Despite there not being any fireworks between us, I thought perhaps kissing Annette might once and for all ignite the spark that had been in hiding up to this point. I was willing to give it a try. It seemed Annette was as well, since she was here.

Annette set her purse down on the coffee table, joining me on the couch. However, she chose to sit on the opposite end of the couch, as far away as humanly possible. Hmm. I was no expert on picking up signals from women, but it seemed if a woman was interested, she would stay close rather than distance herself as much as the length of a couch allowed. Two overweight people and a teddy bear could have comfortably sat in between us. Maybe she was getting a slow start, which I could respect. I remained alert, waiting for the slightest clue Annette wanted me to make a move. I studied the tone of her voice, the look in her eyes, her body language. Nothing. Perhaps in the course of our conversation she would say something suggestive and I could run with it. Nope. She talked about the farmers' market, how she liked to go on Saturday mornings. "You can get really good homemade hummus there . . ."

This was party talk, that's what this was. The same kind of chatter heard at parties in which people held large red plastic cups. I hated parties. The idea of explicitly gathering somewhere to socialize seemed forced. At parties I felt like I was talking to people not so much because I wanted to, but because I *had* to. My general strategy at parties was to pick a comfortable seat, establish that as my headquarters, and speak to whichever guests streamed by until they continued on their way, much as I was talking to Annette at the moment. Only she wasn't leaving.

Annette changed subjects from hummus to snowboarding. "I like to go to Mammoth and snowboard. Do you snowboard?" I told her I did not snowboard. She continued. "I love snowboarding. Except when it's crowded. It's a drag when it's crowded . . ."

I remembered being at a party once, sitting on a couch. Two young ladies took a seat beside me. They'd also enjoyed snowboarding. I believe I had the exact same conversation with these two ladies as I was currently having with Annette. Eventually the ladies and I discussed other activities I also did not participate in. It was draining, talking to them. I'd been certain our conversation ended at least three or four times. But they plodded on. I got the feeling the only reason they kept talking was because they couldn't figure out a natural way to bid me farewell. I tried to help by cordially saying, "You guys look pretty tired. Maybe you should go."

Annette asked if I exercised much. I told her not much, but I was considering taking up yoga. There was a yoga studio nearby and one of these days I was going to check it out. She shook her head in disapproval. "I've tried yoga," she said. "It's too boring. Spinning is good though. I have the most amazing spinning instructor. On Monday, Wednesday, and Friday mornings I take her class at the gym. She always makes us . . ."

That party with the tired girls on the couch, that was a strange party. Two people brought their dogs to that party for some reason. One was a boxer, the other a shepherd mix. The dogs were kept apart for most of the night. But at some point they found each other and they weren't happy about it. An out-and-out dogfight erupted during the party. My friend Bill broke it up by inserting his index finger into the boxer's anus. The boxer was understandably confused, as was I. Bill took advantage of this confusion by picking the boxer up and carrying him into another room. Later, I asked Bill why he had given that dog the finger.

"It's the quickest way to get the dog's attention," he told me. I wondered if Bill even knew the dog. "Yes. He's mine. His name is Calvin. I wouldn't do that to just *any* dog." As if doing it to Calvin was somehow all right. It did break up the fight. But what a strange technique. I wondered if it would be effective on other animals. Maybe I would try it the next time I was attacked by a mountain lion while hiking in the local Southern California mountains. I bet it would work on a mountain lion. I'd probably get injured in the process, but I was sure I could reach around.

"Do you have any brothers and sisters?"

I didn't catch Annette's question. My thoughts had drifted. She asked me again if I had any brothers or sisters. I told her I was an only child.

"I have an older brother and a younger sister," Annette informed me. And then there was talk about her siblings . . .

I looked at the time. It was now half past ten. One way or another I would need to make my move by eleven at the latest. Eleven rolled around. Annette was still sitting far away from me, now going on and on about hip-hop. I felt like I had been on the couch my entire life. "Have you ever taken a hip-hop class? You should . . ."

Midnight. And we were *still* on the opposite ends of the couch. This was a true test of endurance. There were a number of times I thought of giving up. It would have been easy. I could have just risen to my feet, told Annette I was beat and called it a night. But I had invested so much time, I stayed put, holding out hope that sooner or probably later we would end up in each other's arms in an effort to create some heat. My patience had been tested in a similar manner while waiting at the department of motor vehicles. I also considered throwing in the towel there. But after a while so much time had gone by, it seemed a shame to let it go to waste.

I suppose at any moment I could have leaned in for the kiss. Or in my case, I could have gotten up, walked over to Annette's end of the couch, sat down beside her, and leaned in for the kiss. If Annette was repulsed by my actions she could have said so, or screamed, or punched me in the face. Then I would have had my answer. But going in for a kiss with someone who did not wish to be kissed topped my list of all-time scenarios I loathed, at least in theory. Thankfully, I had never attempted such a thing with someone who was not receptive. The very thought made my skin crawl. I'd rather have my neck tattooed. I needed some signal from Annette, some go-ahead. Anything. She was stingy, refusing to reveal her cards. It was like sitting on the couch with a bale of hay. One that talked.

Half past midnight. Annette had been in my apartment since *yesterday.* This was the opposite of speed dating. This was watch-paint-that-is-already-dry-dry-some-more dating. Enough was enough. The fact that she had been in my apartment for so long was ample circumstantial evidence to merit a move being made. I would have to do it quickly because I was getting sleepy.

I tuned back into Annette in time to hear her say, "I'm not a true vegetarian because I eat fish. But that's all. I don't eat flesh. I think it's okay to eat fish because fish are—"

Annette stopped talking when she saw me signal the time-out sign. I cleared my throat and said, "Annette, I don't want to make things awkward, but I'd just like to let you know that one of my least favorite things in the world is making a move on a girl who doesn't want a move made on her. So if you'd like me to make a move, I'd be happy to. If you'd prefer that I not, that's fine. I'll just stay on this end of the couch. But if you'd like me to, just let me know and I will." I held my arms out, offering myself.

Annette was quiet, weighing her options. She spoke after careful consideration. "Well, I would certainly like to get to know you better. If at any point, you feel the moment is right, I'd say go with your instincts." That seemed clear enough. Just as I started to scoot in her direction, she continued speaking. "Maybe we could go out again next week, see what happens." I pretended to stretch as I retreated to my corner of the couch.

"Sure, that sounds good," I replied. "Next week. We can see how that goes." There was a pause. I proceeded. "But if you're giving me the okay to make a move on you, I'm perfectly happy to make one on you right now."

Annette smiled, her face reddening a bit. "Okay," she said.

"Okay?"

She nodded. "Okay."

Before I got up from the couch, Annette beat me to it. She walked over to me with purpose. I remained sitting. Annette bent toward me and we hugged. It was not the most sensual of hugs since I was sitting and she was standing, but we made do. After the hug, she sat next to me on the couch and we began the process of necking. Our arms got momentarily tangled, but we worked out positions for them. My legs also didn't feel comfortable—my legs and my hip flexors. Part of the problem was my body faced east while Annette was sitting north of me. This meant I had to twist my torso north while kissing her. It was inconvenient.

I pulled away from Annette, asking, "Um . . . is it . . . would you . . . would it be all right if we changed positions? I feel a little contorted here. Maybe if we switched?" Annette was happy to comply. She took the east position and I was now to her north. Somehow our bodies were cumbersomely tangled. The struggle to find a sweet spot reminded me of trying to reach the front seat of my car from the back. After a bit of shifting, I basically ended up sitting in her lap. We kissed for several minutes.

The kissing lacked passion. It lacked a lot of things. Passion, emotion, desire, energy.

Annette placed her hands on my knee and left them there while we went at it. This meant that she was basically just sitting there, which was kind of unsettling. Despite my best efforts, a spark still eluded us. Maybe I would have to go out with her a third time to see if the third time was the charm. But how far was I willing to chase this phantom spark? What if there were no results on a third date? Then what? Was I to continuously date this woman? Move in with her? Get engaged? Married? And then after all that, if there was still no spark, would I tell her: *"Annette, I don't think this is working out"*?

"Carlos, I don't think this is working out." Annette said the obvious, saving us years of despair. I nodded, seconding her motion.

"We gave it a shot," I added. She smiled in solidarity. Annette gathered her things and left. While I felt the sting of having gone out with yet another woman who was not for me, it did not compare to the joy of regaining my freedom from the chains of the couch. America. What a country.

I thought about the look on Annette's face as she left my apartment. Her expression was familiar. She was disillusioned, disheartened. I sensed that she had been through this before, many times. Another date with someone who was not right for her. I felt Annette's pain. Neither of us was to blame. It was my mother's fault, although her lack of matchmaking skills wasn't entirely responsible. I had been incapable of finding a love connection on my own for years. Apparently Annette was in the same boat. I surmised a lot of us were. A bunch of single people floating around in the same boat, wondering why it was so hard. It occurred to me that part of the problem was I had cast such a wide net. I thought that was for the best, but it was clearly slowing me down. I should attempt to narrow the field. More precise, specific sets of social circles might be the key—especially ones that weren't necessarily centered around singles events that reeked of desperation. I decided to continue playing pin the tail on the dating donkey, but with the blindfold off. It seemed a much better way to play.

LEILANI FROM TOLEDO, HAWAII

"Would you be interested in going out with a hot Hawaiian girl?"

I was being asked this question by Elaine, a member of the book club I joined at the request of my friend Socrates (Joann). Elaine was not a friend—she was an acquaintance. Most of the book club members were acquaintances. Additionally, most of them were in relationships. The purpose of this book club was to actually read the books. Not exactly what I was hoping for, but I rolled with it. Elaine had been striking up conversations with me over the past few book club meetings, asking me questions as if I were a foreign exchange student. She would often turn to her husband when making a comment and he would nod vigorously in support, like a bobblehead. We were all sitting in Joann's living room, having just finished a discussion about a novel involving a middle-aged Japanese couple who had stopped being intimate, unless the husband thought his wife was asleep. In that case, he would lightly fondle her while she pretended

to remain unconscious. Our book club concurred spousal molesta-
tion was not cool. I privately concluded that neither were book clubs.
I wasn't sure how much longer I wanted to give this club a try. It was
at the end of our latest gathering when Elaine asked if I'd be interested in going out with her friend, a hot Hawaiian girl.

"Is that a trick question?"

"No."

"Then yes." Who was I to turn down a hot Hawaiian girl?

Elaine looked to her husband for confirmation. She asked him,
"Don't you think it would be a good idea for Carlos to go out with
Leilani?" On cue, he nodded with peculiar enthusiasm. That settled
it. We were all in agreement.

When I spoke to Leilani on the phone she quickly vetoed my
suggestion of meeting up for a tea somewhere. She explained it had
been a long week and she was ready to go out, let loose. She felt like
hitting the town, if I didn't mind. I'd never been one for hitting
towns. But Leilani was so adamant about making of evening of
things, I didn't have the gumption to say, "We're going to have a tea,
damn it." I picked Leilani up the following Friday night. Her appearance was about as Hawaiian as a Kentucky barmaid. She looked
more like a Jolene. The kind of Jolene bemoaned in country-western
songs. Thinking perhaps I was being greeted by a roommate, I veri-
fied with uncertainty, "Leilani?" Yes. She wasn't unattractive—she
just didn't look like the Polynesian goddess I had been fantasizing
about ever since Elaine had mentioned her. I wasn't disappointed; I
just needed to mentally adjust—the way I would if I thought I was
about to enjoy a sip of 7UP, only to discover it was mineral water.

Leilani was fair-skinned and thin, with slightly disheveled hair
that might have been intended to appear stylish. She seemed

nervous. In general, she had a frazzled quality, as if she was late for something. Her dress was designed in a colorful floral pattern. It was the only physical characteristic about her that was remotely Hawaiian. Leilani asked if I was ready. She closed her apartment door so quickly, I couldn't help but think she was hiding a corpse. Her energy wasn't quite right. Instinct told me to cancel the date, to tell her something had unexpectedly come up and I just dropped by to let her know I wouldn't be able to go out after all. I didn't think I would be able to express this convincingly so in answer to her question about being ready, I said, "Absolutely."

Leilani was constantly fidgeting in the car, adjusting her seat. She spoke rapidly, trying to get the words out in time to accommodate her next series of thoughts. Most of those thoughts revolved around dancing. She loved dancing. That is why we were going dancing. To make matters worse, we were going *swing* dancing. Upon first hearing Leilani's suggestion of cutting a rug, I told her I wasn't a big of fan of shaking my booty—to put it mildly. She immediately responded, almost snapped, "Oh, don't worry about it—you'll love it." I guardedly asked if she might prefer miniature golfing. No way, no how. "I *have* to get out on that dance floor," she said with a deep exhale. I cautioned her that a scarecrow would make a better dance partner than me, or a giant sock monkey. Or Frankenstein. This did not faze Leilani. "You're going to dance. It'll be fun." The tone of her voice made it clear I did not have a say in the matter. "Don't worry. I'll lead if I have to." Leilani was obviously a take-charge kind of gal. It was best to step aside and let her make the decisions. She'd find out soon enough my dancing skills were beyond repair. I only hoped that when she did, she wouldn't get too upset. I could picture this girl getting upset.

We were stopped at a light. "So, you're Hawaiian?" I asked, trying not to sound too incredulous.

Leilani alleged that she was. She told me she loved the Big Island. The people, the food, the natural beauty. I asked if her parents still lived in Hawaii. "No, they live in Toledo." I wondered why her parents moved from Hawaii to Toledo. "They never lived in Hawaii. They're not Hawaiian. I'm the only who ever lived in Hawaii," she explained.

"Oh. Okay. How long did you live in Hawaii?"

"I've been there the past six months. I just moved to Los Angeles. My birth name is Loni. But once I got to the Big Island I became *Lei*-lani. It's so me; it sounds more like me. I'm definitely going to go back some day. Hawaii is my adopted homeland." So Leilani was from Hawaii by way of Ohio. I had many more questions. But the light turned green. The car in front of us did not start moving right away. Leilani reached over and aggressively honked my horn. "Let's go, asshole! I want to dance." Thankfully, the car in front of us accelerated without its occupant getting out and pumping us with bullets. I made a mental note not to make any sudden movements around Leilani, considering her unpredictable and brash behavior.

The swing dancing club was packed. There was a long line of people waiting to get in. As we stood in line, Leilani decided to give me a few impromptu swing dancing lessons against my wishes. She kept knocking into the person behind us without apologizing. "It's simple. Slow, quick, quick, step," she instructed. I knew what those words meant individually, but together they were gibberish. *Quick, quick?* That didn't make any sense. Leilani started to grow impatient with me. "Move your feet. You've got to move your feet." I suggested we do this inside, rather than in an unhappy line of annoyed spectators. She ignored my comment, pressing on. "Single, single, rock step." The only thing I learned from her lessons was that when we got in the club I was going to have a horrible experience. I was dreading it.

We made our way to the front of the line. The tall, bulky bouncer asked for our IDs in a no-nonsense tone. I showed him mine. He glanced at it and nodded, gesturing for me to proceed inside. Leilani, aka Loni from Toledo, fumbled through her purse in search of identification. She hadn't had time to get her driver's license ready because she was too busy yelling, "Rock step!" at me. Her fumbling became more frantic.

The bouncer prodded, "Come on. We got people in line behind you."

Leilani grumbled at him. "Just a second. I know I have it. I'm sure I brought it." The bouncer told her to step out of the line while she continued looking through her purse. "Hold on. I have it. I have to have it." She didn't have it. Leilani shook her head in frustration, taking a step closer to the bouncer. "I don't know what's going on here. I swear I had it. Look at me. I'm obviously over twenty-one."

The bouncer was unimpressed. "Can't let you in without ID." Oh my goodness, this was music to my ears. I held my breath, wishing upon a star *please pretty please* don't let us in.

Leilani continued to plead her case. "Come on. You must be new. I've been here so many times. Just let us in."

The bouncer matter-of-factly called out, "Next." The couple behind Leilani stepped in front of her, flashed their IDs and were quickly allowed entry. Leilani stood there, simmering. The bouncer glanced at her. "Go back home, get your ID."

"We drove all the way across town. I'm not making the trip twice." Her voice was low and shaky.

"Then you're not getting in." People continued to stream past her.

She squinted at the bouncer, a large vein popping across her forehead. "Why are you being such a shithead!"

The bouncer kept his cool. "I'm doing my job. You don't like it, find another club, honey." He said *honey* in an extremely derogatory manner. I could tell Leilani was not happy about this by the fact that she began to call the bouncer every bad name in the English language at the top of her lungs. She got right up against him, screaming like a baseball coach furious at an umpire. The bouncer gave back as good as he got. Both of them were going at it like maniacs. I looked to the ground, hoping things would blow over momentarily. But they only got worse. Leilani told the bouncer that he'd better watch it, otherwise she was going to do some not nice things to him—only she used different terminology. It looked as if these two were actually going to come to blows. I couldn't believe it; I thought: *My date is about to get into a fistfight with the bouncer? Are you kidding? If they start pounding each other on the pavement, I'm leaving.*

The conflict ended with an enraged Leilani storming off to my car. The bouncer stared at me. I nodded, secretly overjoyed he wouldn't let Leilani into the club. When I caught up to Leilani, she was breathing heavily, pacing on the sidewalk, reeling from her run-in with the bouncer. She stated the obvious. "I'm so angry right now."

"I can tell. You're definitely not passive-aggressive." Leilani ignored my remark, still huffing and puffing. There was an Italian restaurant across the street. I suggested we go there, get some tea or a coffee, maybe a dessert—just chill for a bit.

She studied the restaurant for a moment and then nodded. "Yeah, okay." With that, she quickly jaywalked across the street. I jaywalked a little more slowly, a little more carefully. Inside, I found

Leilani quietly standing near the host's podium. It was unnerving how still she was. A dapper, dignified older gentleman standing behind the podium greeted me with a warm smile. He was a stark contrast to the bouncer across the street. Not that the bouncer couldn't be dapper and dignified, but the way he was roaring at Leilani, he seemed more like a professional wrestler than any kind of dignitary. The host at the Italian restaurant asked if we were a party of two. I told him we were. He said, "One moment please," and then left to find a table for us.

As we waited for the host to return, I commented, "This looks like a nice place."

Leilani began shaking her head. Her entire body started to tremble. She was blowing a gasket. If she suddenly transformed into the Incredible Hulkette it would not have surprised me. "I can't be here; I can't do this. I'm too furious." She marched out of the restaurant in anger.

I jaywalked with care across the street and joined Leilani at my car once again. She was yanking the passenger door handle, signaling me to unlock it. Once I got in the driver's seat, Leilani told me, "There's a dance club in Beverly Hills. I'm friends with the manager, Hormoz. Hormoz will let me in without an ID. He won't be a stupid son of a bitch about it!" She said the last part louder, in the bouncer's direction, even though there was no way he could hear her.

Her anger made me tired. I wanted to go home and go to sleep. Why had Elaine set me up with this person? She must have really disliked me. I must have unwittingly done something to her and this was Elaine paying me back by setting me up with Mount Kilauea. This was truly a setup. The only thing I could remember that might have caused Elaine to seek retribution was a minor, brief spat we had a few months earlier at one of our book club meetings. She mentioned she had seen a bunch of dolphins at the beach. Elaine went on and on about how much she loved dolphins. They were her favorite animals because they were so smart and caring and playful. For the sake of conversation, I pointed out that some dolphins were actually sociopaths who could be as brutal as Genghis Khan. I had read an article about it. Elaine did not appreciate my bad-mouthing dolphins. She insisted there was no such thing as an evil dolphin. I told her we'd have to agree to disagree. I'd thought that was the end of it. But I guess not.

Leilani and I were now driving down a prominent Los Angeles thoroughfare on our way to Beverly Hills, where the guy would supposedly let us in for sure. We were still quite a distance from the club when Leilani suddenly yelled out, "Stop! Stop!" I thought I was about to hit a cat. Before I could pinpoint the emergency, I abruptly pulled the car over. My heart was racing. I asked Leilani what was wrong. She pointed to a French restaurant on the corner and said, "I like that restaurant. Why don't we just eat there instead of dancing?" I didn't question her immediate change of plans; I only hoped I would escape this night unharmed.

We sat at a booth inside the swanky restaurant. There was a large aquarium directly behind Leilani. A huge orange fish positioned himself just to the right of Leilani's head and stared at me with his unblinking eyes the entire time. His mouth kept opening and closing as if he was showing me what he was capable of. The fish was irritating. I did my best to ignore him, but it was difficult. It's difficult to ignore a giant fish opening and closing its mouth while it unceasingly stares at you, just to the side of your unstable, unpredictable date's head.

Suddenly in an inexplicably chipper mood, Leilani decided she was hungry. Because she was hungry, she ordered two appetizers, the special, some kind of chocolate soufflé–type dessert that required at least half an hour to prepare, and a glass of fine wine. "This is turning out to be a pleasant evening after all," she noted with a pleased expression.

"Yeah," I responded as I tried not to stare at the dumb fish behind her.

Leilani excitedly informed me she could read palms. "Would you like me to read your palm? I'm kind of a psychic." Part of me wanted to point out she wasn't psychic enough to remember her driver's license, but I knew that would be treading dangerous ground. I thanked her, telling her it wasn't necessary. She reached across the table and firmly grasped my palm. Her hand felt grimy and rough, like a mechanic's hand. "*Oh*. A lot of stuff going on here," she noted.

There was another girl named Shirley who had read my palm once. She would also do my tarot cards. Shirley was a self-described gypsy in her twenties, who worked along the Venice Beach Board-walk. I was out for a stroll along the boardwalk one day when I saw her and decided to sit down at her booth—mostly because I wanted to rest. She charged five dollars to tell me the future. I thought it was a fair price for letting me in on what to expect the rest of my life, so I went along. When she read my palm she told me I was extroverted as well as egotistic and impulsive. She said this in a friendly way. It made me laugh. I thought maybe she was picking up residue from the last person who had sat down with her. Her tarot card reading was also way off the mark. She would predict such events as my becoming a farmer. I would visit Shirley regularly for the sheer enter-tainment value.

Shirley was by far the worst psychic I had ever met, until Leilani. Leilani made Shirley look like Nostradamus. After carefully studying my palm, Leilani predicted "something significant" would happen to me within the next six years. I took my hand back and thanked Leilani for the heads-up. At least she didn't say *nothing* significant would happen within the next six years. Our waiter came around and delivered the check, which came to a total of nearly one hundred and fifty dollars, fifteen of which accounted for food I had ordered. Leilani flashed a bright smile. "Thank you *soooo* much for dinner." She excused herself to visit the ladies' room, leaving me with an unsympathetic fish opening and closing its mouth as it stared, stared, stared.

We finally returned to Leilani's apartment. The parking gods saw to it that there was a space directly in front of her building. I pulled into it and left the motor running, showing Leilani that I wanted to be on my way. She didn't get out of the car. There was the awkward pause before a couple says good night on a date. I sensed she was going to invite me in to her place. A little voice inside my head—actually *my* voice—told me, "Whatever you do, do not go inside this person's apartment."

"Would you like to come inside?"

"Sure," I said, turning the ignition off. I don't know why I said this. Maybe it was a mixture of fatigue and fear concerning what might happen had I said no.

For all Leilani's frantic and tempestuous nature, her apartment was surprisingly clean. She lived alone. It was just the two of us. I was often uncertain as to whether or not a female wanted me to make a move in these situations. But not in Leilani's case. Her vibe was inviting. The way she sat on the couch, so close. Her gaze, so flirtatious. I did not want to kiss her. Kissing her might open the possibility of having to see her again. She was too volatile. I wanted a girl who never in a million years would honk my horn or get in a huge bouncer's face.

I sat next to Leilani on the couch exchanging polite conversation while I waited for my opportunity to make a natural exit. An hour later, I was still waiting. I'd been here before, stuck to a couch. I wasn't doing it again. Genuinely tired, I stretched my arms out and said, "Well, I think I'm going to go. I'm ready for some sleep."

Leilani rose to her feet with me, a look of disappointment on her face. She asked if I was okay to drive home. An amusing question, considering I hadn't had a drink and lived about fifteen minutes away. "I'll be fine," I assured her. She walked me to the door. I knew this was kind of a cold gesture, but to make things clear I offered her a handshake good-bye, thanking her for a memorable evening. She grabbed my hand and pulled me into her, giving me a powerful smooch on the lips. I smiled and wished her a good night.

She did the same, adding, "Hope to see you again." It's a good thing she could not read my mind because if she could she would have known I was thinking *that's funny, I'm hoping for the opposite.* I did not understand what I had said or done on our date to interest her, other than let her do most of the talking—a big turn-on for certain women.

A few days later, I was awoken from a nap by the sound of my phone ringing. It was Leilani. She was calling to see if I wanted to go out again on Friday night. Half asleep, I told Leilani I was getting ready to travel the world for a year starting on Friday night. This was a bald-faced, not to mention ridiculous, lie. It startled me to hear it come out of my mouth. There was silence on the other end of the line. Then Leilani bitterly told me, "Have fun," before hanging up. I realized if I was going to keep my lie going about traveling the world, I could not return to the book club anymore. Elaine would see me, and she might tell Leilani I was still in the Western Hemisphere. I would have to stop attending the book club meetings. It was a sacrifice I was willing to make.

I did feel bad about lying to Leilani. If I ever saw her again, I'd apologize, explaining, "I'm sorry I said that, about traveling the world. That wasn't true. I got nervous and I was half asleep and I didn't know what to say. The truth is I just don't like you. Not in a hostile way—not anything against you personally—I don't like confrontation is what I don't like. Screaming matches, not my thing. I don't like it when people's veins pop out of their foreheads. And when somebody shouts for me to stop instantaneously as I'm driving, that's not good. That's not good for my health. I don't think you're good for my health. Please don't hit me." Even in my daydreams, Leilani scared me.

I needed somebody more even-keeled, more balanced. Someone calm. That was more my speed. I thought of where I might find somebody with such qualities. It would have to be in a place where people respected and nurtured their inner spirit. A place that not only relished peace and quiet, but thrived on it. Alcohol would be frowned upon, downright prohibited. Tea would be the beverage of choice. Green tea. People would sip it with a smile as it soothed their souls. There had to be a place I could go with like-minded individuals that offered a pleasing tranquillity for body and mind. I knew just the place.

DOWNWARD SPIRAL DOG

The yoga studio in my neighborhood was beckoning. Yoga appealed
to me. Not the naked yoga I had read about, many lazy Sundays ago,
while perusing an Internet list of top ten things to do in the buff.
Being surrounded by a legion of nude, perspiring men in a steamy
room somehow wasn't all that enticing. But the studio in my neighborhood, that one looked promising. After my stressful date with
the hot-tempered Leilani from Toledo, it seemed a relaxing yoga
session would hit the spot. I don't know how many times I had said
to myself I would give that studio a try someday. The day had
arrived. When I showed up, there was a poster on the front window
featuring an extremely attractive yoga instructor smiling brightly
with the words *Honor Yourself* above her. I liked this place. I liked
that instructor. Though hopeful to find a compatible female in this
more relaxed environment, I decided to let things happen naturally.
This didn't seem like the kind of setting where asking a woman,

"Hey, baby, you come here often?" would be successful. As if I would ever ask any woman, anywhere, anytime that question.

Yoga was hard. *I don't know if I can do this—please make it stop—I'm going to cry* hard. It snuck up on me. Bending my knees while standing and holding my arms above me sounded simple enough. But doing this for several continuous minutes was the equivalent of climbing K2 with a refrigerator on my back. Even the simplest actions were a tremendous challenge. One of the instructors asked the class to make our eyes twinkle. I managed to make my right eye twinkle, but only for a second.

A different instructor in another class approached while I was in what is known as Half Moon Pose. This sounded like a pose in which a person exposed half of their bum, but it was nothing of the sort. Half Moon Pose involved balancing on one leg with the corresponding arm on the floor while extending the other arm upward and the other leg parallel to the floor or something like that. I was in my version of this pose when the instructor walked over and said, "You know, yoga is about more than pushing your physical edge. It's also about pushing your emotional edge. Are you ready to push your emotional edge?" I pretended to push my emotional edge to make her go away.

The first few classes nearly destroyed me. I lost approximately two-thirds of my body weight in perspiration. After a class, I'd return home and sleep like a rock. I was sore in parts of my body I didn't think were capable of getting sore. After the initial struggle, I noticed I started feeling better. I started feeling *good*. My refreshed body actually began craving the various yoga poses. It was surprising. I thought, *Body, are you kidding? You want to go back? Every day? You really want us to become a yogi? That's absurd.* But my body was in favor of us becoming a yogi. And so we did.

Of course it didn't hurt that a number of stunningly beautiful women also attended the yoga studio. In any given class I would inevitably see my future wife. Sometimes I would see three or four of my future wives. I was realistic enough to understand these were my future wives in an alternate universe. For the most part, I admired the women as I would fine works of art. I would remain focused on my own practice, only occasionally noticing if a gorgeous yogi nearby happened to twist and bend with jaw-dropping flexibility. There was no denying they were nice to look at. But I was beginning to learn that attractiveness was not the be-all and end-all of things. My last date was a good example of this. Upon hearing Leilani was a "hot Hawaiian," I immediately volunteered to date her, only to end up in a car with someone who had passenger road rage. And of course there was the famous *Playboy* bunny I went out with, too stupid for her own bad. Beauty wasn't everything.

I mostly kept to myself at the studio, doing my stretches and bends and going home. If I happened to strike up a conversation with a girl, and those conversations led to a possible friendship, and that friendship led to perhaps more—so be it. And if I struck up a conversation with the toned beach-blond girl I saw all the time, so be it awesome. Though I never spoke to her, I knew her name was Missy. She regularly attended classes led by the teacher who wanted me to push my emotional edge. That teacher often called her Missy. "Bend that leg, Missy. Straighten those hips, Missy."

At the studio, Missy and I exchanged glances. Glances became smiles. Eventually, Missy felt comfortable enough to join me on the bench in the lobby one night before class. We started talking. She wondered how challenging the class was going to be, mentioning she was in the mood for something low-key. We were talking so much, she decided to introduce herself, saying, "By the way, my name is—"

I cut her off. "MISSY!" I yelled, like a savant. "Your name is Missy."

She gave me a confused look, and then corrected my mistake. "No," she said, "my name is Julia." Missy, it turns out, was the nickname the instructor called her when advising her to adjust a pose. Missy, as in *Miss* or *Ms*. I had failed to notice that this instructor referred to *all* the ladies in her class as Missy when addressing them. Unfortunately, after flubbing Julia's name, I continued speaking to her.

"Nice to meet you, Julia. What's your last name?" I was hoping it would be easy to spell so I could Google her. But her last name was something like Smyrlkolwskigler. I nonchalantly asked her to spell it, still holding on to hope that I could look her up later. She chuckled, telling me I would never remember it. I let it go, introducing myself, "I'm Carlos. You're really good at yoga." The second I heard these words come out of my mouth, I regretted them. The way I told her she was good at yoga made it sound as if all I did was spend the entire class staring at her. In an effort to backtrack, I dug myself a deeper hole, saying, "It's not as if I stare at you the entire class. It's not like I pick a spot in the studio that gives me the best vantage point to check you out. No, I just have a feeling that your practice is solid." The doors to the studio opened and we walked in without saying another word. A terrible performance.

I saw Julia a few days later and decided I would try again. Hopefully she was willing to excuse my first attempt at socializing. She was already in the studio this time, doing a few preliminary stretches before class began. Summoning my courage, I decided I would approach her, compliment her stretching, and then ask if maybe she'd like to grab a bite to eat after class. Little did I know I was walking into the perfect storm. The moment I approached, the moment my words were leaving my mouth—the neurons in my brain had already triggered the message—that was the very moment she decided to go into Happy Baby. Happy Baby is a pose where a person rolls onto their back, lifts their feet, grabs their ankles and spreads their legs. That is what Julia was doing when I walked up, innocently stared at her crotch, and said, "Looking good!" I began taking different classes after that incident.

It wasn't so bad, attending different classes. One of them was taught by an ethereal, lithe woman named Iris. She was the instructor in the poster I'd seen in the front window the very first day I showed up. I enjoyed the hushed tone of her voice. It created a peaceful atmosphere in the studio. She had a less aggressive approach to the poses. Iris became my favorite instructor. Not only because she creatively varied the sequence of her classes, but because her perfect ass made me want to weep. It was truly spiritual. Yes, beauty wasn't everything. But in Iris's case it was a whole heck of a lot.

As one of Iris's regular students, I got to know her fairly well on a superficial level. I tried being clever and witty around her. As usual, however, I would fall victim to self-sabotage. Once, she stuck her tongue out at me and made a funny face. I was going to call her, "Wacky." But at the last second I considered calling her, "Wacko," which led me to unintentionally say, "Wackyio." Rather than amuse her, this confused her. I beat myself up for days, thinking, "Damn it, I meant to say *wacky*."

My subtle charms finally began to wear Iris down like Chinese water torture. She became friendlier and friendlier, until one day, as she was helping me get into a handstand, she grabbed my crotch. It was magic. At the end of that class she hugged me good-bye so tightly I thought she might never let me go, which was fine. Since she was showing me such affection, I asked Iris if she would like to grab a drink. I suggested *a drink* because I was attempting to sound adultlike. She spoke softly into my ear. "Yes," she replied, "but let's be discreet. Let's have a drink at your place." My heart soared. This was amazing! Straight out of the beginning of a *Penthouse Forum* letter!

A few hours later, she was in my living room. We had some wine. One glass and I was plastered. Under the spell of a Cabernet Sauvignon, I did something wild. Something so reckless, so stupid, few have done this before me. I had drunken, unprotected sex. Moments after we finished, as we were still basking in the afterglow, Iris said something unexpected. She said, "If you got me pregnant, I'm keeping our child." This destroyed the mood. I sobered up immediately—and laughed, of course. One problem though. Iris wasn't laughing with me. The expression on her face reminded me of Kathy Bates in *Misery*. *Misery* was probably one of Iris's favorite romantic comedies. Iris continued our postcoital cuddle by informing me she was not on any kind of birth control. Then she draped her arm across my chest and asked, "When did you first realize you loved me?"

I have always wanted to visit New Zealand. Never more so than in that particular moment. I had met women in the past that moved fast, but this was ridiculous. Though Iris and I were in the same bed, we were obviously on different planets. I tried not to sound too frightened when I responded, "The first time I saw you, you made a really strong impression."

This seemed to satisfy her because she quickly jumped out of bed and suggested, "Let's eat!" Her new pregnancy was already giving her an appetite. I hastily served Iris the only food I had—some shredded wheat in a plastic cereal bowl.

Any smart, rational individual would have realized Iris was probably not pregnant just yet. But I, valedictorian of my high school, was convinced there was one in Iris's oven—an embryo soon to be a fetus soon to be a teenager. How was I going to put this kid through college? Iris detected my anxiety. She stopped eating, squinted at me, and sternly stated, "There's more than one person in this situation, you know." I nodded my head, hoping for a moment when I would be able to call 911 without her noticing, so that I could report an intruder.

As it turned out, Iris decided to leave on her own. She said she needed time to think about "the baby." I walked her to her car and spoke my mind, explaining when we slept together, I wasn't visualizing parenthood. I was not prepared, nor planning to raise a child with her. She looked dismayed and let loose a supernatural bellow, followed by a display of tears. Then an unmistakable anger welled up within her. She glared, somberly warning, "Actions have consequences." The only thing missing was thunder and lightning. Iris slammed the door of her car and peeled out into the darkness. How I longed for the days when my greatest concern was having said the word *wackyio*.

The following night, I hung out with my friend Jason, telling him I was possibly going to be a daddy. Jason was a ladies' man. He was a location scout. I'd often receive phone calls from Thailand or Cuba or some such place. It would be Jason, saying something like, "I'm riding an elephant sandwiched between two hot Thai girls.

They're twins." As much as I wanted to settle down with the right girl, he wanted to remain a perennial bachelor. Jason sympathized upon hearing the yoga instructor and I were potentially expecting. "Dude, that's rough. How long after you guys had sex did she say she might be pregnant?"

I told him. "Five minutes." Upon hearing this, Jason nearly lost consciousness due to an inability to breathe due to hysterical laughing. Once he was able to speak, he had two questions. Did we have sex in a mental hospital? Was she dressed as a giant frog?

Probably as a result of stress—I was truly a wreck—I came down with a cold soon after my chilling tryst with Iris. I went down to the general care clinic of my hospital and met with a Dr. Sander, hoping he would give me something to speed up my recovery. The monotone Dr. Sander struck me as a humanoid. His manner was such that I would have been surprised if he knew people were equipped with a sense of humor. Still, he was an anonymous doctor, he was in front of me, and I had a spontaneous sort of meltdown. I told him my situation, of my recent night with the yoga instructor, of how it had gone so very, very wrong.

Dr. Sander was probably attempting to comfort me when he dryly said, "It's natural for you to be upset. You're concerned this woman will approach you on the sidewalk and attempt to assassinate you." This specific thought had not entered my mind until Dr. Sander planted it there.

When I got home, I turned to a doctor I was more familiar with, my Trekkie doctor, Dr. Kovac. When last I communicated with him, it was to determine whether or not an Internet girl had bequeathed genital herpes to me. Now I was e-mailing him about another sexual exploit, asking him what he thought my chances of becoming a father were. Dr. Kovac no doubt considered me a whore. Remembering the jokes he cracked during my herpes visit, I braced myself for his goofy brand of humor. I was hoping for reassurance, for a response along the lines of, "It's actually a lot harder to get someone pregnant than you think." Instead, he wrote, "Anything is possible. Good luck!"

I noticed there was an attachment to his e-mail, an audio file. I downloaded it and discovered it was dialogue from the movie *Toy Story*. It was Buzz Lightyear saying, "There seems to be no sign of intelligent life anywhere."

Considering the circumstances, I found a new yoga studio. I thought it would be awkward if I continued attending Iris's classes. Months went by. Not that I was keeping track, but eight months, two weeks and three days went by, and I had not heard from or seen Iris since our fateful night. I knew she was still teaching at my original yoga studio because her name still appeared on their Web site's schedule. So when my married friends, Todd and Kristy, asked me to recommend a good yoga class, I sent them directly to Iris, requesting a small confidential favor from Todd. I casually asked Todd, "After you take class, could you tell me if the teacher is—"

Todd interrupted, "If I think the teacher is hot?"

"Sure." I went on, "And also one other thing . . ."

When I told Todd what the *one other thing* was he high-fived me. He seemed proud. But he also advised me to be careful because, as he put it, "Yoga teachers can be a little crazy sometimes." Todd gave me a call after taking Iris's class. He'd completed his reconnaissance mission and reported, unequivocally, "There's no way that woman is having a baby."

I never saw Iris again, though I would sometimes expect her to suddenly jump out of the bushes holding a baby, or a machete, or both. Yoga wasn't so relaxing after all. I put in place a strict policy of not sleeping with yoga or Pilates instructors or personal trainers. No matter how many times they might ask, my answer would be the same. "Absolutely not."

Following my experience with Iris, I wanted a break. From everything. I decided to put my search for a soul mate on hold. I still wanted one, very much so. I just didn't want to *look* for one. Bad things happened when I looked. Besides, I had heard on the street that people found their soul mates the moment they *stopped* looking. That was actually the *one* thing I hadn't done in all of this. I hadn't *not* looked. I'd given everything else a try; it was time to give not giving a try a try. I would go about my business, live my life without worrying about being alone or having a date or not having a date. She would have to find *me*.

RUDITY

The one I thing I discovered about doing nothing when it came to finding love was that in return nothing happened. Nothing begot nothing. It kind of sucked. Whoever said, "You'll find someone when you stop looking," was just trying to remove competitors from the dating pool. As a result, I found myself in a battle of wills. I didn't want to do it. Just the thought made me shudder. Part of me fought the idea fiercely. But another part kept encouraging, kept egging me on. What did I have to lose, except a little dignity perhaps? No. I could not do it. I *must* not do it. No matter what, however strong the temptation, I had to resist. There were better ways. Hadn't I learned my lesson by now? In the end, I gave in. I revisited a world of darkness. A world rife with peril, deception, and disappointment. I signed up for another round of Internet dating.

It was my way of sticking my toe in the water. Several months of self-imposed inactivity had passed. My sources had gone dry. I had no prospects. No one was setting me up—not even my mother. The Internet was my only ally. It was still there for me, waiting. My profile was listed as *hidden*. With one click of a button, I was back on the market. I saw a countless number of familiar faces from my previous Internet dating tours. Apparently many of these ladies had yet to find their match either. But there were also plenty of new faces, new possibilities. Enough to dig deep. Once committed, I went all in. I scoured a number of dating Web sites—some familiar haunts, others uncharted territory.

Careful and deliberate consideration was given to each and every profile that caught my eye. I devoted hours to finding my online better half. It's not as if my previous tours of duty were half-hearted exercises; they were not. But this time I was more determined, more focused. When reaching out to a young lady, I would specifically reference something she had written in her profile to show I had taken the time to closely review her words. There would be no cutting and pasting. You don't find a soul mate by cutting and pasting. Additionally, I would only reach out to girls with genuine potential. Whereas before I'd write to any girl who looked attractive, or even moderately attractive, this time I would scale back. If a girl looked pretty in her photos but wrote, "I like 2 parteee!!!! Can u rock wit me?" I would not be attempting to rock wit her. And—this was important—I would not be contacting any girl who posted only a picture of her face, especially if it was in black and white.

During my thorough assessment of online profiles, I noticed a lot of women wrote similar things. I lost track of how many times a girl posed the question, "Is that too much to ask?" or "Is he really out there?" Many of them noted they were just as comfortable in a fancy cocktail dress during a night on the town as they were in their pajamas curling up on the couch. There was a lot of curling up on couches. Most, if not all, were "down to earth" gals looking for their "partner in crime" so long as that criminal was six feet tall or over, could make them laugh, was not bald or balding, did not post pictures of himself shirtless, didn't have any baggage, and kept physically fit. Other than that, they were up for meeting just about anybody. For some reason, a lot of the women posted pictures of themselves wearing fake mustaches, often by simply holding a strand of lengthy hair across their upper lip. If they weren't clowning around in a fake mustache, they were at Machu Picchu in the mountains of Peru or zip-lining in a Costa Rican rain forest. If I drank, I would have made a drinking game out of every time I saw a photo that featured zip-lining, Machu Picchu, or fake mustaches. And I would have gotten plastered.

After a while, the profiles began blending together. Looking through the galleries of anonymous women displaying distant smiles made me feel as if I were sifting through photographs of the missing and exploited. Toward the end of one online session, I became a little punch-drunk due to fatigue. I should have called it a night and started up again in the morning, refreshed. For better or for worse, I kept going, pushing myself. The last message of the night was sent to a pleasant-looking girl named Becca. In the message to Becca, I jokingly ended with, "Becca, if you write back . . . you will make me the happiest man on Earth." Signing off the way one might propose marriage proved ineffective. Becca didn't write back. Regardless of my pointed attention to detail, most of the women did not write back, just as before.

The lack of responses caused me to question my existence, my self-worth, and my Internet connection. How could I be certain my messages were arriving in the first place if none of them were acknowledged in any way? It was a tree falling in the forest situation . . . if an e-mail is sent to someone through a third party, does it arrive? Amongst the thousands of profiles I was surveying, I found one that allowed me to circumvent the system. The profile was posted by a girl whose screen name was Untoxic. Like a lot of other single young ladies, she was loyal to her friends, loved the beach, and enjoyed meeting new people. What set her apart was that she posted her direct e-mail address in her profile. Per her instructions, if anything she had written sounded interesting, I should e-mail her directly. I did, introducing myself as a new person who was loyal to his friends—especially on the beach. Since I was sending a direct e-mail, I let Untoxic know that if she wanted to check out my profile on the dating Web site, my screen name was ChickenWhisperer.

Lo and behold, I received a reply from Untoxic a few days later. It was a short, odd message. I appreciated receiving it nonetheless. She wrote: "HotSurfer69, is this you? If so, I'm not Asian—I'm not your type."

I didn't understand why she thought I might be HotSurfer69. Upon rereading the original e-mail I sent to her, I confirmed that I had clearly identified myself as ChickenWhisperer. Never in a million bazillion gazillion years would I call myself HotSurfer69. First of all, I didn't surf. Secondly, it was up to other people to decide whether or not I was hot. And third, I'd never include a number in my screen name associated with a sexual position in which two people align themselves so that each person's mouth is near the other's genitals.

Maybe Untoxic was tired; maybe she'd had a long day. I wrote back, clarifying my identity. "Hi, Untoxic. No, I am not HotSurfer69 on that Web site. I am ChickenWhisperer. But in all fairness to Hot-Surfer69, give him a chance. You guys might still be a great match even though you are not Asian. How are things going for you lately? I'm doing pretty good. Went to the dentist this morning for a teeth cleaning—still no cavities. Never had a cavity in my life! How about that? Take care, ChickenWhisperer."

I wrote the part about giving HotSurfer69 a chance for the sake of levity. Mentioning my teeth cleaning was an attempt at getting a conversation started, any conversation. I thought my pristine teeth might be a potentially interesting detail. Perhaps it would impress Untoxic. Maybe she would write back in awe and admiration. Or maybe she'd never had a cavity in her life either. That might be one of many clues indicating we should spend our lives together.

Untoxic's next note came quickly, in all caps. "SINCE YOU REFUSE TO TELL ME WHO YOU ARE, AT THIS POINT I'M GUESS-ING YOU'RE RETARTED. I DON'T CARE ABOUT YOUR BORING VANILLA STORIES."

It seemed impolite not to reply. "Hello again, Untoxic! FYI, you spelled retarded wrong. No, I am not retarded. However, I am spe-cial. All of us are special. Especially you, it seems. I'm sure you have friends and family members who would say only kind things about you and who love you with all of their heart. I'm sure you're not a diabolical, self-loathing, vile, explosive, mad cow 24/7. But thank you for the peek into that part of your soul. Though it has been entertaining corresponding with you, regrettably I don't think we're a match. Best of luck in your search for a mate. You might want to try dating a chimpanzee. They have a temperament similar to yours. Sincerely, and as always, ChickenWhisperer.

"P.S. Also consider removing 'Un' from your screen name."

Untoxic never wrote back. Shortly after our brief exchange, a few more e-mails began to trickle in from other potential candidates.

Just as before, for about every five hundred e-mails I sent out, I'd get one in return. After Untoxic came JulesNLA.

JulesNLA was originally from New York City. She thought Los Angeles was an armpit on account of its devastating lack of culture. Despite its culture deficiency, JulesNLA had lived in the city she hated for ten years. This I learned from a phone conversation. We graduated to the phone after two simple inoffensive e-mail messages. JulesNLA suggested she come over to my place for a long walk in my neighborhood. I didn't know her. She could have come over to my apartment, chopped me into little pieces, and stolen all of my belongings. It had a been a while since I'd gotten some action. I was willing to take that chance.

When JulesNLA arrived, she gave me a hug as if I had been deployed at sea for a year. I met her in front of my building, thinking we would start our walk right away. But she asked if she could come inside and pee. She was not threatening, so I let her. Once she finished, she conducted a self-guided tour of my apartment, ending up on the couch. I sat beside her. We had what amounted to a speed date, asking things of each other we didn't get a chance to over the phone such as, "Do you have a criminal record?" She was clean.

JulesNLA's first question was, "Are you on Twitter?" I hesitated long enough for JulesNLA to become concerned. She asked, "You don't know what Twitter is?"

I did know. Of course I knew. It was an online social networking service that allowed people to inform the world they just ate a really good cheeseburger or that the revolution was starting at noon. I was not on Twitter. Organizing revolutions wasn't my thing. And if I wanted to tell my friends I just ate a really good cheeseburger I would call them and say, "Hey, I just ate a really good cheeseburger."

When JulesNLA discovered I wasn't on Twitter it was like she found out I didn't use oxygen. How could someone survive in a world without Twitter? She had a mild panic attack. Her chest started heaving; her eyebrows furrowed so intensely it looked painful. If her head could have swiveled, it would have. In an effort to calm her down, I promised JulesNLA I would join Twitter. That was not good enough. I had to join Twitter *now*. She had me turn on my laptop and immediately registered me as Twitter's newest member. *Then* she calmed down, a deeply satisfied smile on her face. "You'll thank me later," she promised.

We went on our walk. Despite her neuroses about Twitter, JulesNLA turned out to be good company. That is to say, I did not object to her presence. She was personable and cute. It was slightly overcast. The sun was going down. Its waning rays gave the clouds a mystical orange hue across the sky. JulesNLA wanted a picture. She attempted several times to capture the clouds with her camera phone, but the phone was not cooperating. I snapped a photo with my phone, telling her I'd e-mail it to her. This pleased JulesNLA to no end. She went on and on about how wonderful it would be to have that picture. I was such a gentleman to take the picture for her. Whenever she looked at the picture, she would think of our lovely walk. It sounded like being sent the picture was going to be one of the highlights of her year, if not her life. We ended up in front of my building again. JulesNLA gave me a quick, but affectionate hug. I kissed her on the cheek. Both of us thought it would be a good idea to see each other again and made plans to do so.

I e-mailed JulesNLA the picture the very next day, writing, "Here are the orange clouds. Hope they are as exhilarating as when you saw them in person."

Several hours later, JulesNLA sent her reply: "Okay. Thank you." That was it. Quite a contrast from her initial excitement. It made me think perhaps JulesNLA was bipolar. I imagined her huddled in a corner of her apartment, aimlessly flicking her lamp on and off as she responded. Given her terse e-mail, I now wasn't sure if she was interested in getting together a second time. We had planned on going out that Saturday night. After receiving her e-mail, I didn't know. I let Tuesday and Wednesday go by, calling JulesNLA on Thursday to see if we were still on for Saturday.

She sounded jolly on the phone. "Of course we're still on for Saturday. Why wouldn't we be?" I told her I wasn't sure because of her emotionally distant message. She laughed. "What are you talking about?" I explained that her three-word e-mail surprised me because she seemed so passionate about the orange sky. She was so upset when she couldn't take a picture and so happy when I did. "Oh. That's why you sent the picture. I thought it was weird you were sending me a random picture of clouds."

Huh? She was talking as if she didn't remember how gallant I had been snapping that photo, how moving the sky was for her. "You wanted that picture really badly. Remember?"

There was a pause. "Oh yeah. Now I do." To be sure, I asked if I was speaking to the JulesNLA I went on a walk with a few days earlier. She laughed. "Yes, it's me. I'm sorry. I've just been really busy. Don't worry about me writing 'Okay. Thank you.' It's been a hectic week. I'm looking forward to seeing you." I accepted this, with the caveat that at some point in the near or distant future I reserved the right to respond with "Okay. Thank you," to any e-mails she might send me. JulesNLA laughed again, in agreement.

That Saturday night, we went to dinner. She was back to being carefree and full of life. After dinner, we returned to my apartment and wound up sitting near each other on the couch. She told me I was sexy. I smiled with a shrug, pretending I heard that compliment all the time, no big thing. I leaned in and gave her a kiss, which she responded to. We made out. It was enjoyable. After about an hour, she said it was time to go. I walked her to her car, giving her a long good-bye kiss. Then she drove away.

I wasn't over the moon about JulesNLA, but I liked her. Compared to Untoxic, she was the love of my life. Going out with her again would be fun. Perhaps the more we went out, the more I got to know her, the more excited I would become. Maybe this was a slow burn into a meaningful relationship. That would be nice.

The morning after our second date, I received an e-mail from JulesNLA. I expected her to write something about going on a third date. My expectations were off base. "It's been great hanging out with you, but I think we make better friends." That was it. The real-life JulesNLA was quite different from the one who sent me e-mails. The *e-mail* JulesNLA was on lithium. As I was still processing her message, I received another e-mail. This one was from Twitter. Twitter informed me that I was now being followed by JulesNLA. She was my one follower. So after cutting bait, she decided to join me on Twitter. Maybe that was her plan all along. She probably worked for Twitter and bounced around Los Angeles making out with various men and women every night, signing them up. Either that or she was trying to add to her own list of followers.

Since JulesNLA was my sole follower on the Twitter, I contemplated having a pseudo–emotional breakdown one hundred and forty characters in length. She had not shattered my heart—I was not emotionally invested. Still, for my amusement, I thought of posting to my one follower such bulletins as: *Wondering what you're wearing.* / *I'm not wearing anything.* / *How could you do this to me, you heartless wrench?* / *I meant to write "wench" in that last post.* / *Sorry about my angry words. It's just that I'm drunk and I need to be held right now.* In the end, I did no such thing. Mostly because I didn't want the hassle of having to log in to my Twitter account. Who knows what the password was? Instead, in response to her *let's be friends* message, I sent her an old-school e-mail. It simply read, "Okay. Thank you."

Next at bat was Daisy323. She was much more cautious than JulesNLA. We traded a few harmless back-and-forth e-mails before Daisy323 informed me, in an e-mail, the next step would be to have multiple phone conversations, after which we would possibly meet for coffee. If that went well, we would have dinner some other night—but we would meet each other at the restaurant. In the event of a successful dinner, I could pick her up at her place for the next dinner. Fine. Whatever hoops somebody wanted me to jump through was fine. What else was I going to do?

I missed Daisy323's call by a few minutes. Her voice mail was extremely officious. She stated her name, the purpose of her call, and the times she would be available. It gave me a chuckle because it reminded me of the calls I received from my dentist's office to confirm an upcoming appointment. I told her this when I called Daisy323 back. She apologized right away, apparently thinking I was making some sort of negative judgment about her style of leaving voice mails. "Oh no, no. You don't have to apologize," I made clear. "It was just an observation. I just had my teeth cleaned not too long ago. No cavities. I've never had a cavity." She responded with silence. Nobody cared about my teeth.

Daisy323 broke the uncomfortable silence by asking where I

lived. Since we lived a bit of a distance from each other, Daisy323 suggested a popular coffeehouse about halfway between us. I told her that would be fine, though I probably wouldn't drink coffee. I'd have a hot chocolate instead. She wondered why I wouldn't have coffee. "Because I don't like it," I explained. "It's not my cup of tea. I realize a lot of people in the global community enjoy coffee, but I'm not one of them. I've never actually had a cup of coffee. But I've sniffed it. The smell bothers me. And if the smell bothers me, then I'm sure the taste would." More silence on Daisy323's end.

I asked Daisy323 if she went to that coffeehouse often. She did. Not only to drink coffee—which she loved—but to play the guitar. She performed regularly at that coffeehouse. "That's cool. How long have you played the guitar?" I asked. She'd been playing for over twenty years, since she was eight. "Wow, you must be really good."

"I'd say I'm all right. I'm better at playing the guitar than singing, but I do both."

I hoped for her sake she was being humble. Anybody who has played the guitar for over two decades and considers themselves to be just "all right" should probably stop playing. I kept this thought to myself, instead telling her, "When I was a kid, my parents forced me to play the accordion. They signed me up after two door-to-door accordion lesson salesmen came to our house on a Sunday afternoon."

"Carlos, I don't think this conversation is going very well." Daisy323's tone changed dramatically.

"You don't?" I didn't think the conversation was going poorly, or well. It seemed like we were simply engaging in small talk before deciding what day and time to meet for hot chocolate/coffee. I figured once we met in person we'd decide what's what. But I figured wrong.

"No, it's not going well." I guess she had an aversion to people who sniff coffee and were forced to play the accordion as a child.

"I'm sorry our talk isn't meeting your expectations." Now I was the one who was apologizing. It was sincere.

"Yeah, I'm very good at determining these things. I need someone that I'm going to click with. You're not that person. I don't mean to hurt your feelings, but there's really no point in meeting. Have a good night." Click.

I looked at my phone. We had spoken for five minutes and thirty-six seconds. In five minutes and thirty-six seconds, Daisy323 had evaluated my entire being, my essence, my value. I wasn't crazy about the vibe I was getting from her either, but I was willing to give things a try—at least for as long as it took me to drink a cup of hot chocolate. On the other hand, I admired Daisy323's ability to make snap decisions in a limited amount of time based on a limited amount of information. This would surely come in handy later on, and probably already had many times in her life. When she did meet The One, they would probably get engaged in five minutes or less. It would take ten minutes to plan her wedding, fifteen to get pregnant, half an hour to find a house. An hour into their relationship they'd already be celebrating their golden anniversary. Lucky her. And lucky guy who ended up with her. I envied that guy the way I envied someone who had contracted malaria.

Having negative experiences with women I met through the World Wide Web was starting to feel like a job. And I was getting good at it. It made me tired. When I received a response from a *fourth* girl, it deflated my spirits rather than lifting them. Another one? Ah, man. I bucked myself up, remembering to give everyone a chance. All it took was one; all it took was one. That was my mantra. This one's screen name was PlumLuv. So she liked plums. Okay. PlumLuv had no interest in talking on the phone. She cut right to the chase in her e-mail, asking when was a good time to get together for a drink.

We met the following night at one of her favorite restaurant bars. The place was loud. It was difficult to hear what PlumLuv was saying, but I did my best. She had a martini and I had a ginger ale, which she mocked as being unmanly. After a few minutes I found myself wishing this girl had pulled a Daisy323. It would have been nice if she had ended things abruptly over the phone rather than making me sit in a loud bar. "Are you hungry?" she asked. "I'm hungry. How about some food?" The restaurant part of this establishment was quieter, and I *was* kind of hungry, so we grabbed a table.

As I had dinner with PlumLuv I thought of how I considered her a *maybe*. When I first saw her online profile, I wasn't sure. Her picture looked okay—like it could go either way in person, attractive or not so much. She was borderline attractive. Her written words didn't reveal much in the way of a personality. She could have been engaging or, as it turned out, a vessel of stale air. For future reference, I concluded any girl who struck me as a *maybe* online should be considered a *no—definitely not—do not contact this individual under any circumstances.*

In the middle of dinner, PlumLuv asked me what my last name was. I told her. She replied, "Oh, that's a horrible last name."

Unsure how to respond, I said, "Thank you." *She* thanked *me* when the check arrived, she thanked me so much. Dinner was expensive, but it was worth the price of never having to see PlumLuv again.

As we walked out of the restaurant, she suddenly stopped and nonchalantly told me, "I'll be right back. I just have to take a shit."

Internet dating clearly wasn't working out. It was the dregs. I was done. No more Internet dating. I knew the temptation would be strong to log back on, especially in the event of a dry spell. But I promised myself I would not be returning. Under no circumstances. If it meant I had to lock myself in a closet, so be it. I'd inform all of my friends that no matter how loud I yelled for them to let me out, no matter how forcefully I pounded on the door and demanded to be set free so I could get back on the computer and write to more girls, they could not comply. No. More. Internet. Dating.

WAITING FOR THE ONE

Jeez Louise, I was on my way to another Internet date. Dagnabbit, my friends were the worst. They weren't stopping me, mostly because I never got around to telling them they needed to stop me. It was a moment of weakness, this date. The thing was, the girl wrote to me. Unsolicited. A girl writing to me *first* was as rare as a cowardly chicken. I knew what it was like not to receive a response, so I felt compelled to have a beverage with her, if for no other reason than to thank her for making first contact. Plus, even though she was a *maybe* at best, she had great cleavage. (I was only human.) Plus, I hadn't gone out with anyone in a while. Super extra plus plus, what if this girl was incredible? What if it turned out she was much prettier than her pictures and her personality shined? Maybe she purposely made herself look less attractive in photos to weed out superficial men. It made me nervous, the thought that if only I had gone on *one* more Internet date, *that* would have been it. (In all probability, this was going to suck and I knew it.)

For some insane reason I agreed to meet her in her neighborhood, which was located in Glendale, California. Without traffic, it took about twenty-five minutes to get from my neighborhood to Glendale. With traffic, it took about two and a half hours. There was *always* traffic. The only possible way I could have avoided it was if I had scheduled my Internet date for three a.m. But this girl wanted to meet at eight p.m., so I left at five thirty.

Before I got on the freeway, I stopped at a grocery store near my apartment to get some cash from an ATM. I parked my giant car at a curbside meter and dashed inside the market. When I returned, I found someone had parked their car in front of mine, fairly close. I slowly backed out along the curb, giving myself extra room to clear the car in front of me. That's when I heard an agonizing crunch and scrape. I had backed into the car behind me—the car I did not see in my rearview mirror and still could not see as I brought my vehicle to an abrupt halt. I got out to investigate what I had hit, hoping it was a used Gremlin with missing hubcaps. Instead I ended up staring at a beautiful, black, shiny convertible Porsche. At least it used to be beautiful before I dented and scratched the front fender.

I immediately called Internet Girl, explaining I had been in a terrible car accident and was not going to be able to make it. She did not answer. I left this information in a voice mail message. She never answered her phone. I would always leave messages and she would respond with a text. This was highly suspicious. For all I knew the girl wasn't a girl at all. She could have been a trucker named Earl up to no good. Maybe backing into the shiny Porsche was the work of my guardian angel.

The scent of fresh muffins wafted in my direction. I had parked directly in front of a small bakery next to the supermarket. It was still open. Keeping an eye on the street, I bought one of those muffins. Then I took a seat at a sidewalk table and waited for the owner of the Porsche. The owner was probably not going to be happy when he or she learned of the damage I had caused. It was certainly unpleasant to have dented such a valuable car. I felt bad about it. And yet, I couldn't help feeling relieved at the same time. At least I didn't have to go to Glendale.

I enjoyed my muffin, relishing the calm before the storm. It seemed as if the peace was about to be disrupted. A tall, fit, white-haired gentleman dressed for a tennis match began briskly walking toward the Porsche. This was it. I placed my partially eaten muffin on the table and nervously stood up. But the gentleman continued marching up the sidewalk. I sat down again.

It had been a month of unexpected occurrences. Three weeks earlier, I had received an e-mail from a ghost. It was a message from someone I had not seen or spoken to in over twenty years. My very first girlfriend, Yvonne from fifth grade, wrote to me through the social networking Web site Myspace. I was surprised. Not only because Yvonne wrote to me, but because I had a Myspace page. I had completely forgotten about it.

Yvonne still looked like Yvonne—the thirty-something version of herself. She was fit, attractive, and single. Yvonne asked in her message if I remembered her. How could I forget my first girlfriend? I wrote back to Yvonne right away, noting specific things I remembered about her. The time she clapped so proudly when I won glory for our academic team by yelling out the correct answer of "Australia!" The way she laughed when I mistakenly wrote *roffs* on the chalkboard instead of *roofs*. And the badge she wore that read I Love Carlos. At the end of my message, I suggested we have dinner, catch up sometime. I informed her it would be a lot easier to get together because I had a car now. Yvonne never wrote back.

Putting myself in Yvonne's shoes, I kind of understood why she didn't reply after initially reaching out to me. It might have been a little unsettling to have someone list such specific details about mundane activities that took place ages ago. I probably should have played it cool and written, "Yeah, I remember you. What's up?" or better yet, "Yvonne who?" My e-mail was the opposite of playing it cool. After reading it, Yvonne probably assumed I had an altar devoted to her in my bedroom and I had been waiting to hear from her since the last day we saw each other. This was not the case. There were no altars. I had not been pining for Yvonne. I just had a good memory.

My memory was not one of those supercalifragilisticexpialidocious memories in which people can remember every day of their lives down to what they had for breakfast fifteen years earlier on the first Wednesday in January. That would be exhausting. Certain bowls of oatmeal aren't worth remembering. I recalled minute yet random details about everything and everyone. My earliest memory was as an infant, crying and crying in my crib when my parents left me all alone. My mother wanted to check on me but my father decreed, "He needs to learn."

I finally stopped crying. Not because I was tired, but because I was angry. I thought, in my infant way, *Screw them. I don't care anymore.* Once I was quiet, my parents snuck in to check on me. I *pretended* I was asleep. They were too late. If they weren't interested in me, I wasn't interested in them. I was not proud of this passive-aggressive behavior and did my best to curb it as an adult. Whenever I shared this early memory with anyone, it was always met with disbelief. But that did not change the truth.

The downside of having a good memory was being able to remember all the bad dates I'd been on. Never mind that. I shook off the weight of a hundred plus bad dates and finished eating my muffin. It was good. Many people had passed me on the sidewalk, but none claimed ownership of the dented Porsche. I noticed a car cruising down the street. Its driver was listening to a song from a century gone by—Bette Midler's "Wind Beneath My Wings." I hated that song. Nothing personal against Bette Midler, but whenever I heard that song, I instinctively wanted to squirt her in the mouth with a kitchen hose.

Coincidentally, two weeks earlier, I'd created a mix CD of the worst songs ever recorded in the history of mankind. I called this CD *Grocery Store Music.* "Wind Beneath My Wings" was on this CD. It also included the works of Michael Bolton, Clay Aiken, and Amy Grant— to name a few. In my humble opinion, anyone not familiar with these artists has led a charmed life. I'd put this CD together for two reasons. One, to combat boredom. And two, it was sort of a Rorschach test. I kept the CD in my car. When driving with a passenger, I would casually start playing it without comment. If the passenger responded in thirty seconds or less by saying something along the lines of, "What the hell is this crap?" I knew I was riding with a true friend.

Among the first of my unsuspecting passengers was one Aaron Downing. He was a postproduction supervisor on a film I worked on. Aaron was gregarious, always up for a conversation, usually in a lighthearted mood. He enjoyed breaking into spontaneous song. Aaron invited me to a party at his coworker's place. He chose to sit in the back of my tank because we were picking up two female friends of his on our way to the party. With Aaron sitting in back, me acting as his chauffeur, I nonchalantly began playing the *Grocery*

Store Music CD. It took about ten seconds of Aaron hearing Michael Bolton before he yelled out, "Why do you do this? Turn it off!" Aaron was a true friend. I turned the music up.

Since Aaron was sitting in the backseat, he was unable to turn the music off himself. He decided to implement a bit of reverse psychology. Aaron began singing along to the music at the top of his lungs, as if he were celebrating it. On the inside, my choice of tunes was irritating him something fierce. By the third song, Aaron gave up on the sing-along and implored me to stop this madness.

I explained, "These are the worst songs ever recorded in the history of mankind."

"Yeah, I know. That's why you need to turn them off." Something about his demanding tone led me to raise the volume up even louder, and to lower all the car windows. "Don't do this. This is dangerous," Aaron advised. He had a point. We were driving on Venice Boulevard. Certain sections of Venice Boulevard were not the greatest areas to be blasting Celine Dion's "The Power of Love." For example, *all* sections of Venice Boulevard. I was aware of the danger, but continued pumping my Celine Dion jam because it made me laugh until I was out of breath. Meanwhile, Aaron was slumped in the back trying to make himself invisible.

I turned the music off just before we picked up his two lady friends. Hopefully, I'd make a love connection with at least one of them. They were cute, giggly girls who were looking forward to the party. One of them sat in front with me, the other in back with Aaron. As we continued toward the party, I nonchalantly turned the music on, and waited. Aaron said nothing. The girl sitting next to me started singing along to Clay Aiken. I thought perhaps she was in on the joke, that her singing was done in jest. But I soon realized, she was actually enjoying the music. Thoroughly, sincerely enjoying it. And so was her friend.

With each new ditty, the girls' enthusiasm grew. They sang exuberantly. The one in the back complimented me by saying, "This is the best mix CD I've ever heard." Her friend agreed. *They were not kidding.* There would be no love connection with either of these two. I gave the CD to the one in the back, as a gift. She was stunned. "Are you sure?" she asked. It was the right thing to do, considering I would never see her again.

A man approached the damaged Porsche. He sort of stumbled to it before stopping right in front of it. I saw immediately that this man was not the owner. It was the man I privately referred to as Jerry. Good ole Jerry, who regularly performed external monologues in a business suit or bathrobe while ambling up and down the street. Today he was dressed in his bathrobe. He looked slightly more confused than usual, but only slightly. Jerry focused on the Porsche for a moment. It seemed as if he was considering hopping in. Instead he broke into a vibrant operatic aria. It was the first time I'd heard him sing. He was pretty good (although I wasn't a fan of opera). Without giving me so much as a glance, Jerry ended his musical showstopper and continued on his way, mumbling something about piñatas.

I suspected Jerry was single. Perhaps his current mental state was a result of too many Internet dates gone awry. I wondered what his screen name was. And more to the point, I wondered if Jerry was a foreshadowing of my own circumstances. Maybe someday I would end up walking aimlessly along the street in a bathrobe, alone, muttering statements that only I fully comprehended, such as, "A zonkey is a half zebra, half donkey."

I'd lost track of how many times someone had told me there

were seven billion people on the planet and I should be able to find at least *one*. It was not a valid argument. Yes, there were seven billion people. However, half of them were men. That left only three and half billion women for me. Of those three and half billion, about ninety-five percent of them lived in parts of the world I would never visit, such as Uzbekistan. With this in mind, there were roughly one hundred million women I could end up with. The number dropped to around sixty million when I took away all the married women. It went down to fifty million after discounting all the females not within my age range. Subtracting the approximately forty-seven million lesbians living in the United States, I was left with three million available women. Of those three million, about half of them probably enjoyed listening to grocery store music. This meant there were one and a half million women I could end up with in Los Angeles County. Most of the time I stayed within a three-mile radius of my neighborhood. Realistically, there were five women I could potentially end up with—*if* we happened to meet. When it came down to it, I was searching for five people—out of seven billion. No wonder.

What if the owner of the Porsche was The One? How amazing would that be? What a story to tell at dinner parties! "I was on my way to an Internet date when I backed into her Porsche. She wasn't in it. I waited for her. When she finally showed up, she was furious. I told her to calm down—accidents happen—which only made her angrier. There was an undeniable sexual energy between us. At the height of our impassioned argument, I took her in my arms and we kissed with abandon. It started to rain. We didn't care—we kept kissing."

A man in his forties, carrying a bag of alcohol, strolled to the Porsche. He had a curly brown mop, wore a gold chain, shorts, and an open-collared shirt that revealed a briar patch of chest hairs.

The man placed his bag of booze in the passenger seat of the Porsche, instantly destroying my fantasy. He was not The One.

He took his keys out of his pocket. I approached him reticently. "Sir, I assume this is your car?"

The man nodded, seeming to be in a hurry. I gave him the bad news. He inspected the damage and started to fume. His face changed colors. I had only previously seen this physiological effect in cartoon characters. He said the F word for a long time—not repeatedly, just once. "Fuuuuuuu . . ." Then he turned to me and angrily asked, "Why did you do this?" I almost told him it was because I'd been lonely lately, I'd been looking for different ways to meet new people. But the man didn't seem like he could take a joke. "This is all I have!" he yelled. He shook his head incessantly, repeating, "This is the last thing I need. I just ordered a pizza—the place is about to close. How could you not have seen my car?"

I showed him my insurance card, ready to exchange information. He read it carefully and claimed my insurance had expired. I studied the card. He was correct. According to the card, my insurance had expired a month ago. The man continued his head shaking, muttering, "Great. I just ordered a pizza—the place is about to close—and you don't have insurance." He kept referring to this pizza he ordered and the fact that the pizza parlor was about to close; he seemed just as upset about the pizza as he was about his car. I promised the man my insurance was still current—it was just the card that was out of date. I hoped this was the case. In truth, I wasn't sure. But I kept a brave face. "Well, I need to get this pizza," he insisted, calming down a little. "I have to go right now—the place is closing. It's right there." He pointed a block away. We could see the pizza place from where we stood. I told him I would meet him at the pizzeria and began walking toward it. "You're not taking your car?" questioned the man.

I stopped walking. "Well, no, it's right over there. I can see it. It'll take me thirty seconds."

He stared at me with distrust. It obviously wasn't good enough for him that I had waited for him to arrive. Maybe my plan was to confess my crime to his face and then sprint off into the darkness just for the thrill of it—like people who dine and dash. Still giving me an angry stare, he said, "Why don't you get in my car? We'll go together."

The man got his pizza, just in the nick of time. The pizza smelled good, so I ordered a slice as well. We sat at a table and exchanged information. What a turn of events. I began the evening planning to have tea with a buxom girl in Glendale, only to end up having pizza in my neighborhood with a hairy douche bag. He wrote his name on the pizzeria's paper menu. It was Tod, with one D, confirming his douche bag status. "Your insurance is current?" he asked me again and again. I told him I was positive it was, even though I had my fingers crossed, hoping. Tod gathered his pizza along with the menu that had all of my personal information written on it and stood up. "I don't know if they're going to be able to match the black paint you scraped off my car." That was his good-bye.

I walked back to my car, still parked in front of the bakery, which had now closed. They made good muffins in there. I didn't want to, but I called my auto insurance company while standing alongside my car. After pressing the number one on my keypad several times and listening to an interminable amount of hold Muzak, I heard a melodious voice. She said her name was Sophia. She wanted to know how she could help me. When I heard her voice, I wanted to know Sophia.

"I just backed into one of the worst cars I could have possibly backed into," I said to Sophia. She laughed, an alluring laugh, and asked what kind of car. I told her. Sophia comforted me, saying that a Porsche wasn't the worst car to back into. There were worse cars, like a Rolls-Royce, a Bentley, or a car made of pure gold. She was making jokes—she had a sense of humor. I liked it.

Surprisingly, Sophia asked if the owner of the Porsche had been mean to me. She wanted to know if he made me cry. I asked her to repeat the question, thinking I heard wrong. "Did he make you cry?" It seemed she was genuinely concerned.

I replied, "No, I didn't cry. I'm not going to cry, unless you tell me my car insurance isn't paid up." She laughed, assuring me my insurance was fully paid. I had every kind of coverage conceivable. "Including space alien highway abduction?" I asked. Another laugh. Sophia understood me. She told me I wouldn't even have to pay a deductible for the Porsche and that my rate probably wouldn't go up for another month. There was even a good chance the rates wouldn't go up at all because it was my first claim. That's when I told her, "*Now* I'm going to cry." And once again, as if on cue, her laugh. This was going well.

Sophia said there were a few more quick things she needed to take care of while she had me on the phone. I heard the *clickety-clack* of her typing as I patiently waited, in no hurry to end the call. I decided to engage her in a little bit of small talk, unrelated to my insurance claim. "While I was waiting for the guy to show up, someone drove by who was listening to 'Wind Beneath My Wings' really loud in their car."

"Oh my God—I hate that song," Sophia responded, with her laugh. Oh my God, she hated that song. Sophia was on my frequency. Could it be? After all my searching, all of my disappointments, all the meals and drinks shared in vain . . . was Sophia *The One*? "We'll take care of the rest from here. Is there anything else I can help you with tonight?" she asked. I didn't know Sophia. I'd only spoken to her for a few minutes over the phone. Who knew what she looked like, where she lived, how old she was? She was probably at least twenty years older than me, living in India, married with four kids. That was my luck. She asked again if there was anything else she could help me with.

"No. No, there isn't. Thank you very much." She told me to have a good night and we hung up. I got in my car, disappointed in myself. But it was crazy to ask a car insurance agent out over the phone. Nuts. Sure, she was nice. But that was her job. She was nice like a stripper would be nice. What if I did ask her out and she had said yes and then I met her in person and she was a linebacker with hairy moles? This was stupid, to be thinking about her. I was about to start my car and head home when my cell phone rang again. I answered.

"Hi, it's Sophia." I never thought I would be so happy to hear from my auto insurance agent. "I'm sorry. I've given you the wrong information. If your rates do go up, they won't go up for at least another year—not next month, since your policy was just renewed. I wanted to let you know."

"The news keeps getting better every time you call. Hitting the Porsche has been the highlight of my day," I said. She laughed. I told her I looked forward to her next call. *Ask her out, you idiot.* Ask *who* out? She was a complete stranger. Although that hadn't stopped me in the past. And look where going out with complete strangers had gotten me up to this point. Absolutely nowhere. *Ask her out, moron.* Maybe I could sort of make a silly joke of it. I could say something like, "I know this is crazy. But you sound really cool. Would you be interested in going deep-sea fishing with me one of these weekends? We could go on a chartered boat." If she was truly on my frequency, she would know I was kidding about the fishing. She might respond with a suggestion of having drinks instead, if she was single and interested. (If she suggested we meet for a tea, I was done searching.) Drinks would undoubtedly be a life-changing experience and next thing we knew we'd be on the beaches of Bora Bora. Sophia, in her splendiferous voice, told me to enjoy the rest of my evening once again.

"You too," I said. We hung up for the second time. It was insane to fall for my anonymous auto insurance agent after a business call. Or was it? I thought of my parents' light-speed engagement. Perhaps I *should* have asked her out. I knew her name—I could always call the insurance company and request to speak with her. That might seem creepy and desperate, mostly because it was. I decided to leave things up to fate. I'd let this go. If it was meant to be, it would happen. Either I would run into Sophia at a party or the supermarket or a fancy hilltop restaurant and somehow we'd happily put two and two together. Or. She would call back a third time. If she called back a third time, I would ask her out—no ifs, ands, or buts about it. Satisfied, I was about to start the ignition yet again when the phone rang. I caught my breath. It was my mother. There was a girl she wanted me to meet.

ACKNOWLEDGMENTS

Sufficient words do not exist for the immeasurable amount of love and support my parents have provided from the beginning. Thank you for *everything*.

This book would not be a book without Brad Mendelsohn placing the call, Yfat Reiss Gendell taking the call, Hannah Brown Gordon making the sale, Talia Platz being part of the team and asking bold questions, Mark Chait seeing the possibilities and guiding the material through the goal posts, and also without Kara Welsh saying yes. Profound thanks and gratitude to each of them.

And last, but not least, thank you to all the girls who went out with me. I meant well.

ABOUT THE AUTHOR

Carlos Kotkin was born in Mexico City. His father, from Southern California, met his mother, from Mexico, while vacationing in la Ciudad de México. His dad proposed after a few days and the two are still happily married—giving Carlos a stilted, unrealistic view of finding a partner. Carlos is the only known case of a woman traveling *from* the U.S. *to* Mexico so she could have her baby. He returned to Southern California when he was two months old, with the help of his parents.

Before becoming a comedian and storyteller, Carlos had a brief stint in the Sears Hardware Department and then began pursuing a career in Hollywood, where he chauffeured and brought organic beverages to a number of highly acclaimed Emmy- and Academy Award–winning filmmakers.

Carlos is currently a writer and performer who has appeared at the Upright Citizens Brigade Theatre, the Comedy Central Stage, the world-famous Comedy Store, and a number of other venues in the Western Hemisphere. He is a ten-time Moth StorySLAM winner— including two-time winner of the coveted GrandSLAM—and has been featured on NPR's *The Moth Radio Hour*, KCRW's *UnFictional*, and the popular podcast *RISK!* His column *Heavy Breathing* regularly appears in the online magazine *Smalldoggies*, and his essays have been featured in *Fanzine*, *Pop Serial*, and the anthology of humorous essays *Dirty Laundry*. He also wrote and directed the short film *Overcoming Shyness*, which has been viewed over thirty-seven times on YouTube.